William Harvey Quick

Negro Stars in all Ages of the World

William Harvey Quick

Negro Stars in all Ages of the World

ISBN/EAN: 9783337033057

Printed in Europe, USA, Canada, Australia, Japan

Cover: Foto ©ninafisch / pixelio.de

More available books at **www.hansebooks.com**

Negro Stars

IN

ALL AGES

OF

The World,

BY

W. H. QUICK, ESQ.,

ATTORNEY AT LAW,

ROCKINGHAM, N. C.

1890.

D. E. Aycock, Printer,

Henderson, N. C.

red, according to Act of Congress, in the Office of the Librarian, at Washington, D. C., May 25th, 1889, by
W. H. QUICK, ROCKINGHAM, N. C.

INDEX.

Introductory,	5
Preface,	12
Fatherhood of God,	15
Brotherhood of Man,	18
Color of Adam and Eve,	21
The valley of Shinar,	24
Events, Beauty, Valor, Progress,	28
Preeminence, skill of the early African,	31
Genealogy	33
Governments, Rulers, and the Punic Wars,	35
Jethro, Nimrod, and Queen of Sheba,	36
Zipporah, Berosus, and St. Augustine,	37
St. Catharine and Hannibal,	38
Slavery,	41
Social relation of races,	54
Fall and Redemption of Africa,	56
Phillis Wheatley,	63
George M. Horton,	71
William Costen,	76
James Forten, Ignatius Sancho,	77
Hon J. H. Rainey,	79
Hon. E. D. Bassett, Hon. A. J. Ransier,	81
Hon. J. T. Rapier, Hon. J. R. Lynch,	82
Hon. J. M. Turner, Prof. William Chavis,	83
R. P. Brooks,	84
Hon. Edward Jordan,	86
Mrs. F. E. W. Harper,	88
Benjamin Banneker,	89
George M. Williams,	91
Colored Inventors,	93
Hon. J. S. Leary,	95
Hon. J. M. Langston,	97
Hon's W. P., and G. L. Mabson,	109
Hon. J. C. Alman,	113
Hon. W. C. Coleman,	115
Hon. H. R. Revels,	120
Judge M. W. Gibbs,	122
Hon. D. A. Straker, Bishop J. J. Moore,	123
Hon. B. K. Bruce, Rev. R. S. Rives,	127
Denmark Vessie,	130
Hon. F. Douglass,	132
Hon. A. Hanson, Alexandre Dumas,	135
Bishop W. F. Dickerson,	136
Hon. P. S. B. Pinchback,	137
Hon. R. H. Gleaves,	138
Toussaint l'Ouverture,	139
Zerah, Rev. A. E. Quick,	140
St. Chrysostom,	148
Prof. J. C. Price,	149
Hon. R. B. Elliott,	154
Hon. J. F. Quarles,	156
Judge J. J. Wright,	159
Hon. A. J. C. Taylor, Hon. George H. White,	163
Hon. J. H. Collins, Colored Jurors,	164

Judge George L. Ruffin, ... 167
Wealth and business, ... 168
Theory and practice of American Christianity, ... 177
The Romance of the Negro, ... 197
War of 1812, ... 217
Rev. A. M. Barrett, ... 219
War Between the States, 1861–65 225
Negroes as Soldiers, ... 225
Miliken's Bend, ... 232
Capabilities and Opportunities, ... 238
Industry, Emancipation Day, ... 258
Extract from speech of W. H. Quick, ... 266
Correspondence and Addresses, ... 268

DEDICATION.

To the Reading Public of the United States, this volume is Respectfully Dedicated with the Ardent Hope that the Faithful Reader May, upon a Careful Perusal, Join the Author In the Work of Inspiring Race Pride, and in the Vindication of the Rights and Claims of the Negro, and in all that Pertains to his True Physical, Moral and Intellectual Manhood—Growing With the Growth of His Country, Believing that the Development of Each is an Honor to the Other.

WILLIAM HARVEY QUICK, Esq.
BY
Hon. W. P. Mabson.

SKETCH AND INTRODUCTION.

The subject of this sketch was born near the town of Rockingham, North Carolina, November the 14th, 1856, of slave parents, namely: John Quick, who died in the month of August 1861, was a house carpenter of some repute and was claimed as the property B. & H. Quick, of Marlboro county, S. C. For quite a number of years John Quick was "his own hired man," giving for his time $300, per year. In this way he met Elizabeth Covington in North Carolina whom he afterwards married in the year of 1855. Both parents were noted for sobriety, industry, honesty and frugality. His mother being the seamstress for all the white families in the neighborhood had but meagre opportunity to teach her boys otherwise than by counsel and example. On a cool Thursday Morning in the month of March (twas the 9th) 1865, during the passing of "Sherman's Raid," Mr. Quick was accidently wounded in the lower thigh by a heavy charge from a musket. But for the patient care and attention which only a true mother knows he never could have recovered from his unfortunate affliction.

Though a youth, Mr. Quick espoused an inordinate

relish for books and their beautiful contents. * * *
Remembering as he doubtless did that,

> "The heights by great men reached and kept,
> Were not attained by sudden flight;
> But they, while their companions slept,
> Were toiling upward in the night."

At the age of eighteen he entered the Shaw University Raleigh. N. C., this was in 1874, here he proved to be docile, and companionable with his fellow students and enjoyed the hearty commendation of the faculty.

After a masterful effort to fit himself for a broader field of usefulness than was the school room by itself, he commenced the study of the law under the *direction* of first one and another of the white lawyers of his town,—I can't claim that he read under their *instruction*. Subsequently he entered the law office Hon. J. S. Leary, then of Fayettville, N. C., (now Dean of the Law Department in the Shaw University.) During his course of reading Mr. Quick readily found the reason of the Law much to satisfaction of his distinguished tutor. While no one of the white lawyers would directly refuse to explain or untangle a knotty question of law yet all blandishly and politely declined to impart any regular instruction to him even for the money. He, however, in due course of time was examined and admitted by the Supreme Court to practice law, as counsel and attorney, in all the courts of the State Since February 5th, 1884 Mr. Q. has enjoyed the intellectual contentions of the bar to some advantage, pecuniarily and mentally.

In the year of 1876, he stood on the burning deck of the Republican party, hard by his guns, even when victory appeared hopeless to the most sanguine. In that year he canvassed Marlboro Co., S. C., for the success of the grand old party.

The Republicans in convention assembled nominated him for the House of Representatives from his native county to represent their county in the General Assembly. This was in 1884, and he was duly elected by the people at the polls but was counted out by the methods of the prevailing election frauds committed against a fair election. Notwithstanding he holds no position of trust or of public honor, he wields great influence in the Pee Dee Section of the State. Distinguished for sobriety, industry and the fullness of genial spirits, wearing consistency as an honor bright jewell, which serves him with poplular complacency in every turn of affairs.

"*The Advance*," a weekly newspaper, emitted from his heart, head and hand found its way into the domicile of hundreds of his own as well as into that of the white people of his county. On March 1879 the author of these pages unfurled the sails of the *Advance* to the breezes emblazoned all over with the command Advance. Morally, Socially, and educationally and materially.

Such an undertaking for a young man without means or any substantial encouragement from those whose mere sympathy would mould and shape a manly sentiment and brace up the young freedman as he struggles up the hill hill with the burden of slavery's curse upon his back was simply herculean. The humble thrift and the steady perseverance of the Negro afford quite a moral contrast to the proud, haughty, senseless and dark forebodings uttered against the freedom of the black man. Mr. Quick possesses none of that spirit which would drag angels down, but rather works to stimulate and appreciate, in both races, virtue and intellectual attainments.

Oh! that the same could be written in living letters of eternal light upon the life record of every reader of this sketch? Concluding that it was not best to live alone

Mr. Quick choosed for himself an "help meet" in the person of Miss S. A. Morse, who, moved, when quite young, with her parents from Cheraw, S. C., to Rockingham, N. C. On the 22nd of April, 1880, they married she being then only 15 years and 6 months old. Rev. John Hooper officiating. Freddie D. and A. Evans (their sons) bless this union of hearts and hands with the promise of future usefulness.

Mr. Quick was a shining star in the Colored Mens' State Convention, held March 29th, 30th and 31st, 1882, in the town of Goldsboro, N. C. Hon. J. C. Dancy, of the *Star of Zion*, was president, with Hon. A. S. Richardson, as secretary. This was the greatest body of colored men that ever assembled in North Carolina. The claims and sufferings, the rights and wrongs of the race were very forceably set forth in its address to the people of the State.

In all great economic questions of the day he may always be found on the moral and equitable side. The great Prohibition movement in North Carolina in 1881 brought him prominently before the public again. In this struggle he crossed swords with some of the leading Anti Prohibition orators of the State.

While he does not aspire to the rank of an orator yet Mr. Quick is a profound thinker and good speaker. Rising as the occasion demands to force and eloquence. He is a regular correspondent to many of the leading newspapers in, as well as out of, the State, all of which bear the impress of his mature thoughts on the now strained, yet hopeful, future relations of the dual races of America. Mr. Quick wields a very trenchent pen and generally under a *nom de plume*. (See appendix.)

There is a something vastly agreeable in the first days of professional life. For this agreeableness, and his adaptability this Negro Star very naturally loves the law and is therefore an honor to the Bar. The Bench and Bar are uniformly courteous toward him. In this feature of honorable endeavor the colored lawyer labors under disadvantages and moves among environments not encountered by those of his race who are in other callings of public life. For instance: the minister of the gospel enjoys the kind words, approval and hospitality of his flock with no one to cross swords with him in the pulpit. And there is the technical physician whose diagnosis is treasured up not only in the peripatetic casket of memory but also in bottles. His nostrum is put down as golden and his vain verbosity is often reckoned as wisdom's vehihicle—on which the poor, hopeful, confident, yet languishing patient is to ride around to the ever refreshing springs of health, strength, longevity and new life, from a pill of some unknown and uncertain quantities is to issue virtue that will roll back the dial of time for a number of years, as in Hezekiah's case.

But this is not so with the practicing lawyer. He is like the mighty oak amidst the fury of a terrific storm, but still blooming, unbroken, undaunted, without the loss of a single limb or leaf—or he is comparable to an egg shell at the mercy of a "tempest in a tea kettle"; ever and anon tumbling and being tumbled, by Court and Counsel, by law, facts and false witnesses, into the daedalian crucible tempered as it were by the raging Greek fire. Fighting for every point he wins. Herein is a dangerous rival hanging upon and analizing every word uttered by him, and hence his battles and laurels, the colored lawyers as well as those of the whites, must win by force of intellect, logic and equity. The nobler part of his nature is now and then mortified, insult is added to injury, when some brainless fop of the Bar or an unmanly blusterer, confused in the miasmatic maze of color-prejudice and ignorance and who cannot comprehend the pristine beauty of honorable consistency of principle, even in Courts of Justice, and cannot discuss an issue of fact or law without lugging into its vituperous trend race scintilations when a colored man, women or child is a party. For the purpose of his case such a legal blather skite will refer unkindly to the whole race the world over, though it be only one Negro out of nine millions this species of jealous fasile attempts to impeach.

In the year of 1884-86, the subject of this sketch was Secretary of the Executive Committee of the Sixth Congressional District of North Carolina. This District runs East and West from Wilmington to Charlotte, joining the east of the Atlantic ocean to the Blue Ridge Mountain. The distinguished son of Robeson county, Dr. R. M. Norment, was president of this Committee. Mr. Quick is an aggressive debater and a christian gentleman, devoted always to his family, his friends, his country and his God

> "To virtue and her friends a friend,
> Still may his voice the weak defend
> And never prostitute his tongue,
> By protecting the villain in his wrong,
> Nor wrest the spirit of the laws,
> To santify the villain's cause."

There is this intrinsic dignity in the honorable career of Mr. Quick, void, as it is, of selfishness, or narrowness, in the discharge of its duties, it serves, though it may be in an humble way—that Eternal Justice which is earlier than time and older than all creeds, and whose decrees will be executed when all human sytems shall have spent their force.

There is nothing that more earnestly and vehemently inspires the honest, thoughtful man to shun the breakers and race drawbacks or to imitate or re-act the nobler traits that have moved men to deeds of love and humanity than does the true record of on's race, as chronicled by the historian.

The correct historian is a reflector of the Nation's greatness or incapacity. He paints the drama of its existence upon the canvas before the eyes of thousands of eager gazers at a glance, as it were. The history of the Negro has been for more than twenty centuries garbled, distorted and misrepresented by the "Caste-marked Brahmen" of prejudice, only for the purpose of winning a popular verdict from the jury of the world against him and to brace up the interest of the slave trade and race domination. Color-prejudice will foster, inculcate and precipitate all the trouble this class of men desire and more. Such are swallowing whirl-wind.

"He that soweth to the wind shall reap the whirl-wind."

Mr. Quick has, in his laborious researched for the almost lost golden grains of truth, unearthed "Negro Stars In All Ages of The World," that sparkles all over with examples of honor and ability in a race, somewhat, hitherto-groping in a long, painful darkness. In this he heralds its forthcoming, all-conquering and all-redeeming spirit from the murderous slough of despondency. The characters here portrayed are a beautiful group of personified stars, rising gradually, like the morning star, floating through a sky, alternately fair and clouded, presenting a cluster of shooting orbs and planets, onward and upward, to the meridian of Godly grace and glory.

W. P. MABSON.

PREFACE.

Joineriana well says, "books, like friends, should be few and well chosen," so true is this remark that the author deemed it as a debt due the present and future race of readers that much labor, great care and an overflowing heart of race pride and national honor should be devoted, unsparingly, to the consideration of this subject.

It is the all-consuming purpose of the writer to inspire the Negro youth of this country with the higher qualifications of race pride, self respect, founded in a due sense of moral engagements and a proper appreciation of our civil manhood. In order, therefore, to accomplish this end he seizes, the broom of research and with it endeavors to sweep from our sky and our golden horrizon, that dark, miasmatic, sickly, heathenish mists, Avalancheon fog-falls, rayless clouds of criminal custom, selfish policy, color prejudice, check the oppressor, break the sinews of his entangling-man-catching liberty, destroying web, that spreads wide its baleful vail between man and man. In this we shall hope to exhibit to every "seeker after truth," in full view, an immense canopy of human stars, myriads of bright orbs, in clusterings and configurations of exceeding beauty, smiling in the vast blue ocean of space, chanting among themselves and other nations and races, under adverse as well as favorable circumstances, the harmony of truth and honorable service to God and man in all the rounds of Father Time. The history of man forms one-world-wide page and on it all will find that :

"Full many a gem of purest ray serene,
　The dark, unfathomed depths of ocean bear,
　Full many a flower born to blush unseen
　And waste its sweetness on the desert air."

To illustrate, let the reader choose a clear, calm night, summer or winter, when the thunder storms are rolled up in the hollow of the hand of the Almighty and the sweeping waves of dark clouds have hid themselves in the yawning mouth of the roaring ocean, let him take his position and scan the cerulean vault—with the aid of a telescope or with the naked eye, and behold apparently in his reach, almost, hangs that silver crescent, of light, the moon, shining, calm, clear, mild in a meridian of lovely blue, surrounded by an array of bright attendants, and here we discover a miracle of God's power. Such is a true semblance of the Negroes history when honestly written in the light of truth and not in the fog of hate and falsehood—by friends and not enemies of the human species. "As one star differeth from another" so does one Negro genius differ in capacity and brilliancy from another. The starry heaven does not display its glittering, glorious constellations in the glare of day, neither is real merit always shown when life is smooth, but rather in the dark hour of adversity. This work is made up of bright, and pointed biographical illustrations—catechetically arranged, of men and women who have achieved distinguished success in the various directions in which they turned their respective energies.—In every case the success won and honors attained were the direct result of extraordinary industry, economy, sobriety and the cultivation of a high moral principle.

If Napolean, "the child of destiny," beheld a star continually before him, leading him over the bloody field and on to victory, the subjects briefly noticed in these pages saw also their star beckoning them upward and onward to victory and to glory, compared to whose moral and intellectual worth Napolean and his armored deputies fades into an insignificant bauble. And some of us are following our luminous semble of hope yet.

It is equally as impossible to name and delineate the character and service of each prominent Negro Star in America as for the Astronomer to enumerate all the heavenly bodies through one lens. For the want of space, indeed, all cannot be related of these Negro Star lights that otherwise might be.

I shall assay to prove by portraying individual character and merit and racial durability that:

"*Fleecy* locks and *black* complexion
    Cannot forfeit nature's claim,
    Skins may differ but affection
        Dwells in black and white the same."

And but for the desire to extend the rays our of Stars of Hope farther into the wilderness of minds and hearts I should not have consented to indict these investigations and conclusions and offer them to the public.

Being aware of the environments of lively critics, but fearing little from that source, the author tenders this little volume to you as a memorial of Negro genius, trusting that the reader may gird about himself the sword of truth, marching forward, fighting and conquering for man his brother, and God, his father, following on after your star (these stars) whether it (or they) lead through crimson light or Egyptian darkness, ever holding up the hands of the right, until you are called hence to rest "where just men are made perfect."

W. H. QUICK.

Rockingham, N. C.

CHAPTER I.

THE FATHERHOOD OF GOD.

"In the beginning God created * * * * *man* in his *own* image, in the image of *God* created he him; male and female, create he them. And God blessed them and said unto them: Be fruitful, and multiply, and replenish the earth, and subdue it; and have dominion over the fish of the sea, and over the fowl of the air, and over every living thing that moveth upon the earth. And God said, Behold, I have given you every herb bearing seed, which is upon the face of the earth, and every tree, in the which is the fruit of a tree, yielding seed; to you it shall be for meat. And to every beast of the earth, and to every fowl of the air, and to every thing that creepeth upon the earth, wherein there is life, I have given every green herb for meat; and it was so."

"God hath made of *one blood all nations of men* for to dwell on all the face of the earth."

"And the Lord God formed man of the dust of the ground and breathed into his nostrils the breath of life; and he became a living soul."

How can poor silly man, acknowledging the *common Fatherhood of God*, fail to honor the divine authorship and love his brother because his brother is darker? Claim a heaven-appointed right to domineer, to Have and to Hold all rights, privileges and appurtenances belonging to public con fidence, private pleasures and social happiness, refinement and an exclusive christian worship and fellowship—when he can look out into emmensity itself and behold the matchless bow of many colors, call it a providence, a promise and a blessing—Then listen how this crawling worm, called man, lauds the Deitys praise upon observing the *gorgeous rings* of Saturn—hear him sing His infinite skill and love when He dots our fields and gardens with pinks, jasmines, geraniums, violets, lillies and all the varigated, charming features of the vegetable kingdom—the countless shades, hues and tints of our fruits—the piebold diversity of the beasts of the forest—the party-colors of the winged family that makes the very ethereal space in itself one measureless amphitheatrical orchestra of song—atuning their tongues to repeat after Solomon: "praise ye the Lord. Praise God in His sanctuary: praise Him in the firmament of his power: praise Him for his mighty acts: praise him according to his excellent greatness. Praise Him with the sound of the trumpet: praise Him with the psaltery and harp. Praise Him with the timbrel and dance: praise Him with stringed instruments and organs * * * * * Let everything that hath breath praise the Lord. * *"

Here are the green, brown, black, white, yellow, speckled and striped colors in the *finny* tribe under the *water*—the *black* storm cloud laughing at the lightning, marshal around and hug the *white* caps of bellowing thunder—the hazy atmosphere gives place to the calm blue canopy. In these divine attributes can't we see the wisdom and glory of God in giving the world and everything therein a diversified existence. "Time cannot wither it nor custom stale its infinite variety." His power and mercy are too great for one eternal sameness or stagnant monotony, in things animate or inanimate.

This shows God's greatest power while diversity is man's greatest lesson. Why should we consider a black skin a curse—or look on it with indifference and claim a natural superiority because we are white or educated or have black or blue eyes—long or short hair? as if there was virtue in external attributes? "There is neither Greek or Jew, Barbarian, Scythian, bond or freed for ye all are one." Can any christian feel and know of the reality of the religion of the Lord Jesus Christ or can any infidel possessing the slightest rudiments of knowledge—historical truths, or abstract science, and

" Find his fellow guilty of a skin
Not colored like his own, and having power
Doom and devote him as a lawful prey?"

Will sensible, honest men mount the wings of skin aristocracy and sail through realms of hate to distant, dangerous heights, and perch on a rotten bough, beyond the limits of human comprehension and there blurt at the incomparable symmetry of the All Wise as manifested in the formation of Worlds and elements? Fixed in utter astonishment, we gaze upon such a doleful creature as he appears to be just blasted by a hot stroke from heaven, yet alive: in dreadful looks—a monument of God's wrath and offended mercy!

"The wicked in his pride doth persecute the poor. He hath said in nis heart, God hath forgotten; He hideth his face; He will never see it. Thou *hast* seen it; for thou beholdest mischief and spite, to requite it with thy hand. The poor committeth himself unto thee; thou art the helper of the fatherless. Lord, thou hast heard the desire of the humble. Thou wilt cause thine ear to hear; thou wilt prepare the heart. To judge the fatherless and the oppressed, that the man of the earth may no more oppress."
—*10th chapter of Psalms.*

God gave to Africa's sons
  A brow of sable dye ;
And spread the country of their birth
  Beneath a burning sky.
With a cheek of olive He made
  The little Hindoo child ;
And darkly stained the forest tribes,
  That roam our Western wild.
To me He gave a form
  Of fairer, whiter clay ;
But am I, therefore, in his sight,
  Respected more than they ?
No :—'tis the hue of *deeds* and *thoughts*
  He traces in his book ;
'Tis the complexion of the *heart*
  On which He deigns to look.
Not by the tinted cheek,
  That fades away so fast,
But by the color of the *soul*,
  We shall be judged at last.

THE BROTHERHOOD OF MAN.

"We hold these truths to be self-evident, that all men are created equal ; that they are endowed by their Creator with certain unalienable rights; that among these are life, liberty and the pursuit of happiness. That to secure these rights, governments are instituted among men, deriving their just powers from the consent of the governed. That whenever any form of government becomes destructive of these ends, it is the right of the people to alter or abolish it, and to institute new government, laying its foundations on such principles and organizing its powers in such form, as to them shall seem most likely to effect their safety and happiness."

Declaration of Independence of The American Colonies Against the power of Great Britain In convention Assembled at Philadelphia, July 4th, 1776.

"As the member of an empire, as a philanthropist by

character, and, if I may be allowed the expression, as a citizen of the great republic of humanity at large, I can not help turning my attention sometimes to this subject, *how man ind may be connected, like one great family, in fraternal ties.* I indulge a fond, perhaps an enthusiastic idea, that as the world is evidently much less barbarous than it has been, its melioration must still be progressive; that nations are becoming more harmonized in their policy; that the subjects of ambition and causes for hostility are daily diminishing ; and, in fine, that the period is not very remote when the benefits of a liberal and free commerce will pretty generally succeed to the devastations and horrors of war." GEORGE WASHINGTON.

From what common stock sprang all mankind ?

From Adam and Eve, dwellers and tenants in the garden of Eden, of whom was required

  *   *   * "No other service than to keep
This one, this easy charge, of all the trees
In paradise that bear delicious fruit
So various, not to taste that only tree
Of knowledge, planted by the river of life ;"
 *   *   *   *   *   *   *   *
"How beauty is excelled by manly grace,
And wisdom, which alone is truly fair,
So spake our general mother and with eyes
Of conjugal attraction unreproved,
And meek surrender, half-embracing leaned
On our first-father ; half her swelling breast
Naked met his under the flowing gold
Of her loose tresses hid ; he in delight
Both of her beauty and submissive charms,
Smiled with superior love, as Jupiter
On Juno smiles, when he impregns the clouds
That shed May flowers ; and pressed her matron lip
With kisses pure. *   *   *   *   *   *   *
 *   What thou seest,
What there thou seest, fair creature is thy self ;
With thee it comes and goes ; but follow me.

And I will bring thee where no shadow stays
Thy coming, and thy soft embraces, he
Whose image thou art ; him thou shalt enjoy
Inseparably thine, to him shalt bear
Multitudes like thyself, and thence be called
Mother of the human race.   *   *   *   *
—*Paradise Lost, Book IV.*

CHAPTER II.

WHAT WAS THE COLOR OF ADAM AND EVE?

Adam was red or earthy, while mother Eve was white Rev. J. F. Dyson, B. D., in his recent desertation on the "*Unity of the Human Race And The Origin of Color*," has this to say on this subject: "The word which we translate Eve is *Chavvah* in Hebrew and means simply *life*, and no one who is familiar with Holy-writ will deny that life and immortality are symbolized by *white*, from the Pentatench of Moses to the Apocalypse of John, and in human experience from Nimrod until now. Therefore, Eve's *color* indicated that she was the "mother of all living," or the source of all living, as much as her *name*. In order for the woman to engage the attention of the man she must have been attractive. What color is more attractive than white? For her to claim her protection she must have a delicate appearance. What color is more delicate than white?

To draw upon his affection she must have been fair, or in other words white; and I do not think it more poetic than truthful for me to say that Eve's color also denoted virtue, the brightest gem in the diadem of her priceless womanhood, and the most glorious and the most valuable legacy left her to her posterity."

When we remember that father Adam was of the color of the substance out of which he was created—*Red*, how can we escape the logical conclusion that Mother Chavvah was of the color of the substance out of which she was made—a *White* rib.

Who was Cain ?

He was the oldest son of Adam and Eve. He dwelled in the land of Nod, a short journey East of Eden. He a tiller of the ground, (a farmer.) Cain founded a city in Nod and named it for his oldest son, to-with: Enoch. Over the inhabitants of this place Cain was Prince and Ruler. This is the first city mentioned in the Bible—the most venerable monument of antiquity. It was for his condition and circumstance as well as for the murder of his brother Abel that brought him into distinguished prominence.

What was the color of Cain ?

It is supposed by some writers on ethonological questions that he was swarthy, dark or brown, indicating a sanguinary cross between his red father and white mother. We do not entertain even a vage idea that Cain of Nod was black no more than we do that he was the progenitor of the Negro, but insert this digression by way of parenthesis in answer to some wicked aspersions cast upon the Negro in order to degrade him by associating the two.

Is there any scriptural authority, precedent or abstract reasoning for associating the mark of Cain with the color of any race of people or for imputing color as a signal of criminal instincts or divine displeasure ?

There is not. Neither is the Mark of Cain, nor Curse of Canaan the cause of the Negroes swarthy hue, nor is it the nucleus of the texture of his hair, any more than Miriam's fearful doom was the cause of the color of the white race. (She was smitten with a deadly malady—her flesh half consumed by living fire, her bones began to rot, and she driven out of Israel's camp and burnt in effigy—as one dead. She angered God by the perpetration of one of the greatest of sins—hatred on account of color—jealousy and prejudice.) This malediction was imposed because she attempted to impugn the moral excellence of Zipporah, her brother Moses' wife, on account of her color, she (Zipporah) being an Ethiopian.

What can you say of Cain's posterity indicating skill, contentment and plenty?

Their tented fields—sporting herds and waving barley—their proverbial vintage plains all indicate beauty of natural scenery, and social happiness. There, too, in the dim vista of the past can be seen the hardy sons and daughters of Lamech, of Adah and Zillah, grouped under those wide spreading vines and willows in the balmy breezes of autumn on the banks of the famous Nile, chanting rapturous strains of love, victories and religion upon their well attuned harp and organ. The master workmanship of Tubal in those primeval founderies and mines and shops, fashioning iron, brass and gold, show superior knowledge of metallurgy, mineralogy, sciences and arts, and are, indeed, *marks* and *curses* of which their lineage need not be ashamed.

CHAPTER III.

FROM MT. ARMENIA TO THE VALLEY OF SHINAR.

Who was Noah?

A descendant of Adam in the tenth generation, born 1656, B. C.

Who were Shem, Ham and Japeth?

Sons of Noah, born in the order named.

What sects or tribes make up the semetic race?

The Persians, Asyrians and Lydians, and the Joktons, the fourth in descent from Shem and perhaps the Indians of America.

Who were the Hamites?

The Ethiopians, Egyptians, Philistines, Babylonians, Colchians, Lybians, Canaanites, Sidonians and the Phenicians.

Who were the chileren of Japheth?

The Cimbri, Gauls, Germans, Scythians, Tartars, Medes, Ionians, Iberians, Muscovites and the Thracians.

At what place did the dispersion commence?

Somewhere North of Persia, in the land of Khiva, was probably the second cradle of the human race. This land is now the central meeting point of mighty Empires, here, Russia from the North, England, through India, from the

South and the vast European powers from the West come together. This was the point of departure whence the nations started for their future homes, where each were, in time to achieve wonders and astonish the world.

When did distinctions between these families take place?

From the Armenian Mountains, where Noah landed from the Ark, the streams of population poured forth to Asia Minor, Southwest to Egypt and Africa, South to Arabia, Southeast to Persia and India, and East to China. Then the people began to differ, in color and language, from each other; they gradually changed their habits of life and worship according to their surroundings.

Was this done suddenly?

No. It took ages for the nations to reach the more distant lands; ages for them to become settled in their new homes; ages for them to people these lands densely.

After the float and final rest of the Ark upon Mt. Ararat what became of this isolated family of vari-colored children?

Shem drifted into and settled in the East and South Asia—Ham peopled Syria, Arabia and Africa—while Japheth replenished the North and West Asia and Europe.

Is the climate of the same temperature in each of these countries?

No. In Asia, generally, it is warm, but variable—in Europe it is milder and more uniform, while in Africa it is warmer and sultry, yet healthful as any other part of the continent.

Does the climate exercise any influence over the color of the skin of human family in any degree whatsoever?

Yes. It modifies the color of man; qualifies the habits of beasts, as well as operating very visably upon the nature, growth and properties of vegetation in its regions.

What is the tendency of this color-progression in different climates?

Under the impulse of incompatable temperatures the

color man undergoes a change, becomes intensified, according to food and habits of life and climate.

Thus we see the families of the ark become more and more dispersed, growing and solidifying until they have reached and formed into distinct, specific complexions.

Thusly situated Shem adorns a cuticle of a sallow, warm hue—in Africa Ham becomes darker while Japheth, settled in Europe, is regaled in a paler cutaneous wrapping.

"I assume as a matter of course," says, Mr. Dyson, "that the white complexion did not exist after Eve's death until centuries after the confusion of tongues at Babel, and the dispersion of the three grand divisions of mankind thence upon all the face of the earth; as the Hebrew has it, nor was the very black complexion known until the people distinguished thereby had subordinated themselves to the circumstances which produced it."

This coloring matter was instilled into the blood of the human race while in the garden of Eden. And going out from here encountering heat and cold, "the influences of the chemical solar rays, * * the difference of geological formations, magnetism and the agencies of electricity, atmospheric peculiarities, miasmatic exhalations from vegitable and mineral matter, difference of soil, proximity to the ocean, variety of food, habits of life and exposure." these children acquired this beautiful human bouquet of varigated colors.

It is a pleasure to the author of these pages to conclude this chapter with an extract from a recent poem written by the Rev. Geo. C. Rowe, colored, of Charleston, S. C., entitled, "Historic Truth," (See Rev. Haynes "Negro in Sacred History &c.") the last lines of which I adopt and offer the readers of this Catechism as a living monument, worthy, alike, of both the young, gifted poet and his pristine subject:

"* * * * And early in these parts,
Flourished the noblest sciences and arts;
Vast pyramids, constructed with wondrous skill,
Which stand to-day a questioning wonder still!
What men are these, who built this mighty pile,
With labyrinths most marvellous in style?
What men are these who fully understand
Geometry and mathematics grand?
Who through the summit opening afar,
Can ev'n at midday spy the Polar- star?
What men are these? most superb, it is plain,
Men of rich culture, intellect and brain.

These are the men to whom we look with pride—
Our ancestry; in sciences the guide
To all the world—no need is there of shame,
No reason why we should despise *our* name
Then let us all scan well the historic page,
Tracing the line direct from age to age;
Thus gaining light, encouragement and zeal,
That in life's work, our hearts may always feel
A conscious power, a manhood pure and free,
Which is in truth the highest liberty!

CHAPTER IV

ANCIENT EVENTS, BEAUTY, VALOR AND PROGRESS.

What can you say of the Statesmanship and military genius of Babylonia?

Sacred and secular historians, writing on the subject, tell us that Babylonia was "the glory of kingdoms"—Kingdom of Kingdoms—"and the beauty of Chaldean excellency"—"a people terrible from their beginning." "The golden city." "The capital of the world."

This city was a veritable redoubt—a fortification invulnerable to the approach of an enemy. She was the capitol of the most powerful municipal and social government among the then living nations and empires whose decimated dust now long since the winds have blown as mist, in like manner as Father Time has nearly obliterated all that our fathers did to challenge praise, through the long line of by-gone days.

Who is ranked as the Monarch of the Old World?

Nimrod. Rev. Hayne, in his recent work on "The Negro in Sacred History or Ham and his immediate descendants," tells us that "cities rose at his command behind him, and around him a glorious empire stretched. Nations fled before him as did the wild beasts of the forests.—*Page 98.*

Describe the unique beauty and unrivaled splendor of Babylon

Babylon is the one city known to history which could

have served as a model for St. John's description of the New Jerusalem.—Ibid 100.

This celebrated city was situated on the Euphrates. Some speak of Semiramis and others of Nebuchadnezar as being the founder of this city. It laid in a vast and fertile plain watered by the famous water course above mentioned. Its walls was sixty (60) miles in circumference and three (300) hundred feet high and seventy-five (75) feet wide. In each of the four sides were 25 brazen gates from which roads crossed to the opposite gates. Here were the mysterious temples, gardens and palaces of our fathers. Here you will see what our parents did to challenge praise, through the long line of other days. Hence instructions draw, for here faith was linked with love and Liberty with Law." This city was one great palace. Her queen, Amytis, boasted of a "hanging garden" 400 feet high, sustained by arches upon arches, terraces for trees and flowers, watered by means of machinery, from the river. Now, Babylon had reached her glory and was at the summit of her greatness and splendor. This was about 580 B. C., and was renowned for learning. Her location gave her to a great extent the control of the traffic by navigation and caravan transportation, between all the progressive countries then in existence. Under the reign of Nabonidus it was besieged and taken by Cyrus. This was affected by the consumation an opportune midnight stratagem—a genuine military *coup d'etat*. Yes, by means of an artificial inundation of that stupendous wall that had withstood the ravages of many centuries. Babylon had forgot God—under the administrations of a long succession of Kings Babylon continued to decline. She revolted from time to time against the rule of her late conquerers but to no avail. It was Nebuchadnezar's question that rang in the ears and fed the covetous ambition of the Persian warrior. When he (Nebuchadnezar) exclaimed as follows: "Is not this great Babylon, that I have built for the house of my kingdom, by the might of my power and for the honor of my majesty." The most ancient name of this country was Shinar, it being founded in the year 1998 B. C. Afterwards it was known as Babel, then Babylon and next by the name of Chaldea, successively—according to the whim of the prevailing rulers, assuming different names and forms of government at different ages. Babylon fell 538 years before Christ.

Describe the public career of Nebuchadnezar ?

"That monarch, a brilliant general, an able statesman, a magnificent patron of the arts and sciences, was a profoundly religious man. He united in himself the functions of General, King and Pope. His ambition equaled his ability. Inheriting a kingdom scarcely larger than Portugal, he extended its limits over most of the then known world * * * He strove to retain in cords of silk the nations which Nineveh had bound in fetters of iron. His supreme ambition was to make Babylon what Napoleon labored to render Paris, the incomparable metropolis of the world."—*Ibid. 104.*

In one of his expeditions against Jerusalem Nebuchadnezar captured 42,362 Jews, made them prisoners of war and domestics—confiscated hundreds and thousands of gold and silver, money and wares—almost endless trains of ammunition—horses, cattle and corn and wines.

What was the most remarkable building in Babylon?

It was the temple of Bel, which was pyramidal in shape, having eight stages or circular seats around the tall, wide central, elevating column. The lowest stage was 200 yards square, that is to say, it was 28,800 feet square. On the summit a golden statue of Bel, 40 feet high, stood in a shrine. There were also two other golden statues and a golden table in this shrine. At the bottom of this pyramidal-temple stood a chapel with a table and two images of gold within it.

PRE-EMINENCE AND SKILL OF THE EARLY AFRICAN.

What about the civilization of Northern Africa?

In those remote ages, when the Mesopotamian plain is represented in scripture history as little more than a wide and open common, the Northern shores of Africa sustained a powerful and splendid civilization.

What about Thebes?

When Greece was under the tumultuary sway of a number of petty chieftains, Homer, in song and history celebrates the hundred gates of the city of Thebes and her contributary resources, her mighty hosts which in warlike array issued from them to battle, 572 B. C.

What of the learning and arts of the inhabitants in the valley of the Nile?

Before the faintest dawn of science had illumed the regions of Europe the valley of the Nile was the abode of learning and distinguished for its incomparable works in sculpture, painting and architecture.

What of Egypt and Carthage?

While Egypt was thus pre-eminent in knowledge and art Carthage equally excelled in commerce and in the wealth produced by it, it rose to a degree of power that enabled her to hold long suspended between herself and Rome the scales of universal empire.

What were the varying fortunes of Carthage and Egypt?

She sank amid a blaze of glory in her grand struggle

with Rome, toward which falling kingdoms of all later time have looked with envy. And the land of the Pharaohs, whose alternate splendor and slavery had been the admiration and astonishment of the ages, came also at length under the hand of the Ceasars.

Did their institutions survive the tide of war?

Yes. The fostering republic soon rekindled the fire which the tide of war had extinguished, and Northern Africa was still opulent and enlightened, "boasting its sages, its saints, its heads and fathers of the church, and exhibiting Alexandria and Carthage on a footing with the greatest cities which owned the emperial sway."

Did this power and glory penetrate far into the continent?

No. There was only a narrow strip of light fringing the sea and river, back of this there was the mysterious and unknown.

A civilization and social compact thus founded was not easily destroyed by the Roman horde—war and flames and tyranical persecution.

There was MAURITANIA, though at one time seemed doomed, by the invasion of Ceasar, to be forever the inheritance of a barbarous nomadic race, became a distinguished school of learning Paths were opened through wilds which had defied, hitherto, all human effort, and a trade in gold was formed with countries which had been unknown.

There is GHANA boasting unrivaled splendor. There is *Kaugha* famous for its industries and arts, and celebrated alike for its ingenuities, manufactures and for its witty and *polite women.*

What about the Alexandrian School and Library?

This was an Academy literature and learning of all

kinds, instituted at Alexandria by Ptolemy, son of Logus, and kept up and supported his successors—*The celebrated Alexandrian Library* was founded for the use of the Alexandrian Academy; and by continual additions by successive instructors and managers, it became at last the finest library in the world, containing no less than 700,000 volumes. The method followed in collecting books for the library was, to seize all those which were brought into Egypt by Greeks or other foreigners. The books were translated in the museum, by persons appointed for that purpose, the copies were given to the proprietors and the originals laid up in the library. This was about 332 B.C.

GENERALOGY.

What nations sprang from the loins of Shem?

The Persians, Assyrians and the Lydians, the Jokton, 4th in descent from Shem. The extreme East and perhaps America were peopled by him.

What can you say of the intellectual growth and influence of the Hamitic race?

The children of Ham took the lead in culture, social refinement and national progress, which made Africa the scientific light of the world and from whom learning and polity were imported to and copied by the sons of Shem and Japheth.

What were their natural resources and marks of grandeur?

"THE GOLD OF ETHIOPIA AND HER MERCHANDISE"— "THE QUEENS OF SHEBA"—THE "CANDACES" AND KINGS of whose GREATNESS the prophets spoke—"THE BLAMELESS ETHIOPS" of whom Homer sang and with whom the holiest of the Gods did mingle.

We have seen the prowess of Africa, as we moved along down the line of time, shining forth in all her symmetrical beauty from the planting of Nod down to the crowning act of humanity of SIMON, a Syrenian, and father of Alexander and Rufus.

CHAPTER V.

GOVERNMENTS AND RULERS—THE PUNIC WARS.

From what period may we date the beginning of progress in civilization?

From the founding of the city of Enoch by Cain, where Tubal, who was a refiner, wrought brass and iron with skill.

Who were the Phenicians?

They were a sect of the black race who between the years 2000 and 750 B. C., were at the pinnacle of power and were the instructors and civilizers of the whole Western World.

Describe the delightful climate and sceneries in Syria and Palestine and their production?

This can be the better answered in the poetic deduction of Thomas Moore, which I here lay before the reader.

SYRIA.

Now, upon Syria's land of roses
Softly the light of eve reposes,
And, like a glory, the broad sun
Hangs over sainted Lebanon;
Whose head in wintry grandeur towers,
And whitens with eternal sleet,
While summer, in a vale of flowers,
Is sleeping rosy at his feet.

To one, who looked from upper air
O'er all the enchanted regions there,
How beauteous must have been the glow,

>The life, the sparkling from below!
>Fair gardens, shining streams, with ranks
>Of golden melons on their banks,
>More golden where the sun light falls;—
>Gay lizards, glittering on the walls
>Of ruined shrines, busy and bright
>As they were all alive with light;—
>And, yet more splendid, numerous flocks
>Of pigeons, settling on the rocks,
>With their rich restless wings, that gleam
>Variously in the crimson beam
>Of the warm west,—as if inlaid
>With brilliants from the mine, or made
>Of tearless rainbows, such as span
>The unclouded skies of Peristan!
>And then, the mingling sounds that come,
>Of shepherd's ancient reed, with hum
>Of the wild bees of Palestine,
>Banquetting through the flowery vales;
>And, Jordan, those sweet banks of thine,
>And woods, so full of nightingales!

Who was Jethro?

He was a Midian Priest and father-in-law of Moses. Hence Moses and Jethro were the leading christian spirits of their day and time, they raised, cultivated and directed the two greatest and most renowned families of the world.

Who was Nimrod?

He was the son of Cush "and he began to be a mighty one in the earth. He was a mighty hunter before the Lord; wherefore it is said, even as Nimrod, the mighty hunter before the Lord." He founded the provinces of Babel, Erech, Accad and Calneh, in the land of Shinar— These were formed into one great Empire. Here was maintained *the first organized government of the world.*

Who was the Queen of Sheba?

She was the much honored Ethiopian queen of Sheba who visited King Solomon in all his glory and was by him royally entertained. She was among the most celebrated women of bible history.

The tradition of this visit of the Queen of Sheba to Solomon has maintained itself among the Arabs, who call her Balkis, and affirm that she became the wife of Solomon.

Who was Zipporah ?

She was the daughter of Jethro. She, like the heavenly minded Rachel, tended the flocks and as pious Rebecca bore her pitcher. She was the faithful wife of Moses, the worlds first historian and prophet. He was learned in all the wisdom of the Egyptians and was mighty in words and in deeds. The learning and wisdom of the Egyptians, especially of their priest, was then the profoundest in the world. Zipporah, "had a hand" in all the splendid, yet pious, divinely pious achievements of Moses.

Who was Berosus ?

He was a Chaldean priest who lived in the time of Alexander, the great. He was a very learned man and translated the history of Babylonia into the Greek language. His history commences with the creation and is carried down to his own time. He drew from the records of Babylonia, from the tradition of the people and also from the inscriptions on monuments. It is wonderfully in agreement with the bible record. At first his statements were questioned and disputed, but the researches of modern scholars in many respects confirm their complete accuracy. He wrote many years before Christ.

Who was St. Augustine ?

He was Bishop of Hippo and one of the great doctors of the christian church. His writings are read with reverence at the present day by members of the Greek, Roman and protestant communions. He an African, and was converted from heathenism by St. Ambrose at Milan. On his return he was chosen Bishop of Hippo, in Africa and died at the age of seventy-seven. 430 A. D.

Who was St. Catherine ?

She was an African—was born at Alexandria, and early in life displayed a passion for polite literature. On her conversion she spared no pains in publishing the truths of christianity, and openly rebuked the Pagans for their idolatry. Naturally this gave offense and she was condemned to suffer death by being torn to pieces by wheels having hooked spikes. Tradition has it that her would-be torturers were disturbed by direct interposition from heaven, and, being foiled in this they were content to behead her outside of the city.

Who was Hannibal ?

Hannibal was a common name in Carthage. He was the son of Hamilcar Barca and his name means the gift of Baol. He was the most renowned of that celebrated family of warriors and rulers and statesmen, of whom there were 14 or 15 in all. He was the great invincible Carthagenian general, who commanded the brave Numidians, the Cisalpine Gauls, the Cicillians, the Germans and all the African Cavalries. These were formerly held in subjection by the Roman power, but by the *coup d'etat*, superior generalship and humane statesmanship of Hannibal these minor governments were relieved and the able bodied men enrolled in his army.

He was the greatest general that ever drew sworn or commanded an army.

The unexampled battles on the banks of the *Rhone*, the heroic struggle in the early morning breezes on the green shores of *Trebia*—on the plains of *Campanium*,

Camea, Thraosymenus, Cannea, Ariminum and hundreds of other battles of no less importance. The decisive action was fought at a place called Naragara, not for from the city of Zama; and here Hannabal, according to the express testimony of his antagonist, displayed, on this occasion, all the qualities of a Consummate general. But he was now deficient in that formidable cavalry which had so often decided the victory in his favor. Prior to the meeting of these mighty, before unheard of and since unequaled, wariors he swept all, head long, before him, like a firery flood, dethroning Kings and despoiling governments from Tifata to the shores of the Ionian sea. Hannabal was born 247 B. C., at Carthage and died by his own hand by poison at Libyssa and was buried there on the Coast of Bithynia. Alexander the Great was born at Pella 356 B. C., 109 years before Hannabal was born. The former commanded 500,000 soldiers but the latter commanded only 102,000 soldiers while Napoleon many hundred years afterward commanded a body of 300,000, braves, yet no strategem or heroism of theirs will bear a comparison to the military splendor and invincible engagements of Hanabal.

On many occasions, too, his generous sympathy for his fallen foes bears witness of a noble spirit, and his treatment of the dead bodies of Flaminius, of Grocchus and of Marcellus contrasts most favorably with the barbarity of Claudius Nero to that of Hasdrubal. He was only nine years old when his father, Hamilcar, made him swear upon the altar eternal hostility to Rome. Child as he was then, he never forgot his vow, and his whole life was one continued struggle against the power and domination of Rome. He was about 47 years of age when he tasted of the "poisoned Chalice."

He was was a fluent speaker, and at an early age he

mastered several other languages; he composed, during his residence at the court of Prusia, a history of the expedition of Cn. Manlius Vulso against the Galations. Dion Cassius bears testimony to his having received an excellent education, not only in Punic, but in Greek and latin learning and general literature. During his residence in Spain, Hannibal married the daughter of a Spanish Chieftain; but we do not learn that he left any children. He was a man of high moral character. His marches, tacticts and engagements with his enemy stand out like a full orb in the constellation of warfare with no one to match, equal or dim its lustre. He was a born commander—Hannabals genius may be likened to the Homeric god, who in his hatred of the Trogans rose from the deep to rally the fainting Greeks, and to lead them against the enemy—so the calm courage with which Hannabal met his more than human adversary in his countries cause utterly eclipses the admiration of the world and that Carthagenian Army of conquorers, led forward into the jaws of death, has won for the Negro a niche in the observatory of fame that shall never dim while recorded history is read.

Who was Mahabal ?

He was the best officer of finest Cavalry service in the world.

Who was Hasdrubal ?

He was the manager of Commissariat of the army for a great many years in the enemies Country, under Hannabal.

Who was Mago ?

He was Hannabals younger brother, so full of youthful spirit and military enterprise that he was put in command of the ambush at the battle of the Trebia.

CHAPTER VI.

SLAVERY IN EUROPE AND AMERICA FROM 1441 to 1879.

"Defeat may be Victory in disguise
The lowest ebb is the turn of the tide.'

"Man, proud man,
Robed in a little brief authority,
Plays such frantic tricks before high heaven,
As make angels weep."

When and where was the the first Negro slavery introduced among other nations?

In 1441 Prince Henry, third son of John I., King of Portugal being engaged in Maratime expeditions against Africa, captured some Moors, whom he took to Portugal. The next year they were allowed to ransom themselves and among the goods they gave in exchange for their liberty were 10 African slaves. These were the forerunners of the millions who have since been brought from their native land and sold as slaves during more than four hundred years.

What effort was then put forth to advance the enterprise?

In 1444, a company was formed at Lagas which openly began the African slave trade by seizing and bringing to Europe 200 Negroes who were sold as slaves. Thus the slave traffic was begun about 447 years ago by the then powerful Maratime nation of Portugal.

What relation did America bear to this new industry?

This being before the discovery of America, there was dull market for slaves, therefore, when America was discovered it opened up an illimitable quantity of fertile lands, the demand for labor became great and the trade in human flesh, grew to an enormous proportion.

How many slaves were there in the United States (or colonies) before the Revolutionary War?

It was estimated that there were 300,000 brought and sold into this country alone.

How many were first brought and where landed?

In December 1620 the small number of 20 slaves were landed on the banks of the James river in Virginia.

To what number had the slave population grown up to close of the Revolutionary War?

They had increased to the number of over 700,000.

What was the popular feelings in the colonies regarding the institution of slavery?

A few of the colonies remonstrated against the inhuman butchery, but in vain. The mother country believed in it and, therefore, carried it on in spite of the wishes of the colonists.

How long did it exist in the United States?

From the time of its introduction in 1620 down to the close of the late war in 1865, 245 years.

After the overthrow of the British power in the American colonies did the Constitution of the United States permit the traffic to continue as it had been by the English authorities in the colonies?

Oh, yes, it was permitted by the organic law or constitution. In 1808 the importation of African slaves to the American shores was forbidden under the restraints of heavy penalties.

Where else on the continent was chattel property to be had in human beings?

On all the West India Islands—under the French in Hayti and St. Domingo—under the English in Jamaica—under the Spanish in Cuba.

Which of these governments were the first to restrain the importation feature of the traffic?

The United States, but it was not the first to abolish slavery itself.

Which was the first of these great powers to purge itself of this barbarous, featis practice in modern civilization?

England was the first government to liberate her slaves. This was done in August 1st, 1834. A bill for this purpose was introduced April 23rd, 1833 and after some delay it passed both Houses of Parliament and received the royal assent August 28th, 1833.

Who were the chief agitators in England for the gradual abolition of slavery in all the British dominions?

A Mr. Clarkson, an English Philanthropist began to agitate the matter. Soon afterwards the honorable William Wilberforce, a member of Parliament joined him. The signs of the times seemed to say:

> Oppression shall not always reign,
> There dawns a better day,
> When freedom burst from every chain.
> Shall have triumphant sway;
> The right shall over might prevail,
> And truth like Hero, armed in mail,
> The hosts of tyrant wrong assail,
> And hold eternal sway.

What results attended their humane efforts?

For many years the Christian efforts of these apostles of liberty were fruitless until 1823 a society was organized whose patent object was the final and complete extinction of this nefarious system.

Did this barbarity obtain over the whole area of the United States?

It was confined only to that part of this country known as the Southern States, to wit: The Carolinas, Virginia, Tennessee, Georgia, Alabama, Maryland, Florida, Louisiana, Kentucky, Mississippi, Texas. Missouri and Arkansas.

Upon the admission of what State was the question of the limitation of slavery hotly contested?

Upon the admission of the then Western territory Kansas was the ever memorable debate between the leaders in Congress of the Democratic or slave faction and the free soil parties.

The one faction desired her admission with slavery as a condition precedent, while the other contended that she should be admitted upon terms void of that element. This discussion led both parties to great lengths in the maintainance of their respective positions on the question, even to feuds and riots which was not circumscribed to the boundaries of Kansas.

What was the terms of her admission?

She was admitted in 1861 upon terms of constitutional freedom, in keepin with the provisions of the 13th, 14th and 15th, amendments to the constitution of the United States.

Who were the most prominent leaders in this glorious crusade for human rights?

Chief among the long array of invincible knights of liberty and christian civilization was the nations first martyred president, Abraham Lincoln; behind him is a bright legeon of Spartan braves, each of whom was able to sway Senates by unrestrained eloquence and, who by virtue of conviction and moral courage, would wade througe fields of slaughter to the throne of Justice and Truth.

Among these were the Giddings, Greeleys, Summers Garrisons, Phillips, aided by such heroic patriots as the Sewards, G. Smiths, the Lanes, Mortons, Blaines, Butlers, Shermans, Andrews and last but not least Frederick Douglass himself, an escaped slave, struck a blow more terrible in its effects than the masterful phillipics of Demosthenes against the crown of Macedonia.

> These are a few whose names will live,
> Not in the memory, but in the hearts of men;
> Because those hearts they comforted and raised,
> And where they saw Gods image cast down
> Lifted them up again and blew the dust
> From their worn features and disfigured limbs.

What internal local disruptions shocked the tender sensibilities of the country during thsse ysars of the slave question ?

Nat. Turner's insurrection at Southampton, Va., in 1832.

Denmark Vesseys insurrection and plot to capture Charleston, S.C., and seize the national arsenal at that place, in 1840.

And John Brown's raid at Harper's Ferry in 1849, were all lion-like strategies set in motion to break the jaws of the ferocious slave monster; and each, as a consequence, gloriously failed. But the result of each attempt was to arouse the whole country while these outbreaks all togehter sufficed to present the issue of slavery or freedom tersely, forcibly before the gazing, bewildered world.

Humanity sweeps onward,   *   *   *   *   *
> While the hooting mob of yesterday in silent awe return,
> To gather up the scattered ashes into history's golden urn.

Which of the field officers, in the Union ranks, were the more conspicuous in the late civil war ?

Generals Grant, McLelland, Sheridan, Sherman, Mede, Rosecrans, Butler.

Who were the chief staff of officers in the opposing army?

Generals Lee, Jackson, Hood, Johnson and Hampton.

How many men were put in service for the Union?

The aggregate number of men credited on the several calls and put into service of the United States Army, the Navy and Marine corps during the late war was 2,656,553.

How many colored men enlisted in the Union army as soldiers in the late war between the States and how lost their lives in that ever memorable struggle?

186,017 colored men joined the army for the love of freedom and Union; therein 30,000, of this black phalanx sealed their devotion to the cause with their lives?

When was the institution of American Negro bondage and rebellion overthrown?

In June the 19th, A. D. 1865, this double-headed hydra for 245 years nestling and rankling, brooding and poisoning the fair bosom of our American civilization, was at last cast off as was the viper from St. Paul's hand on the isle of Melita and crushed forever.

In 1865 how many Negroes were there in the United States?

There were 3,938,000.

How many are there now, (1889.)

There are now more than 9,000,0o0.

The inborn impulse, the life, the soul of the Freedmens Jubilee cannot fail to find a glorious lodgment in the appreciative sense of every patriotic man, woman and child in the "land of the brave and the home of the free," and especially those of us who are humble recipients of heaven's copious tidings of relief from the hell of all social institutions.

The scene on this eventful occasion was something more than captivating—see the mother, no longer a chattel slave, with her darling infant clinging to her swelling breast, as she shouts—

JUBILEE!

Lift aloft the starry banner,
 Let it wave o'er land and sea,
Shout alud and sing Hosanna!
 Praise the Lord who sets us free!

Here we stand amazed and wonder
 Such a happy change to see;
Slavery's bonds are burst asunder!
 Praise the Lord weo set us free!

Long we lay in darkness pining,
 Not a ray of hope had we,
Now the sun of freedom's shining!
 Praise the Lord who set us free.

In one loud and joyous chorus,
 Heart and soul join will we,
Freedom's sun is shining o'er us!
 Praise the Lord who set us free!

While the poor, old, wornout, decripit, ex-slave father leaps out of his chains—heart full of gratitude to God and his northern warriors—waving his callous hand toward the emblem of independence—the flag of his country—which to him for centuries prior, had been only an instrument of penal stripes, void of a single star of hope in the stormy night of 424 years (all told) of servitude.

To him there is nothing annoying in Bryant's poetic flight:

The grand old flag, forever let her fly ;
Lightning rolled in evere fold and flashing victory.
God breathe all round it, and when all time is done,
Let freedom's light that knows no night
Make every star a sun!

A more benefitting and transcendent weight of terrestial glory have crowned the brow of no man in ancient or modern times than the grateful wailings and expressions of the colored people upon the untimely demise of the noble souled Wendell Phillips:

It is not enough to win rights from a King and write them down
    in a book;
New men, new lights; and the fathers' code the sons may never
    brook.
What is liberty now where license then; their freedom our yoke
    should be,
And each new decade must have new men to determine its liberty.
Mankind is a marching army, with a broadening front the while;
Shall it crowd its bulk on the farm paths, or clear to the outward
    file?
Its pioneers are the dreamers who heed neither tongue nor pen
Of the human spiders whose silk is wove from the lives of toiling
    Men.

Come, brothers, here to the burial! But weep not, rather rejoice.
For his fearless life and his fearless death; for his true unequaled
    voice,
Like a silver trumpet sounding the note of human right;
For his brave heart always ready to enter the weak one's fight;
For his soul unmoved by the mob's wild shout or the social sneer's
    disgrace;
For his freeborn spirit that drew no line between class or creed or
    race,

Come, workers; here was a teacher, and the lesson he taught was
    good; .
There are no classes or races, but one human brotherhood;
There are no creeds to be hated, no colors of skin debarred;
Mankind is one in its rights and wrongs—one right, one hope,
    one guard;

    While he lived, there was one man endowed with a strong sense of justice "who would be heard," and his voice always made the oppressor tremble. He was so fearless, so pure, so simple, and so truthful and unselfish that the poisoned arrows of hatred and malice never reached the height he stood upon.

    When my mind goes back to the days of my boyhood and I see such an one standing on the stage of old Music Hall, New Haven, the seat of Yale College, before a maddened crowd of men, who thought him an enemy because he denounced slavery as a crime if it was lawful, and hear him say in that rich silver tone, "Howl and hiss, but neither your howls nor your hisses can change the unalterable facts of history," and then see that one man awe that angry crowd into respectful silence, I find it hard to keep back the tears. He seemed like Paul at Ephesus, only grander, if possible. During all that thirty years' conflict with chattel slavery, he never once hesitated or doubted, and never once sheathed his blade of more than Damascus keenness until the last slave market and pen was demolished.

The same may be said of the hundreds of others who championed the cause of the oppressed, and the thousands who sacrificed their lives for the sake of humanity.

When and by what means were the slaves of the West India Islands liberated?

In 1790 the slaves of St. Domingo insurrected or rebelled against their French masters, and claimed their right to freedom. The French manned and dispatched strong, active fleets of war to lay the rising insurgents. They were met by the determined brow and hard hand of the long-suffering victim. The slave was fighting for liberty and manhood, while the trained, well-disciplined French soldier was demoralizing these patriotic, sable sons with the mailed paraphernalia of war for filthy lucre— a bargain and sale in human blood.

Which party was victorious?

The slaves banished the masters from the province, and spirited their ships from its shores.

Who was the immortal leader of this great revolution?

Touissaint L'Ouverture lives.

What political character did the Haytians assume?

They immediately organized a representative form of

government, making Touissaint L'Ouverture Emperor. After his misfortune in being captured and carried away as a prisoner to Paris, tried and executed, the form of government was changed to the form of a Republic, and Desalines elected as President. On this Island their were 600,000 slaves at that time.

How many slaves were there in Cuba under the Spanish, and how and when did they obtain their liberty?

There were 574,102 slaves in Cuba up to 1879 when an act of gradual emancipation was passed, which in 1885 culminated in an act of general and immediate emancipation.

How about Brazil?

Slavery in Brazil has been completed. The government did the work gradually and compensated the owners measurably for the value of their human chattel property. —(See Hawkins, Africans in Africa, &c.)

The Queen Regent of Spain has done an act which the friends of humanity all over the world will rejoice at—she has signed a decree freeing the slaves in Cuba from the remainder of their term of servitude. This reform was begun over seventeen years, ago in the law of February 10th, 1869, which provided for the conditional liberation of certain classes of slaves in Cuba, and for the payment of recompense to the owners of the men and women freed. In 1879 a bill was passed by the Cortes for the gradual abolition of Cuban slavery. This law at once liberated slaves from 55 years old and upward. Slaves from 50 to 55 were set free in 1880, from 45 to 50 in 1882; from 40 to 45 in 1884, and from 35 to 40 in 1886. The intention of the law was to set free those from 30 to 35 years old in 1888 and those under 30 in 1890. In the seven years between 1876 and 1877 the number of slaves in Cuba was decreased by 136,000, but the population showed a falling off in the same period of 20,500. In December, 1878, Cuba still had 227,602 negro slaves. We may conclude, therefore, that Queen Christine has bestowed upon upward of 200,000 slaves the rights and privileges of freemen, and the act is none the less magnanimous because it has anticipated by four years the emancipation in 1890 contemplated by the Cortes itself. Thus by a step, and by an act as noble as well-timed, Spain rids herself of the reproach of being the only European State permitting slavery in its colonies, and gives one more promise of the new and vigorous life which seems to be returning to her in these latter days.

Does slavery exist in any part of the civilized world?

No, except in cases of penal servitude where the party stands guilty of some crime. "Now the banners of freedom, civilization and Christianity float high in the breezes which fan those beautiful Islands."

Who was M. Schoelcher?

He is a venerable and highly distinguished member of the French Senate, who in the first hours of the revolution of 1848 drew up the decrees and carried through the measure of emancipation to the slaves in all the French colonies.

Speaking of him the Honorable Frederick Douglass, who had the pleasure of an interview with him when on a recent visit to Paris, said in a private letter published in the Boston *Transcript*:

A splendid testimonial of the gratitude of the emancipated people of the French colonies is seen in his house, in the shape of a figure of Liberty, in bronze, breaking the chains of the slave. The house of this venerable and philanthropic Senator has in it many of the relics of slaveholding barbarism and cruelty. Besides broken fetters and chains, which had once galled the limbs of slaves, he showed me one iron collar with four huge prongs, placed upon the necks of refractory slaves, designed to entangle and impede them in the bushes if they should attempt to run away. I had seen the same hellish implements in the States, but did not know until I saw them there that they were also used in the French Islands.

What conclusions may be drawn from the observations in this chapter?

Two important facts are suggested, and a few humane political lessons learned upon a careful study of this brief chapter: First, we may note, with no little degree of national pride, the stout tenacity—the unifying principle—the conventional machinery constituting the genius of our ancient country.

For more than two centuries the experiment of a great democratic republic, like ours, for the first time in the history of the world, has been looked on by all lovers of our constitutional government with the most kindly curiosity and the most hopeful sympathy. Though internal fermentations as well as external forces have somewhat disturbed the even tenor and checked the progress of our national life, yet our self-reliant, strong, sober-minded, intelligent, and patriotic Anglo-Saxon stock, well trained in the process of ages to the difficult art of self-government, and the steady hand and forgiving heart of the colored laborers and late victims held their own during a long, bitter and bloody civil war—then shook hands across the gory chasm —recognized and opened up the avenues of industry and citizen life. This was, no doubt, a difficult and slippery problem to solve.

The slave-ocracy of the fertile Southland, assuming the attitude of a dangerous Titanic Confederacy threw her fiery forces against the Republic of the United States, but by great energy and a hot passage at arms, the rebellion was put down, and out of the clash of arms grew freedom and national unity—upon this fabric was builded the plebeian and patrican elements of our body politic, who no longer are arranged in a hostile demeanor, but confronting each other with equal rights before the law, and adjusting their individual differences in a fairly-balanced equilibrium. These are all forces largely operating in the present day, which justify us in hoping that the improved tone of social feeling in all the relations of man to man, which we owe to the great Christian principle of living as brother with brother, as sister with sister, under a common father-hood, may be crowned in the near future with glory and illustrious success.

The holy evangelist furnishes us with many beautiful illustrations of strength and harmony.

"They shall be as one in my hand."

* * * * * . * *

Moreover I will make a covenant of peace with them; it shall be an everlasting covenant with them; and I will place them, and multiply them, and will set my sanctuary in the midst of them forever more." This relates with peculiar aptitude to the cosmopolitan races of America as it did many centuries ago to the refractory tribes of Judah and Ephraim.

CHAPTER VII.

SOCIAL RELATIONS.

What was the moral religious condition of the people in Africa during this long and brilliant career ?

While she was thus moving along in the enjoyment of her magnificent proportion of acquirement and possession, she was also "sinning in high places."

Was a person's civil or social rights denied or questioned in any of the ancient States?

No. That question developed only as the *depravity* of man increased. *This monster* is a child of *slavery* and *ignorance* and whose home is limited to the radius of the territories where these conditions are adhered to and worshiped.

What distinction, if any, is there between the American and the Hindoo caste?

The *American caste* is founded on the *color* of the individual. If he is *black* or *swarthy*, or does not come up to what is supposed to be the *standard whiteness* he is *ostracised, denied* equal social and civil rights with those whose skins are *brighter*. The *color* of the individual is the *measure* of his *manhood* to a very large extent, especially and particularly in the *Southern States*. *Caste* in the *Hindoo* sets up the *social rank* or *material condition* of the individual as a measure of recognition.

During the days of dazzling refinement and enviable splendor, while the storm of rivalry was rife, there was no such heresy among our ancients as color-phorbia or race prejudice to lend its baleful influence to ostracise, imprison, convict or to slaughter any individual or class of persons. Not even did the untutored heathen, the unsophisticated barbarian, dream of such a subterfuge, but it was left, it appears, by the gods of the lower world, to civilized, Christian America to spurn the principle of the brotherhood of man and the Fatherhood of God. Can a soul believe in and feel the force of the teachings of his Savior, when he said, "there is neither Greek nor Jew, Barbarian, Scythian, bond or free, for ye are all one." And then

> Find his fellow guilty of a skin
> Not colored like his own, and having power,
> Doom and devote him as his lawful prey?

CHAPTER VIII.

THE FALL OF AFRICA.

Did these African empires withstand their own civil feuds and public sins?

No. The pleasing grandeur of the macrobiotic Ethiops whom the great *Cambyses* or the Persian could not conquer, surrendered to fate and passed away. A condition of social poisoning permeated the whole compact, inflaming, agonizing wherever it touched, and sinking into a festering barbarism.

Prophet Isaiah, speaking of these peoples as individuals and as bodies politic, said. her "strong cities shall be as a forsaken bough * * * and there shall be desolation."

The prophetic language of Isaiah very fittingly and eloquently and terribly describes the present condition of the once renowned institutions of Africa:

"The (these) nations shall rush like the rushing of many waters: * * * and they shall flee far off, and shall be chased as the chaff of the mountains before the winds, and like a rolling thing before the whirlwind."

"It shall never be inhabited, neither shall it be dwelt in from generation to generation; neither shall the Arabian pitch tent there; neither shall the sheppards make their fold there."

"But wild beasts of the desert shall lie there; and their houses shall be full of doleful creatures; and owls shall dwell there, and Satyrs shall dance there. And the wild beasts of the island shall cry in their desolate houses and dragons in their pleasant palaces."

And it came to pass—To-day Babylon is lost in forest and rubbish and the seat of Syria is a waste.

"*Because thou hast forgotten the God of thy salvation, and hast not been manifoed of the rock of thy strength.*"

This was their "arraignment before the bar of public retribution.

The greater part of this stupendous fabric had thus dwindled down to and by "pride, haughtiness and arrogance."

It appears to have been a part of His divine economy to purge, reform and rebuild this long favored race; with respect to these nations He said, through his immortal mouthpiece, "I will make a man more precious than fine gold, even * * the golden wedge of Ophir."

BABYLON was first threatened, but still stood, under weight of series of moral mistakes, flashing forth her towering brilliancy like a resisted sun, then paled, quivered and fell.

SYRIA was dashed to pieces and ruins merciless plow share turned her into dust and debris forever.

ETHIOPIA, then "Egypt" is thrown into confusion—her people whipped in battle—captured and led away in captivity, old and young, naked and barefooted amidst the greatest desolation by the Asyrian king.

What great phenomena transpired after this warning?

"When the end come the heavens shook and the earth moved out her place—in the wrath of the Lord of hosts and in the (that) day of his fierce anger."

What of the military struggle between these distant countries

They became involved in civil war—"they shall fight

every one against his brother," while the Roman and Grecian arms were brought to bear against them.

What was the result?

Her enemies were victorious. Her kingdoms divided and destroyed and her people scattered and peeled. They remained under this worse than subjugation for many generations.

Describe their condition under Saracens?

Then followed a moral and mental gloom of impenetrable darkness, measured only by millenniums of disappointment and reduced the land of ancient glory into paganism while feticism and slavery have continued to feast on its vitality and made it an object of pity to the civilized world. With these deteriorating environments Africa has made amazing progress backwards.

What nations overrun and spread their prowesses over the wastes of Africa?

The Romans and Greeks and Assyrians.

What can you say of the Saracen sway in Africa?

When they overpowered the effeminate decendants of the Greeks and Romans, and when they had firmly established themselves among the splendid relics and smouldering fires of African supremacy, they wrought a marvelous change in the social system there.

What was the effect of this system?

An auspicious day seemed to be dawning on the continent, the arts and sciences were revived on that consecrated soil

CHAPTER IX.

AFRICA'S REDEMPTION.

What are the prospects of Africa's early redemption ?

There are a number of growing governments on her borders, which may yet, viewing from the present outlook, spread their banners, all lit up with Christian light, over that vast continent and bring Africa back to her olden beauty of conventional symmetry.

Name a few of her leading civilized governments of to-day ?

Liberia.
Natals.
Sierra Lone.
Zullu.

All blessed with great trade centres as Monrovia, Natal and Cairo—and Queenstown and hundreds of smaller towns spreading over her fertile plains and along the coast.

Give me an idea of Zullu character ?

There is very much to admire in the Zulu character. They belong to the great Caffre family, and stand complimented in history.

What is their Capitol town ?

Natal. In and around which abounds plenty and contentment, amidst excellent schools and churches.

What of their humor or disposition ?

They are a good humored, generous and independent people. These manly individuals are proud of their "dark hue."

When asked, "what is the finest complexion," what is their reply ?

"Like my own, 'black' with a little tinge of red"— They love to number amongst the excellencies of their king, that "he chooses to be BLACK."

What can you say of the government of Liberia as it is, its form and etc ?

It is a constitutional government on the western borders of Africa—was organized about the year 1822 by the American Colonization Society and was modeled upon the plan of the United States Government. Time and industry will, eventually, develop it into a powerful sovereignty.

What is her capitol ?

Monrovia. And has a population of about 13,000.

What other places evince and confirm Africa's advancing redemption ?

Tripoli and Sierra Leon, are both noted for their morality, learning and material progress. Egypt is steadily grasping and cultivating a national influence.

Every where Africa's day is breaking—ever changing event presents a bright phase, all over the to-day's historical sky we see the promise plainer written and in the process of fullfilling—every war, every armistice, every great enterprise, every church and school (untrammelled by brotherly hatred) moves the Negro "forward" and raises him on plains higher and more beautiful than Princess Amytis "elevated groves."

To-day we see, where jungles that once furnished a lair for the ravenous beasts, colleges, academies, churches abound and some of the purest men and women, ripest scholars, and the ablest divines of the world.

Therefore, she will live another day among the peoples of the earth, and play her second part in the theatre of the world, then indeed, shall her sun leap forth in the effulgence of a full orb of light, heralding her restoration fixed in and based upon a foundation of the highest Godly civilization.

What is our duty, as Negro Americans, respecting the growth, developement and final triumph of African civilization over African paganism?

While Ethiopia is "to-day" suppliant and stretching forth her bruised hands unto God, it is the duty of us sojourning here yet in America to speedily prepare ourselves as actors, intelligently, honorably, and steadily join heartily in the great crusade, against mental and spiritual darkness.

CHAPTER X.

BIOGRAPHICAL SKETCHES OF CELEBRATED MEN AND WOMEN.

A PERTINENT QUESTION BY FREDERICK DOUGLASS.

Is it not astonishing, that while we are ploughing, planting, and reaping, using all kinds of mechanical tools, erecting houses and constructing bridges, building ships, working in metals of brass, iron, and copper, silver and gold; that while we are reading, writing, and ciphering, acting as clerks, merchants, and secretaries, having among us lawyers, doctors, ministers, poets, authors, editors, orators, and teachers; that while we are engaged in all manner of enterprises common to other men, digging gold in California, capturing the whale in the Pacific, breeding sheep and cattle on the hillside: living, moving acting, thinking, planning; living in families as husbands, wives, and children; and, above all, confessing and worshipping the Christians God, and looking hopefully for immortal life beyond the grave;—is it not astonishing, I say, that we are called upon to prove that we are men?"

MRS. PHILLIS WHEATLEY.

Who was Mrs. Phillis Wheatley?

At about the age of seven this child was stolen from Africa and forced into American slavery.

She could not tell how long it was since the slave-traders tore her from her parents, nor where she had been since that time. The poor little orphan had probably gone through so much suffering and terror, and been so unable to make herself understood by anybody, that her mind had become bewildered concerning the past. She soon learned to speak English; but she could remember nothing about Africa, except that she used to see her mother pour out water before the rising sun. Almost all the ancient nations of the world supposed that a Great Spirit had his dwelling in the sun, and they worshipped that Spirit in various forms. One of the most common modes of worship was to pour out water, or wine at the rising of the sun, and to utter a brief prayer to the Spirit of that glorious luminary. Probably this ancient custom had been handed down, age after age, in Africa, and in that fashion the untaught mother of little Phillis continued to worship the God of her ancestors. The sight of the great splendid orb, coming she knew not whence, rising apparently out of the hills to make the whole world glorious with light, and the devout reverence with which her mother hailed its return every morning, might naturally impress the child's imagination so deeply, that she remembered it after she had forgotten everything else about her native land.

A wonderful change took place in the little forlorn stranger in the course of a year and a half. She not only learned to speak English correctly, but she was able to read fluently in any part of the Bible. She evidently possessed uncommon intelligence and a great desire for knowledge. She was often found trying to make letters with charcoal on the walls and fences. Mrs. Wheatley's daughter, perceiving her eagerness to learn, undertook to teach her to read and write. She found this an easy task, for her pupil learned with astonishing quickness. At the same time she showed such an amiable, affectionate disposition, that all members of the family became much attached to her. Her gratitude to her kind, motherly mistress was unbounded, and her greatest delight was to do anything to please her.

When she was about fourteen years old, she began to write poetry; and it was pretty good poetry, too. Owing to these uncommon manifestations of intelligence, and to the delicacy of her health, she was never put to hard household work, as she was intended at the time of her purchase. She was kept constantly with Mrs. Wheatly and her daughter, employed in light and easy services for them. Her poetry attracted attention, and Mrs. Wheatley's friends lent her books, which she read with great eagerness. She soon acquired a good knowledge of geography, history, and English poetry; of the last she was particularly fond. After a while, they found she was trying to learn Latin, which she so far mastered as to be able to read it understandingly. There was no law in Massachusetts against slaves learning to read and write, as there have been in many of the States; and her mistress, so far from trying to hinder her, did everything to encourage her love of learning. She always called her affectionately, "My Phillis," and seemed to be as proud of her attainments as if she had been her own daughter. She even allowed her to have a fire and light in her own chamber in

the evening, that she might study and write down her
thoughts whenever they came to her.

Phillis was of a very religious turn of mind, and when she was about sixteen she joined the Orthodox Church, that worshipped in the Old-South Meeting-house in Boston. Her character and deportment were such that she was considered an ornament to the church. Clergymen and other literary persons who visited at Mrs. Wheatley's took a good deal of notice of her. Her poems were brought forward to be read to the company, and were often much praised. She was not unfrequently invited to the houses of wealthy and distinguished people, who liked to show her off as a kind of wonder. Most young girls would have had their heads completely turned by so much flattery and attention; but seriousness and humility seemed to be natural to Phillis. She always retained the same gentle, modest deportment that had won Mrs. Wheatley's heart when she first saw her in the slave market. Sometimes when she went abroad, she was invited to sit at table with other guests; but she always modestly declined, and requested that a plate might be placed for her on a side table. Being well aware of the common prejudice against her complexion, she feared that some one might be offended by her company at their meals. By pursuing this course she manifested a natural politeness, which proved her to be more truly refined than any person could be who objected to sit beside her on account of her color.

Although she was tenderly cared for, and not required to do any fatiguing work, her constitution never recovered from the shock it had received in early childhood. When she was about nineteen years old, her health failed so rapidly that physicians said it was necessary for her to take a sea-voyage. A son of Mr. Wheatley's was going to

England on commercial business, and his mother proposed that Phillis should go with him.

In England she received even more than had been bestowed her at home. Several of the nobility invited her to their houses; and her poems were published in a volume, with an engraved likeness of the author. In this picture she looks gentle and thoughtful, and the shape of her head denotes intellect. One of the engravings was sent to Mrs. Wheatley, who was delighted with it. When one of her relatives called, she pointed it out to her, and said, "Look at my Phillis! Does she not seem as if she would speak to me?"

Still the young poetess was not spoiled by flattery. One of the relatives of Mrs. Wheatley informs us, that "not all the attention she received, nor all the honors that were heaped upon her, had the slightest influence upon her temper and deportment. She was still the same single-hearted, unsophisticated being."

She addressed a poem to the Earl of Dartmouth, who was very kind to her during her visit to England. Having expressed a hope for the overthrow of tyranny, she says:—

> "Should you, my Lord, while you peruse my song,
> Wonder from whence my love of Freedom sprung,—
> Whence flow these wishes for the common good,
> By feeling hearts alone best understood,—
> I, young in life, by seeming cruel fate,
> Was snatched from Afric's fancied happy state.
> What pangs excruciating must molest,
> What sorrows labor in my parent's breast!
> Steeled was that soul, and by no misery moved,
> That from a father seized his babe beloved.
> Such was my case; and can I then but pray
> Others may never feel tyrannic sway."

The English friends of Phillis wished to present her to

their king, George the Third, who was soon expected in London. But letters from America informed her that her benefactress, Mrs. Wheatley, was in declining health, and greatly desired to see her. No honors could divert her mind from the friend of her childhood. She returned to Boston immediately. The good lady died soon after; Mr. Wheatley soon followed; and the daughter, the kind instructress of her youth, did not long survive. The son married and settled in England. For a short time Phillis stayed with a friend of her deceased benefactress; then she hired a room and lived by herself. It was a sad change for her.

The war of the American Revolution broke out. In the autumn of 1776 General Washington had his headquarters at Cambridge, Massachusetts; and the spirit moved Phillis to address some complimentary verses to him. In reply, he sent her the following courteous note.—

"I thank you most sincerely for your polite notice of me in the elegant lines you enclosed. However undeserving I may be of such encomium, the style and manner exhibit a striking proof of your poetical talents. In honor of which, and as a tribute justly due to you, I would have published the poem, had I not been apprehensive that, while I only meant to give the world this new instance of your genius, I might have incurred the imputation of vanity. This, and nothing else, determined me not to give it a place in the public prints.

"If you should ever come to Cambridge, or near headquarters, I shall be happy to see a person so favored by the Muses, and to whom Nature had been so liberal and beneficent in her dispensations.

"I am, with great respect,
"Your obedient, humble servant,
"GEORGE WASHINGTON."

The early friends of Phillis were dead, or scattered abroad, and she felt alone in the world. She formed an acquaintance with a colored man by the name of Peters, who kept a grocery shop. He was more than commonly intelligent, spoke fluently, wrote easily, dressed well, and was handsome in his person. He offered marriage, and in an evil hour she accepted him. He proved to be lazy, proud and harsh tempered. He neglected his business, failed, and became very poor. Though unwilling to do hard work himself, he wanted to make a drudge of his wife. Her constitution was frail, she had been unaccustomed to hardship, and she was the mother of three children, with no one to help her in her household labors and cares. He had no pity on her, and instead of trying to lighten her load, he made it heavier by his bad temper. The little ones sickened and died, and their gentle mother was completely broken down by toil and sorrow. Some of the descendants of her lamented mistress at last heard of her illness and went to see her. They found her in a forlorn situation, suffering for the common comforts of life. The Revolutionary war was still raging. Everybody was mourning for sons and husbands slain in battle. The country was very poor. The currency was so deranged that a goose cost forty dollars, and other articles in proportion. In such a state of things, people were too anxious and troubled to think about the African poetess, whom they had once delighted to honor; or if they transiently remembered her, they took it for granted that her husband provided for her. And so it happened that the gifted woman who had been patronized by wealthy Bostonians, and who had rolled through London in the splendid carriages of the English nobility, lay dying alone, in a cold, dirty, comfortless room. It was a mournful reverse of fortune; but she was patient and resigned. She made no complaint of her unfeeling husband; but the neighbors said that when a load of wood was sent to her, he felt himself too much of a gentleman to saw it, though his wife was shivering with cold. The descendants of Mrs. Wheatley did what they could to relieve her wants, after they discovered her extremely destitute condition; but, fortunately for her, she soon went "where the wicked cease from troubling, and where the weary are at rest."

Her husband was so greatly disliked, that people never called her Mrs. Peters. She was always called Phillis Wheatley, the name bestowed upon her when she first entered the service of her benefactress, and by which she had become known as a poetess.

THE WORKS OF PROVIDENCE.
BY PHILLIS WHEATLEY.

Arise, my soul! on wings enraptured rise,
To praise the Monarch of the earth and skies,
Whose goodness and beneficence appear,
As round its centre moves the rolling year;
Or when the morning glows with rosy charms,
Or the sun slumbers in the ocean's arms.
Of light divine be a rich portion lent,
To guide my soul and favor my intent.
Celestial Muse, my arduous flight sustain,
And raise my mind to a seraphic strain!

Adored forever be the God unseen,
Who round the sun revolves this vast machine;
Though to his eye its mass a point appears:
Adored the God that whirls surrounding spheres,
Who first ordained that mighty Sol should reign.
The peerless monarch of th' ethereal train,
Of miles twice forty millions is his height,
And yet his radiance dazzles mortal sight.
So far beneath,—from him th' extended earth
Vigor derives, and every flowery birth.
Vast through her orb she moves, with easy grace,

Around her Phœbus in unbounded space ;
True to her course, the impetuous storm derides,
Triumphant o'er the winds and surging tides.

Almighty ! in these wondrous works of thine,
What power, what wisdom, and what goodness shine !
And are thy wonders, Lord, by men explored,
And yet creating glory unadorned ?

Creation smiles in various beauty gay,
While day to night, and night succeeds to day,
That wisdom which attends Jehovah's ways,
Shines most conspicuous in the solar rays.
Without them, destitute of heat and light,
This world would be the reign of endless night.
In their excess, how would our race complain,
Abhoring life ! how hate its lengthened chain !
From air, or dust, what numerous ills would rise !
What dire contagion taint the burning skies,
What pestilential vapor, fraught with death,
Would rise, and overspread the lands beneath !

Hail, smiling Morn, that, from the orient main
Ascending, dost adorn the heavenly plain !
So rich, so various are thy beauteous dyes,
That spread through all the circuit of the skies,
That, full of thee, my soul in rapture soars,
And thy great God, the cause of all, adores !
O'er beings infinite his love extends,
His wisdom rules them, and his power defends.
When tasks diurnal tire the human frame,
The spirits faint, and dim the vital flame,
Then, too, that ever-active bounty shines,
Which not infinity of space confines.
The sable veil, that Night in silence draws,
Conceals effects, but shows th' Almighty Cause.
Night seals in sleep the wide creation fair,
And all is peaceful, but the brow of care.
Again gay Phœbus, as the day before,
Wakes every eye but what shall wake no more :
Again the face of Nature is renewed,
Which still appears harmonious, fair, and good.
May grateful strains salute the smiling morn,
Before its beams the eastern hills adorns !

THE DYING CHRISTIAN.

BY FRANCES E. W. HARPER.

The silver cord was loosened,
   We knew that she must die ;
We read the mournful token,
   In the dimness of her eye.

Like a child oppressed with slumber,
   She calmly sank to rest,
With her trust in her Redeemer,
   And her head upon his breast.

She faded from our vision,
   Like a thing of love and light :
But we feel she lives forever,
   A spirit pure and bright.

Who was George Moses Horton?

Mr. James Horton, of Chatham county, North Carolina, had a slave named George, who early manifested remarkable intelligence. He labored with a few other slaves on his master's farm, and was always honest, faithful and industrious. He contrived to learn to read, and every moment that was allowed him for his own he devoted to reading. He was especially fond of poetry, which he read and learned by heart, wherever he could find it. After a time, he began to compose verses of his own. He did not know how to write; so when he had arranged his thoughts in rhyme, he spoke them aloud to others, who wrote them down for him.

He was not contented in slavery, as you will see by the following verses which he wrote:—

    "Alas ! and am I born for this,
      To wear this slavish chain ?
    Deprived of all created bliss,
      Through hardship, toil, and pain ?

"How long have I in bondage lain,
 And languished to be free!
Alas! and must I still complain,
 Deprived of liberty?

"O Heaven! and is there no relief
 This side the silent grave,
To soothe the pain, to quell the grief
 And anguish of a slave?

"Come, Liberty! thou cheerful sound,
 Roll through my ravished ears;
Come, let my grief in joys be drowned,
 And drive away my fears.

"Say unto foul oppression, Cease!
 Ye tyrants, rage no more;
And let the joyful trump of peace
 Now bid the vassal soar.

"O Liberty! thou golden prize,
 So often sought by blood,
We crave thy sacred sun to rise,
 The gift of Nature's God.

"Bid Slavery hide her haggard face,
 And barbarism fly;
I scorn to see the sad disgrace,
 In which enslaved I lie.

"Dear Liberty! upon thy breast
 I languish to respire;
And, like the swan unto her nest,
 I'd to thy smiles retire."

George's poems attracted attention, and several were published in the newspaper called "The Raleigh Register." Some of them found their way into the Boston newspapers, and were thought remarkable productions for a slave. His master took no interest in any of his poems, and knew nothing about them, except what he heard others say. Dr. Caldwell, who was then President of the University of North Carolina, and several other gentlemen, became interested for him, and tried to help him to obtain his freedom. In 1829 a little volume of his poems, called "The Hope of Liberty," was printed in Raleigh, by Gales and Son. The pamphlet was sold to raise money enough for George to buy himself. He was then thirty-two years old, in the prime of his strength, both in mind and body. He was to be sent off to Liberia as soon as he was purchased; but he had such a passion for Liberty, that he was willing to follow her to the ends of the earth; though he would doubtless have preferred to have been a free man at home, among old friends and familiar scenes. He was greatly excited about his prospects, and eagerly set about learning to write. When he first heard the news that influential gentlemen were exerting themselves in his behalf, he wrote:—

"'T was like the salutation of the dove,
Borne on the zephyr through some lonesome grove,
When spring returns, and winter's chill is past,
And vegetation smiles above the blast.

"The silent harp, which on the osiers hung,
Again was tuned, and manumission sung;
Away by hope the clouds of fear were driven,
And music breathed my gratitude to Heaven."

It would have been better for him if his hopes had not been so highly excited. His poems did not sell for enough to raise the sum his master demanded for him, and his friends were not sufficiently benevolent to make up the deficiency. In 1837, when he was forty years old, he was still working as a slave at Chapel Hill, the seat of the University of North Carolina. It was said at that time that he had ceased to write poetry. I suppose the poor fellow was discouraged. If he is still alive, he is seventy-five years old; and I hope it will comfort his poor, bruised heart to know that some of his verses are preserved, and published for the benefit of those who have been his companions in Slavery, and who, more fortunate than he was, have become free men before their strength has left them. —*From The Freedman's Book.*

UNIVERSITY OF NORTH CAROLINA,
CHAPEL HILL, N. C., April 7th, 1888.
MR. W. H. QUICK, DEAR SIR:—

I send you the number of the back Magazine asked for by you. I saw a letter from Mr. Collier Cobb to the Chronicle from Cambridge, Mass., reviewing the work of Horton. I think you may get a copy from the editor, unfortunately we have no copy of the book.

I remember Horton. He used to write acrostics for the students at twenty-five cents each. He was a rather small man, nearly black—no white blood in him—inclined to whiskey-drinking, very polite and respected by all, except as to his inclination to strong drink. He was allowed by his master to "have his own time," as it was called, i. e. he paid an annual sum to his master and was allowed the privileges of a free man. I regret much that I did not reserve a copy of his poems.

Occasionally for one acrostic of special poems he would get fifty cents

Yours truly,
KEMP P. BATTLE.

PRAISE OF CREATION.

BY GEORGE HORTON.

Creation fires my tongue !
Nature, thy anthems raise,
And spread the universal song
Of thy Creator's praise,

When each revolving wheel
    Assumed its sphere sublime,
Submissive Earth then heard the peal,
    And struck the march of time.

The march in heaven begun,
    And splendor filled the skies,
When Wisdom bade the morning sun
    With joy from chaos rise.

The angels heard the tune
    Throughout creation ring ;
They seized their golden harps as soon
    And touched on every string.

When time and space were young,
    And music rolled along,
The morning stars together sung,
    And heaven was drowned in song.

THE COLORED MOTHER'S PRAYER.

Great Father ! who created all,
    The colored and the fair,
O listen to a mother's call ;
    Hear thou the negro's prayer !

Yet once again thy people teach,
    With lessons from above,
That they may practice what they preach,
    And all their neighbors love.

Again the Gospel precepts give ;
    Teach them this rule to know,—
Such treatment as ye should receive,
    Be willing to bestow.

Then my poor child, my darling one,
    Will never feel the smart
Of their unjust and cruel scorn,
    That withers all the heart.

Great Father ! who created all,
    The colored and the fair,
O listen to a mother's call,
    Hear Thou the negro's prayer

What can we say of William Costin?

Mr. William Costin for was twenty-four years porter of a bank in Washington, D. C. Many millions of dollars passed through his hands, but not a cent was ever missing, through fraud or carelessness. In his daily life he set an example of purity and benevolence. He adopted four orphan children into his family, and treated them with the kindness of a father. His character inspired general respect; and when he died, in 1842, the newspapers of the city made honorable mention of him. The directors of the bank passed a resolution expressive of their high appreciation of his services, and his coffin was followed to the grave by a very large procession of citizens of all classes and complexions. Not long after, when Honorable John Quincey Adams was speaking in Congress on the subject of voting, he said: "The late William Costin, though he was not white, was as much respected as any man in the District; and the large concourse of citizens that attended his remains to the grave—as well white as black—was an evidence of the manner in which he was estimated by the citizens of Washington. Now, why should such a man as that be excluded from the elective franchise, when you admit the vilest individuals of the white race to exercise it.—*From Freedmen's Book.*"

Upon the force of character and sterling worth, established by Mr. C. and others of like susceptibilities, hundreds of colored men have engaged the confidence of statesmen and have been appointed to as many places in the Treasury and other departments under the United States Government.

Strain every nerve, wrestle with every power God and nature have put into your hands, for your place among the races of this Western world.—WENDELL PHILIPS.

Who was James Forten, of Philadelphia, Penn?

He was a soldier in the Revolutionary struggle (being at the time of enlisting only fourteen (14) years of age) and a mechanic of the rarest skill. He was born 1766 and at fourteen entered into the service of the Colonial Navy, in the ship Royal Lewis, commanded by Captain Decatur, father of the celebrated Commodore. After the close of the war he joined the march of peace, whereby dint of intelligence, honest and industry he soon established a good character in business and private life. He invented an improvement in the management of sails, for which he obtained a patent. As it came in general use, it brought him a good deal of money. In process of time he became owner of a sail loft, and also of a good house in the city.

He married a worthy woman, and they brought up a family of eight children. But though he had served his country in its first and great struggle for independence, though he had earned a hundred thousand dollars by his ingenuity and dilligence and though his character had rendered him an ornament to the Episcopal church, to which he belonged, yet so strong was the mean and cruel prejudice against his color, that his family were excluded from the schools, even, where the most ignorant and vicious could place their children. He overcame this obstacle, at great expense, by hiring private teachers in various branches of education.

He died in 1842, at the age of seventy-six. His funeral procession was one of the largest ever seen in Philadelphia; thousands of people, of all classes and all complexions, having united in this tribute of respect to his character.

Who was Ignatius Sancho?

He was an English gentleman of the highest character. His mother and father were pure blooded Africans of the original stock. His parents were captured in 1729 by a company of the numerous man-stealers who frequented the Western coast of Africa, and placed aboard a slave ship. Ignatius Sancho was born during their passage from Africa to America. His poor, feeble exasperated mother died in the deck amidst the ocean's storm. Therefore, the life of ambitious Sancho was eventful and no less instructive. His father whose noble asperations for personal and political freedom such as he and his people had enjoyed for six hundred centuries ushered upon his mind and character and its power was more than a match for human endurance; he plunged beneath the surging billows of the sea rather than suffer the consequences of slavery. Thus died young Sancho's father. In this wild waste of bondage and mental darkness and political oppression dear little Sancho cried and crawled about for help in a strange land—he had no parents—and only slavery and a master as a legacy—I cannot say, he had no friends, for little children—sweet innocents, always have friends. As he grew up to the estate of boyhood he gave evidence of an inquisitive and brilliant intellect. This love for learning he successfully retained and was such a diligent reader that he was well acquainted with the current literature of his time. He was regarded as a man of the highest intellectual discernment coupled with the purest moral worth. He had such lively manners and uttered so many pleasant jokes that his company was much sought for.

He enjoyed the friendship and confidence of the best English blood.

A faithful and effectionate husband, who honored his good wife for her noble-minded, womanly character. With him as with Bulwer: "To a gentleman, every woman is a lady in right of her sex." On one occasion writing a friend, speaking of his (Sancho's) wife, he said: "If a sigh escapes me, it is answered by a tear in her eye. I often assume gayety to illume her dear sensibility with a smile, which twenty years ago almost bewitched me and which still constitutes my highest pleasure. May such be your lot, my friend. What more can friendship wish you than to glide down the stream of time with a partner of of congenial principles and fine feelings, whose very looks speak tenderness and sentiment."

His children appear to have been the chief delight of his great heart. He called them "Sanchonettas," the Italian word for little Sanchos. He managed to acquire his freedom by the power of his massive intellect and by the same influence he endeavored to move heaven and earth to effect the emancipation of his race in all the provinces of the British Empire. His good wife, who was his Sunday—not his repose only, but his joy, the salt of his eventful life, stood by his bedside, during his illness, and watched and served him as a guardian angel until he was beyond her helping hand and his glorious spirit "shouted the harvest over" and entered "the rest of the final faithful." He was both author and merchant. His writings were very popular with the public. He wrote many magazine articles for the publishing companies and newspaper editors. After his untimely death, which occurred at the age of fifty-two, were all reproduced in a little volume with an engraved likeness of him.

What can you say of the Honorable Joseph H. Rainey, of Georgetown, S. C.?

He was born at Georgetown, South Carolina, (where both his parents were slaves, but by their industry obtained their freedom,) June 21, 1832. Although debarred by law from attending school, he acquired a good education, and further improved his mind by observation and travel. His father was a barber, and he followed that occupation at Charleston till 1862, when, having been forced to work on the fortifications of the Confederates, he escape to the West Indies, where he remained until the close of the war, when he returned to his native town. He was elected a delegate to the State Constitutional Convention of 1868, and was a member of the State Senate of South Carolina in 1870, resigning when elected to the Forty-first Congress as a Republican to fill the vacancy caused by the non-reception of B. F. Whittemore; was elected to the Forty-second Congress, and was re-elected to the Forty-third Congress as a Republican, receiving 19,765 votes being all that were cast. He represented the First District of his State. He ran for Congress in 1876, but was defeated as was the entire Republican ticket, State and nation. He died in Georgetown in the spring of 1888.

What about the Honorable Richard H. Cain, of Columbia, S. C?

Richard H. Cain, of Columbia, was born in Greenbriar County, Virginia, April 12, 1825; his father removed to Ohio in 1831, and settled in Gallipolis; he had no education, except such as was afforded in Sabbath school, until after his marriage; entered the ministry at an early age; became a student at Wilberforce University, at Xenia, Ohio, in 1860, and remained there for one year; removed at the breaking out of the war to Brooklyn, New York, where he discharged ministerial duties as a pastor for four years; was sent by his church as a missionary to the freedmen in South Carolina; was chosen a member to the constitutional convention of South Carolina; was elected a member of the State Senate from Charleston, and served two years; has edited a republican newspaper since 1868; and was elected to the Forty-third Congress as a Republican, receiving 66,825 votes against 26,394 votes for Lewis E. Johnson.

He represented his State at large in the Forty-third Congress. After the defeat of his party he returned to the ministry and was elected Bishop by the General Conference of the A. M. E. church

Who is Ebenezer D. Bassett?

He was a minister Resident and Consul General to Hayti; appointed by President Grant in 1870.

Who was Alonzo J. Ransier, of Charleston, S. C.?

He was one of the colored members of Congress durring the days of Republican power—was a modest' and honest man—a safe and intelligent leader of the people—an earnest, faithful representative of his constituency. Representing the 2d District. He was born at Charleston, South Carolina, in January, 1834; was self-educated; was employed as shipping clerk in 1850 by a leading merchant, who was tried for violation of law in "hiring a colored clerk," and fined one cent with costs; was one of the foremost in the work of reconstruction in 1865; was a member of a convention of the friends of equal rights in October, 1865, at Charleston, and was deputed to present the memorial there framed to Congres; was elected a member of the State Constitutional Convention of 1868; was elected a member of the House of Representatives in the State Legislature in 1868-'69; was chosen Chairman of the State Republican Central Committee, which position he held until 1872; was elected a Presidential Elector on the Grant and Colfax ticket in 1868; was elected Lieutenant Governor of South Carolina in 1870 by a large majority; was President of the Southern States Convention which nominated Grant and Wilson in 1872; and was elected to the Forty-third Congress as a Republican, receiving 20,061 votes against 6,549 votes for W. Gurney. Independent Republican. He died in the winter of 1887–'8 in his native city, ripe in years and full of honors beloved—by all who knew him.

Who is Hon. James T. Rapier, of Montgomery, Alabama?

He was, in 1874, a member of the Forty-third Congress, representing the Second District of his native State. He was born in Florence, Alabama, in 1840; was educated in Canada; is a planter; was appointed a notary republic by the Governor of Alabama in 1866; was a member of the first Republican Convention held in Alabama, and was one of the committee that framed the platform of the party; represented Lauderdale County in the Constitutional Convention held at Montgomery in 1867; was nominated for Secretary of State in 1870, but was defeated with the rest of the ticket; was appointed assessor of internal revenue for the second collection district of Alabama in 1871; was appointed State Commissioner to the Vienna Exposition in 1873 by the Governor of Alabama, and was elected to the Forty-third Congress as a Republican, receiving 19,100 votes against 16,000 votes for C. W. Oates, Democrat.

Who is John R. Lynch, of Natchez, Mississippi?

He was also a member of the Forty-third Congress, and was re-elected to the Forty-eighth Congress, but lost his seat by Democratic fraud—representing the Sixth District. He was born in Concordia Parish, Louisiana, September 10, 1847, a slave, and he remained in slavery until emancipated by the results of the rebellion, receiving no early education; a purchase of his mother carried her with her children to Natchez, where, and when the Union troops took possession, he attended evening school for a few months, and he has since, by private study, acquired a good English education; he engaged in the business of photography at Natchez until 1869, when Governor

Ames appointed him a justice of the peace; he was elected a member of the State Legislature from Adams County, and re-elected in 1871, serving the last term as Speaker of the House; and was elected to the Forty-third Congress as a Republican, receiving 15,391 votes against 8,430 votes for H. Cassady, sen., Democrat.

Mr. Lynch was made President of the National Conference of colored men of the United States, held in Nashville, Tennessee, May the 6th, 7th, 8th and 9th, 1879. Was also nominated and elected temporary president of the National Republican Convention held in Chicago, June, 1884, which nominated James G. Blaine for President. Was a delegate to the National Republican Convention at the same place in 1888 which nominated General Benjamin Harrison for President of the United States. He is a man of high character and enjoys considerable of the world's goods. He enjoys the reputation of being an excellent presiding officer. As a speaker he ranks high among the foremost orators of the country.

Who is J. Milton Turner, of Alabama?

He is a practicing lawyer in the town of —— Alabama. Was appointed in 1870, by President Hayes, as Minister-Resident and Consul-General to Liberia, Africa. His life, character, public services, scholarly attainments, moral attributes and industrial talent, stand out *alto-relieve* indicating Negro capacity under the influences of opportunity, training, development and intelligence.

Who was Professor William Chavis?

He was a classical scholar and the Christian gentleman, who taught a school for white boys in Chatham county, North Carolina, in 1822. Among his pupils who subsequently became eminent statesmen were Kenneth Raynor, who represented the Raleigh District in Congress before the war. After the war he became a Republican and was Solicitor General of the United States Treasury when he died. Honorable **Abraham** Rencher, a distingtished North Carolinian who **was also a** pupil of Prof. C. He was at one time Governor of Arizona, appointed by President Pierce in 1852. Honorable Jacob Thompson, of Chatham county, North Carolina, was born 1810. He graduated at Chapel Hill (N. C.) University in 1831—studied law and was admitted to the bar in 1834. He, too, was a pupil of Professor Chavis, and was classmate of Messrs. Raynor and Rencher. He early became a Mississippi pioneer and settled in Chichasaw county—was a member of Congress in 1839–'51. In this body he was chairman of the committee on Indian Affairs. He was a zealous defender of of the rights, interests and reputation of his State—was a strong partisan and worked indefatigably for the honor and success of the Democratic party—was appointed Secretary of the Interior Department by President Buchanan in 1857; he held this office four years and resigned in 1861 for reasons connected with re-enforcement of Fort Sumter. He was one of the commissioners from Mississippi to North Carolina to urge her to adopt the ordinance of secession. He afterwards became Governor of his State and aid to Beauregard. Professor Chavis was a native of one of the West India Islands and upon coming to the United States he applied for and obtained a certificate of his naturalization, thereby become a citizen of this country. It is but reasonable to presume that Prof. C. implanted within the mind and character of these white youths the seed of glory and fame.

Who was Robert Peel Brooks?

The subject of this sketch was born 1857 in the city of Richmond, Virginia. He received an academic education in the city schools, and subsequently entered the college and law departments in the Howard University, Washington, D. C., where he graduated from both departments with high honors. At the Richmond bar he won quite a distinction for legal ability and purity of character. For some years he edited a weekly newspaper known as the *Virginia Star*. He was a brilliant orator as well as a trenchant writer.

He died at his home in the month of February, 1885, at the early age of 28.

The reader may draw a fitting estimate of the admirable qualities of young Robert upon a careful perusal of the following lines, which appeared in the columns of the *Progressive American* soon after the death of Mr. R. Brooks, the father of young Robert Peel Brooks:

"We can but regard as fallacious the common idea of what constitutes greatness in men. Mighty achievements and brilliant deeds of themselves are no evidence of superior greatness. Deeds and surroundings must be considered together before there can be a computation of a man's great qualities.

Southey said there are more poets who never sang than there are who have; so we believe that there are more great men whom the world does not know, than there are whom it does, and Mr. Albert R. Brooks, who died recently in Richmond, Va., a sketch of whose life is published in the Virginia *Star*, was one of them.

Mr. Brooks was born a slave in June, 1818. In his childhood he was sold, and with his second master he was connected till the close of the war. In 1827, Mr. Brooks, then nine years of age, commenced work in a tobacco factory in Richmond. In 1836 ha became a member of the Baptist church.

In 1838 he was married to a young slave woman, who

was owned by a planter other than his master, and because of this he was taken from his wife by his master, and he so remained for eight years; at the expiration of that time he was again allowed to go to Richmond. This time he was employed by a Mr. Reeves, a Presbyterian church member. Mr. Brooks was coachman to Mr. Reeves for eight years. During that time his employer, with the consent of his master, banked for him all the extra money he made. It amounted to $1,000. Mr. Reeves died, and about this time one of Mr. Brooks' brothers was placed on the auction block, and his $1,000 went to purchase his freedom, while he himself remained a slave.

In 1852 he was permitted to hire his own time, and he sat up a grocery store and boarding house. In 1858 he commenced the hack business; in the same year his wife's master died, and in the following year she ane her six children were sold. Mr. Brooks purchased his wife and his daughter. He made strenuous efforts to buy his eldest daughter, but he was unable. She was sold the second time, and soon died. His eldest son was, during the war, to be sold the second time, and his father bought him. His own freedom he did not enjoy until the close of the war. When the wife of his former master died he was applied to for assistance, and did furnish the means to bury her. Mr. R. P. B. was one of the most polished orators in the State of Virginia.

Who is Hon. Edward Jordan, of Jamaica?

He is the most eminent politician of Jamaica and said to be the principal member of Governor Darling's Cabinet. He is also Mayor of the city of Kinston.

Who was the venerable Bishop Richard Allen?

He was the founder of the African Methodist Episcopal church of America. For many years he was its foremost minister and its first bishop.

This reverend gentleman was born, a slave in Philadelphia, on the 14th day of February, 1760, sixteen years before the Declaration of American Independence. In his early childhood he was carried to the State of Delaware, where he was held a slave until he reached his majority, or thereabout, when at the suggestion of his owner he bought himself, paying sixty pounds of gold and silver for his freedom. After his conversion, he, with a number of others worshiped at the St. George's church, in Fourth street, Philadelphia. When the colored attendents began to get numerous some feelings of unchristian, jealous, race hostility began to manifest itself in the conduct of the white part of the congregation toward the colored brethren. Which spirit of hate grew to such proportions as to deny the colored members sents in the body of the church. Several of these members were actually assaulted by the white officers in the midst of the congregation, on the Sabbath, while all were engaged in the service of prayer. This led to the withdrawal of the colored members who went to work and built for themselves a church where freedom should find a home and beneath whose fostering and protective care free principles should grow and expand in the full amplitude of their nature. Possessing solid, rather than brilliant and dazzling powers of mind, and hence properly classed among the thinkers of logical, mental bias Bishop Allen was, nevertheless, a pulpit orator, whose style was marked by a tender and lively sensibility, a vigorous and vivid imagination, a deep and moving pathos.

The power of his eloquence was demonstrated in the effect produced upon the multitudes moved and converted through his preaching before and after election to the bishopric.

Some time during the year 1784 he preached for several weeks in Radnor. His congregation was composed mainly of white persons; but few colored people lived in the neighborhood. In connection with his labors here this beautiful testimony is borne. Some said: "This man must be a man of God; we never heard such preaching before."

He was strong in his earnest and abiding faith in his heavenly Father, upon whose ability and purpose to fulfill his promises to be relied with the confidence of a child. A thorough and careful study of the character of Bishop Allen will convince us that he possessed all the qualities of mind which distinguished him for real greatness. He was intelligent, docile, sagacious, judicious, earnest, fearless. humane, patient, industrious, self-reliant and self-sacrificing, conscientious and just.'"

The author is largely indebted to Honorable J. M. Langstone, LL. D. for this note on the career of Bishop Allen (see Prof. L's eulogy an the life of Bishop A.

To his memory was the first monument ever erected over the dust of any colored man by the colored people in the United States, which stands out to-day an everlasting beacon light to the honor, public and Christian services of one of the purest, best and noblest of our Redeemer's latter day Disciples.

Who is Mrs. F. E. W. Harper?

She is is a poetess of the purest gem, and of the most exquisite charm and elegance. She has written many poems that evinced rare genius. "*Poetr nascitur' non fit.*" applies with beautiful force to Mrs. Harper.

BY FRANCES E. W. HARPER.

It shall flash through coming ages,
It shall light the distant years;
And eyes now dim with sorrow
Shall be brighter through their tears.

It shall flush the mountain ranges,
And the valleys shall grow bright;
It shall bathe the hills in radiance,
And crown their brows with light.

It shall flood with golden splendor
And the huts of Caroline;
And the sun-kissed brow of labor
With lustre new shall shine.

It shall gild the gloomy prison,
Darkened by the nation's crime,
When the dumb and patient millions
Wait the better-coming time.

By the light that gilds their prison
They shall see its mouldering key;
*   *   *   *   *   *

Though the morning seemed to poise,
O'er the hill tops far away,
Now the shadows bear the promise
Of the quickly coming day.

Soon the mists and murky shadows
Shall be fringed with crimson light,
And the glorious dawn of freedom
Break refulgent on the sight.

Who invented the first clock ever made in this country?

Bejamin Banner, a colored man, who lived near Baltimore, Maryland. This was accomplished in 1762. He was about 30 years old at the time of its construction.

It kept time exactly and people everywhere discussed the matter as being a wonderful thing for a man to do without previous instructions.

By whom was the first almanac made in this country?

Benjamin Banneker calculated and made the first almanac ever made in this country.

It contained much useful information of a general nature, and interesting selections in prose and verse.

His manners were those of a perfect gentleman. He was kind, generous, hospitiable, humane, dignified, and pleasing. He abounded in information on all the various subjects and incidents of the day; was very modest and unassuming, and delight in society at his own house. Go there when you would, by day or night, there was constantly in the middle of the floor a large table covered with books and papers. As he was an eminent mathematician, he was constantly in correspondence with other mathematicians in this country, with whom there was an interchange of questions of difficult solution. His head was covered with thick white hair, which gave him a venerable appearance. His dress was uniformly of superfine drab broadcloth, made in the old style of a plain coat with straight colar, a long waistcoat, and a broad-brimmed hat. His color was not jet black, but decidedly negro. In size and personal appearance he bore a strong resemblance to the statue of Benjamin Franklin, at the library in Philadelphia."

The good which Banneker did to the cause of his colored brethren did not cease with his life. When the Abbe Gregorie pleaded for emancipation in France, and when Wilberforce afterward labored for the same cause in England, the abilities and character of the black astronomer were brought forward as an argument against the enslavement of his race; and, from that day to this, the friends of freedom have quoted him everywhere as a proof of the mental capacity of Africans.

THE GREAT COLORED INVENTOR.

BY REV. H. A. CROMARTIE, A. M.

Mr. George Morsel Williams, of Newark, Newcastle county, Del., has made seven original discoveries in mechanical art. His first invention was the corn-planter, with all necessary implements for opening the furrow, dropping the corn and fertilizer in the same hill, at intervals of three feet, and covering the same, leaving a beautiful elevation; said planter is drawn be two horses. This wondeful discovery will save the labor of at least two men according to the old system of corn planting.

The second invention was the drill-tube, for seeding machines. This is an admirable piece of mechanism for simplicity, durability and general efficiency, by the use of which the seed can always be planted at an even depth. The construction is of such a nature that clogging is impossible. The drill-tube contains the seed, and opens the furrow and makes a smooth surface, scattering the seed up it, and the returning surface covers them at an even depth.

The third invention was a new and useful improvement in the manufacture of mover knives. This consists chiefly in giving them spiral shape.

The fourth invention is in paul ratchet mechanism. This consists of a paul and ratchet mechanism in which the mechanism when applied moves in reverse direction, or runs back, as a lawn mover, the paul being automatically raised to prevent noise.

The fifth invention in paul-and-ratchet mechanism was by means of a shaft which passes through a pinion and a circular ratchet box and firmly connected with the end of the shaft is a pin, whose ends pass freely through widened opening in the tooth portion of the paul; serving to retain the paul on the shaft and to guide it in motion.

The sixth invention was the lawn mower. It consists of a cylinder or rotary; it has a grass gatherer and dropper. The driving wheels have an internal tooth, rim, which by means of paul-and-rachtet mechanism and gerring usual in lawn mover, imparts motion to the cylinder or rotary cutter, and serves to render said cylinder inoperative when the mower is to run backward. There are always two knives in operation on the bed-knife; this makes rapid and thorough cutting of grass. It will cut long or short grass. The bars, which are elastic, are forced from the arm, so that they clear the pin, after which they may be raised or lowered at will. The bars are sprung into engagement with the pin and the parts held firm. It will cut high or low grass with the same rapidity.

The seventh invention has an advantage over the other lawn mowers, chiefly in the adjustable bed-knife, vertically adjusting the cutting mechanism, and the novel grass receiver; said receiver carries the grass until it has a sufficient quantity and then dumps it wherever desired.

We make no attempt here to to describe these valuable additions to mechanical art, but simply to call attention to them. These works have all been patented at a cost of four hundred dollars of the hard earnings of Mr. Wiliiams. They have been on exhibition at Franklin Novel Institute, Philadelphia, Pa., and at the Agricultural

Society Exhibition in Burlington, N. J. At both of these places Mr. Williams took first premium on them in '85. Well done for a colored man; but he does not stop there: he has invented a bird trap. This is an ingenious contrivance; the bird lights upon a ballance, it will ease him down and the bird is caught.

These are only forerunners of the inventive genius and fertile brain of the sons of ebony hue. And let it be written upon the golden hills and sounded along the fiery shores of caste, ostracism and oppression, that the despised and rejected sons and daughters of Afric's clime must wear the same inventive crown worn by discoverers and inventors of other races.—In Christian Record, Pottstown, Pa.

COLORED INVENTORS.

LIST OF COLORD INVENTORS WHO SECURED PATENTS.

The People's Advocate, Washington, D. C., has secured through Mr. Henry E. Baker, the following list of colored inventors which is a feature of much interest just at this time. In a note Mr. Baker says of the difficulties of obtaining a complete list: "The records of the Patent Office do not in any way indicate whether a patentee is white or colored, and having had to secure these names through personal inquiry mainly among the examiners in the office and attorneys who practice before it, the list is necessarily incomplete. Colored inventors have not always been able to obtain a patent, inasmuch as the oath contains a clause reciting the citizenship of the applicant, colored inventors in *ante bellum* days were compelled to go through the form of assigning their inventions to their masters, who afterwards secured patents for the inventions of their slaves, and reaped all the benefits resulting from the manufacture and sale of such articles."

Joseph Hawkins, West Windsor. N. J., March 6th. 1845, Improved Gridiron.

Wm. Murray, Alexandria, Va.. Feb. 1, 1870, Cornstalk Harvester.

Horde Spears, Snow Hill, N. C., Dec. 27, 1870, Shield for Infantry and Artillery men.

T. J. Martin, Dowagiac, Mich., March 20, 1872, Fire Extinguisher.

E. H. Sutton, Edenton, N. C., April 7, 1874, Cotton Cultivator.

David A. Fisher, Jr., Washington, D. C., April 20, 1875, Joiner's Clamp.

Alex. P. Ashbourne, Oakland, Cal., June 1, 1875, Process for preparing Cocoanut for Domestic Use.

Henry M. Nash, Baltimore, Md., Oct., 1875, Life Preserving Stool.

David A. Fisher, Jr., Washington, D. C., March 14, 1876, Furniture Castor.

Alex. P. Ashbourne, Oakland, Cal., August 21, 1875, Treating Cocoanut.

Wm. A. Lavalette, Washington, D. C., Sept. 17, 1878, Printing Press.

Joseph R. Winters, Chambersburg, P., April 8, 1879, Fire Escape Ladder.

Wm. Bailiss, Princeton, N. J., Aug. 6, 1879, Ladder Scaffold Support.

Alex. P. Ashbourne, Oakland, Cal., July 27, 1880, Refining Cocoanut.

Traverse B. Pinn, Alexandria, Va., File Holder, Aug. 17, 1880.

Powell Johnson, Barton, Ala., Nov. 2, 1880, Eye Protector.

James Wormley, Washington, D. C., May 24, 1881.

Life Saving Apparatus.
R. W. Alexander, Galesburg, Ill., April 18, 1882, Corn Planter Check Rower.
H. H. Reynolds, Detroit, Mich., April 3, 1883, Window Ventilator for Railroad Cars.
Jonas Cooper, Washington, D. C., May 1, 1883, Shutter Fastener.
Leonard C. Bailey, Washington, D. C., Sep. 1883, Combined Truss and Bandage.
Luckrum Blue, Washington, D. C., May 20, 1884, Hand Corn Shelling Device.

Who is the Honorable John Sinclear Leary, of Fayetteville, N. C.?

He is one of the leading lawyers of the Fayetteville Bar—was born in 1843 in the city where he now resides.— His industry and energy enable him to live in comfortable circumstances while he continues to enjoy the confidence of the best people in his city and State.

In the years 1885–'86 he was president of the State Colored Industrial Association, under his administration, by force of the happy faculty of grit and grace, this institution has developed into one of the chief features of the commonwealth. The father of this subject was ever vigilant of the rights of his race and seized each opportunity lustly to improve the moral and political condition of his people. In 1841 when the defendant Manuel in the State vs. Manuel, 4 D. and B. Law Reports of North Carolina, was denied certain rights belonging to him as a free person of color. Mr. Matthew Leary, referred to above, engaged counsel to appear for him, to wit: Honorable Robert Strange (afterwards Judge). The able attorney was requested to exhaust the judiciary of the State if necessary in the defence of his client, it was done, since the defendant was cast at *nisi prius,* an appeal was taken to the Supreme Court of the State, where presided the distinguished legal trio, the Honorable Thomas Ruffin, *Chief Justice*, crowning genius with virtue and sterling ability—there sat the Honorable William Gaston, Associate Justice, master of a broad comprehensive mind, thoroughly trained in the unfathomable riches of legal lore, with these forensic giants were associated the elegant, accomplished Joseph J. Daniel, with a **vigorous intellect** rooted in a profound knowledge of law and human nature. The rendition of the opinion of this high tribunal devolved upon Judge Gaston. The question of the rights of free colored persons at that time had not been adjudicated upon and was therefore unprecedented by any court of competent jurisdiction in this country—the decision forsooth, inadvertently and immediately became the leading—patern case—the great national controlling case. This great reform in the law governing colored people was set in motion by the venerable father of Sohn S. Leary—Young J. S. L. was a saddler by trade before he chose the law. In 1874 he was elected to the General Assembly of his State by a very flattering majority vote. He was married the first time in Raleigh, N. C., December the 9th, 1874 to Miss Alice B. Thomas—married a second time, after the death of his first espouse to Miss Nannie E. Latham, his present wife, at Charlotte, N. C., July 14th, 1886. Both these lady companions were well educated, possessing culture and the most polite refinement. Emerson in one of his flashes of emotion and tenderness says: "A beautiful woman is a practical poet, taming her savage mate, planting love, hope and eloquence in all whom she approaches."

In 1881 Mr. L. was appointed by President Garfield as Deputy Collector for the Third District of North Carolina, which position he held through the administration of President Arthur when he (President A.) was succeeded by President elect Cleveland in 1885. In the summer of 1888 he was invited and solicited to accept the chair as Dean of the Law Department in Shaw University, Raleigh, North Carolina.

It affords the author pleasure to add by way of parenthesis that, in 1881, he read law with Mr. L. in his office at Fayetteville. Like the novi homines among the Romans, who were such persons as by their own personal merit, had raised themselves to curule dignitaries without the aid of family connections. It was at first addressed by Cataline to Cicero and intended as a reproach. But now in the light of a higher godly civilization 'tis a much coveted honor to be able to merit fame and fortune by one's honorable efforts. Mr. Leary enjoys all the comfort that can be obtained through prudence and integrity.

(*What is said of Professor Langston below was extracted, principally from Rev. Dr. Simmons Men of Mark.*)

HON. JOHN MERCER LANGSTON, A. B., A. M., LL. D.

Lawyer—Minister Resident and Consul-General—Charge de Affaires—President of the Virginia Normal Collegiate Institute —Formerly Dean and Professor of Law in Howard University.

One of the greatest Negroes in America is the subject of this sketch. His name has become a household word, especially among the younger generation, and his deeds shine brightly alongside of those of even older men. My personal acquaintance with him dates from the time I was a student attending Howard University, in 1870, to the present day. I remember him well as a man who did not fear to speak his opinions. In those days there were many colored men who bowed and scraped to any kind of bloated, shoddy aristocracy. We all had faith in him, and

I remember distinctly that of all the six hundred students at that time, not one could have been found who believed Langston thought himself less than the best citizen of the country. At present, however, we have to deal with his distinct acts which, developed him into the great man we now find him.

He was born in Louisa county, Virginia, December 14, 1 29, and is, in blood, Indian, Negro and Anglo-Saxon. He has the fortitude of the first, the pride of the second and the progressiveness of the third. He was born in slavery and takes, since his father was his owner, the name of his mother's family, which was Indian and Negro mainly, and was closely related to the family of Pocahontas. In this he can make the boast that he belongs to the F. F. V's. Emancipated when a mere child upon the death of his father, by his will and testament he was sent to the State of Ohio, where he grew to manhood, and was educated and pursued a professional and official life to the year 1 67.

In 1 4 he entered Oberlin College, located at Oberlin, Ohio, and graduated after five years regular collegiate study in 1849. He then sought admission to a law school conducted by Mr. J. W. Fowler at Ballston Spa, New York, but was refused admission on account of his color. He was advised to edge his way into the school, claiming he was a Frenchman or Spaniard coming from the West Indies, Central or South America, for he could pass for either, but his own manly nature scorned a trick even for success. He next tried to gain admission to a law school in Cincinnati, Ohio, conducted by Judge Timothy Walker, but he was refused here too, with the kind assurance from the Judge that he being a young colored man could not find himself at home with white scholars. That man never made a greater mistake in his life.

He was forced to seek a situation as a student in some lawyer's office, and his success in this direction was poor enough, as few white lawyers in our country were ready in 1849 to take a Negro law-student in their offices. Only the Hon. Sherlock J. Andrews, of Cleveland, Ohio, would consent to furnish Langston books with an occasional opportunity for explanation of law doctrines and principles, so that no interference was made in ordinary office business. Of course there was little accomplished in this way, and the attempt under such cruel embarrassments only served to discourage him, so he abandoned the study for a while, and entered the Theolgoical Department of Oberlin College, from which he graduated in 1853. Then he entered upon the study of law under the tuition of Hon. Philemon Bliss, of Elyra, Ohio, at the time one of the first lawyers of the Ohio bar, distinguished especially for his excellent culture, and his anti-slavery sentiments and utterances, as well as his large and commanding influence in the community. About one year later Mr. Langston appeared by order of the court for examination, with reference to his admission to the bar, before a special committee appointed by the court, composed of two Democrats and one Whig. The matter of admitting colored men to the bar was novel. No one of this class up to that time had the termerity to offer himself as a candidate for such an honor. Mr. Langston was in the lead so far as the western part of the country was concerned, but his erudition in law was so apparent, and his general knowledge, classic and scientific, so profound, that he at once won the favor of the committee; but here again was the ghost of color. "Shall a Negro or mulatto be admitted to the Ohio bar?" "Can he be, legally?" At once the answer was made to these questions in the negative and in the judicial phrase with emphasis. The old Whig member of the committee, a man of generous and manly sentiment suggested to his colleagues and the court composed of five distinguished lawyers, that it might be well in view of the late decision of the Supreme Court of the State of Ohio to enquire whether Langston was either a Negro or mulatto; "for," he urged, "Judge Bliss is taking care of his case;" whereupon the color of Langston was inquired into and when it had been decided that he had more white than Negro blood, as it was phrased, he was ordered to be sworn by the court as a lawyer, October 24, 1854. Constant and uninterrupted scholastic labors including school teaching during the winter season from 1844 to 1855, eleven consecutive years, had considerably disturbed Mr. Langston's health. At the suggestion of his physician, he went, therefore, as soon as he was admitted to the bar, upon a farm in Brownhelm, Lorain county, Ohio. This was a rich, popular, intelligent and progressive community of white people in one of the best sections of the Western Reserve. He was the only colored person residing in that part of Ohio, but he no sooner purchased his farm and settled among these good people, than he was cordially welcomed with opportunity for the employment of all the ability, legal and otherwise, which he possessed. One week, just after he had moved into this new home, a leading Democrat lawyer of the community called upon him to assist in a trial of a very important case involving several questions of possession and occupancy of land, requiring consideration and verdict of a jury. Mr. Langston was, of course, delighted with such a call, and he hastened to accept it. It was well he did so, for no man ever gained a greater advantage and more various than that which came to him from the call of his friend, Mr. Hamilton Perry. For the first time, in the fall of 1854, on a beautiful Saturday afternoon, a colored lawyer appeared in an important suit as the assistant of a white attorney. The court, the witnesses, the lawyers, except Langston, were all white. Such was the success of the colored lawyer in connection with this case that he found himself at once surrounded by numerous clients with fat retainers. From that time he grew in business and influence rapidly and solidly. The spring election in 1875 in the State of Ohio was signalized for the first time by the nomination and choice to the clerkship of one of the most advanced townships of the State, of a colored man, upon a total white vote. For the first time, too, in the history of our country, a colored man had been elected to an office of responsibilities and emoluments upon a popular choice. The fortunate colored man was Lawyer Langston. He was immediately called in view therefore to take part as one of the orators of the May meeting of the American Anti-slavery Society, held in 1855 in New York City.

The speech on that occasion was of such character in sentiment, delivery and effect as to secure its full report and publication in the daily papers of New York and the leading journals and periodicals of the Anti-slavery societies of the times. Those who heard the speech of the young orator never can forget how his first sentences were uttered. His words were these:

A nation may lose its liberties and be a century in finding it out.
Where is the American liberty?
In its far reaching and broad sweep, slavery has stricken down
 the freedom of us all;
And American slavery itself has gone glimmering into the things
 that were,
A schoolboy's tale, the wonder of an hour.

In his capacity as clerk in Brownhelm township, Mr. Langston was given special opportunities in connection with his profession, but he was, by reason of his peculiar relations to the Board of Education of the township, given special duties as regarded its common schools. Indeed he was ex-officio school visitor. In the fall of 1860, Mr. Langston was engaged in looking after the school interests of the colored youth of Ohio, organizing schools among them and supplying teachers thereof, traversing the entire State from Lake Erie to the Ohio river. When the war came, Mr. Langston signalized his conduct by loyal patriotic labors in favor maintaining the authority of the government, and although he did not go into the field as a soldier, he engaged actively in recruiting troops and did more, perhaps than any other single man to recruit the Fifty-fourth and Fifty-fifth regiments, to the latter of which regiments he gave the colors. He also recruited Fifth regiment of colored troops of Ohio, to which also he gave colors, and finally when he thought the colored American should be given the full recognition which he had won, as introduced to Secretary Stanton by General James A. Garfield, he asked of that great war officer a commission as colonel, with permission to recruit and command a colored regiment officered by colored men who had already won distinction in the service. Such proposition was taken under discussion by the government, but it was not decided in time to give Mr. Langston his commission before the war closed.

Moving to Oberlin in 1856, Mr. Langston was at once elected clerk of the township of Russia; next year a member of the council of the incorporated village of Oberlin for two years, and a member of the Board of Education in that village, successively for eleven years. In this time he became especially distinguished for his skill in examining witnessed and his eloquence and power in addressing courts and juries.

Mr. Langston was an able, bold, determined advocate using tongue, pen, and all the force of his nature and learning in behalf of the enslaved and oppressed colored Americans, demanding for them freedom, legal rights, and educational advantages. In 1867 Mr. Langston was invited by General O. O. Howard, through the influence of the Chief Justice of the Supreme Court, Hon. Salmon P. Chase, to act as general inspector of the schools of the freed people of the country. It was in July of the same year that he made his first trip southward on the errand indicated. He went entirely through the State of Mississippi on his trip, visiting and speaking in every prominent place in the South. On his return he found President Johnson declaring at the White House and through the Journals of the country, that he intended to relieve General O. O. Howard of the commissionership of the "Bureau of Freedom, Refugees and Abandoned Lands," to which he had been appointed by President Abraham Lincoln, and that he would appoint thereto Langston, if he would consent to take the place. Langston would not consent to such a change, claiming that General Howard should be retained and supported in his position, going even so far as to tell General Howard all that the President held and said against him, and tendering his services in his support, to the extent of a call upon and an argument to General U. S. Grant in his behalf. He did call upon General Grant, then Secretary of War, whom he found altogether ready and willing to hear all that could be said in General Howard's favor. In his interview with General Grant, Mr. Langston became enamored of him and made bold to say to him that the advocacy of such sentiments as he had so clearly and eloquently expressed with regard to the reconstruction, the rights, the education and the care of the newly emancipated classes, would make him the next President of the United States. General Grant was elected to the position. About this time President Johnson offered to Mr. Langston the mission to Hayti. This he declined, preferring to remain at home.

This same year, 1867, he was admitted to practice in the Supreme Court of the United States, on the motion of Hon. James A. Garfield. He continued to act as general inspector of Freedmen's schools, traveling throughout the South during the time, to 1869, when he was called to a professorship in the Law Department of Howard University. He at once became Dean of that department, organizing it, and for seven years he was at the head of what was recognized as one of the finest law schools in the country, and graduating therefrom many of the first white and colored male and female students of the law that ever went from such an institution. It was from this school, while under his charge, that the first female of the law in the world, a young colored lady, Miss C. B. Ray, of New York, was awarded a diploma. During the last two years that Professor Langston remained at Howard University he was, by especial request, made vice-president and acting president of the institution. He filled this position with such marked efficiency and success, that at the close of his first year of such service the Board of Trustees of the university conferred upon him by special arrangement and in an especial and impressive manner, with addresses by General Howard, the degree of LL. D. During this time he was appointed by President Grant a member of the Board of Health of the District of Columbia. For seven years he acted as attorney of the board and for one year as its secretary. As a sanitarist, he was able and efficient.

In 1877 Mr. Langston was appointed by President Hayes United States minister resident and consul-general to Hayti. In this position he served his country in an acceptable and conscientious manner, as the records of the State department will show, from September 1, 1877, to July, 1885, almost eight years. As a diplomat he was an entire success, and the citizens always found him ready to serve them, as well as the officers; and the people of the country, near whose government he resided, united in bearing testimony to the fact. Besides being the Dean of the Diplomatic and Consular Corps, he was most of the time while in Hayti a personal and great favorite in general society. It was as the Dean of the Diplomatic Corps that, during the yellow fever in the country when the very popular representative of the French government died of such disease, he pronounced the eulogy upon him at his tomb, in the French language, of such character and order of elegance and beauty that it found its way into the public journals of Paris and brought to him, through the French government, the acknowledgments of the family and friends of the deceased ambassador. In the government of San Domingo, was *charge de affaires* of our government, and his relation with the officers of that government, though many of the matters he had to deal with were like most of those in Hayti, difficult and trying, he won the warmest respect and consideration from all parties concerned. On the 30th of January, 1885, Mr. Langston, of his own choice, resigned the position of United States Minister resident, to President Arthur, having resolved on the expiration of his administration to return to this country and enter again upon the practice of his profession. After considerable delay, in July, 1885, he returned, and was at once employed by one of the first business houses of the country to attend to its interests in the West Indies. He made a single trip in such service, when, upon his return in the same year, he found that he had been elected by the Board of Education of Virginia, President of the Virginia Normal and Collegiate Institute, which was founded by the government in 1882, and supported by popular appropriations of twenty thousand dollars annually. The faculty, as at present constituted, is composed of ten well educated, scholarly persons, four ladies and six gentlemen. In addition to the ordinary departments and courses of study established and pursued in the institute, covering all the branches of the higher mathematics, philosophical, scientific and classical studies, the law provides for and creates a summer school for the public school teachers, which was attended at the last session by over two hundred teachers. The estimate put upon President Langston in his present position by the officials of the educational department of the government of Virginia, is discovered in the following words of the late superintendent of public instruction of Virginia, Hon. J. B Farr, in his annual report for 1885:

After considering the applications of all who presented their claims for the place, the board determined not to confine its selections to applicants, but to seek out a man that would add most dignity and weight to the position, and whether he had applied or not to tender him the appointment. After taking into consideration the education, intelligence, honesty, energy and general ability, Hon. John Mercer Langston, ex-minister to Hayti, was considered pre-eminently fitted for the great work, and the Board of Education, November 19, 1885 unanimously elected him President of the Virginia Normal and Collegiate Institute. This was done without solicitation on the part of Professor Langston or his friends. Indeed he knew nothing of it until the official announcement of the action taken by the board was made. This was one of the extremely rare cases on record where the office sought the man, and we believe the quest was well rewarded. Fortunately for his race and State, he is a Virginian by birth, and he had patriotism enough to accept the honor and assume the responsibilities of building up an institution which has in its compass the grandest possibilities, and which reaches a wide and untilled field of usefulness. President Langston's reputation is national, and he not only enjoys the highest esteem and confidence of his own people, but by his education and ability commands respect of all with whom he is thrown in contact.

The following resolutions show how the president is appreciated by those over whom he presides: At the close of his usual Thursday lecture, on the 20th of January, 1887, Professor D. B. Williams, on behalf of the faculty of the institute and its two hundred students, presented the following preamble and resolutions:

WHEREAS, The Hon. J. M. Langston, LL. D., did at a very critical period in the history of the institute, accept the presidency unanimously tendered him without his solicitation by the Honorable Board of Education at much personal pecuniary sacrifice, and

WHEREAS, He has succeeded so well not only in placing it upon a solid foundation, but is rapidly making it one of the leading institutions of the country; therefore be it

Resolved, first: That we regard our president as being fully equipped for the great work in which he is now engaged, in everything that pertains to intellectual ability, high moral purpose and religious culture.

Resolved, That his coming into Virginia as an educator has proved a great blessing to the people of the commonwealth and is indicative of great future results for good.

Resolved, That in these resolutions we voice the sentiment of the people of the State by asserting that his administration of its affairs has been entirely successful, and has caused the sons and daughters of Virginia to turn their faces toward this fountain of learning.

Resolved, That a copy of these resolutions be handsomely engrossed by the committee and presented to the president.

He is amongst the most scholarly, refined and ac-, complished gentlemen of the race. Surrounded as he is by wealth, and even luxury, he is a good parent, and owes much to his charming wife, who has been a great help to him in reaching this eminence. She has made his home pleasant and entertained his guests well, all of which goes a great distance towards a man's promotion. He has many testimonials of all kinds, that show his standing among men and testify to the worth of his character. What a beautiful picture is the engrossed resolution of the Board of Health of the District of Columbia, awarded President Langston as he took his leave of it in 1877, as the same hangs upon the wall of the broad and magnificent passage of his residence, and his certificate of life-long membership of a fellow of the great English philosophical association, the Victoria Institute, composed of the distinguished scholars and thinkers of the world. Then still how beautiful and interesting to witness the fact that a great library, law, scientific, literary, commercial, industrial, in the French, Spanish, Hebrew, Greek, Latin and English languages, gathered by him during the thirty-five years of his student life, occupying cases located in every part of his house, inside and outside the library room proper—every available nook and corner thereof.

It seems only a question of time when Mr. Langston will be made member of Congress from Virginia, and may it be so. He would be heard from on the most important questions of the day, nor would the matters pertaining to the race be neglected.

Let me close with the opinion of the Montgomery, (Alabama) *Herald*, concerning President Langston:

> It is impossible for the Fourth Virginia Congressional District to elect a man that would reflect more credit upon his constituents and race, or American statemanship, than Mr. Langston. He is undoubtedly the highest type of Africo-American citizenship. All through his long, eventful, venturous course, leaping with giant-like strides, from the valley of obscurity to the summit of human grandeur and manly excellence, not one act of his has tended to reflect dishonor upon himself, his people, or his country.

At the Republican Congressional Convention held in the Petersburg District, Virginia, in the summer of 1888,

Professor L. was duly nominated for to represent that District in the 51st Congress of the United States. At the subsequent election he was elected by a flattering majority. It is to be hoped that his life may be spared by the All-wise and immutable God, to round up a life's drama in the glorious service of his God and country.

William Patrick Mabson, of Tarboro, N. C., was born November 15, 1845, in the city of Wilmington, North Carolina. Although his mother, Eliza Mabson, was a slave, and his master-father, Geo. W. Mabson, a white gentleman of means and influence of the last above mentioned, whatever advantage could be derived from hereditory gifts and educational attainments fell to young Williams' lot. Grave and studius as he was in youth there was no school in the city, nor in the Southland, open to the colored boy or girl, yet at the age of twenty, when the fall of Fort Fisher made it possible, he entered the Lincoln University, Oxford, Chester county, Penn., which was the leading, if not the only institution of like character and facilities open to "God's image cut ebbon." In this institution he remained three years, graduating with high honor.

For twelve years thereafter he labored in the school room as teacher, training and educating something more than 3200 pupils, alternately in Rockingham, Abbottsburg, Rehobeth, Washington, Leggetts, Tarboro and other places. One hundred and fifty or more of these grateful students have reached the stage of active public service. The writer can never forget those halcyon winter days, a source of so much joy, during which were laid the foundation of serious reflection and an earnest endeavor to leave the world better than he found it.

Aside from his daily routine of business and lesson exercises, Prof. M. gave a portion of his time and talent to lecturing in different places in the State. The sentiments advanced and the inspiration, shedding forth like a halow of morning light, cherished and preserved in the mind and character of his pupils, seem also to have flowed gently into the musical mind of the poet and filled his soul with celestial fire:

> Love thou thy land, with love far-brought
>   From out the storied past, and used
>   Within the present, but transfused
> Through future time by power of thought.
>
> Make knowledge circle with the winds,
>   But let her herald, Reverence fly
>   Before her to whatever sky
> Bear seed of men and growth of minds.
>
> Watch what main currents draw the years,
>   Cut prejudice against the grain;
>   But gentle words are always gain;
> Respect the weakness of thy peers;
>
> Not clinging to some ancient saw;
>   Not mastered by some modern term;
>   Not swift nor slow to change, but firm,
> And in its season, bring the law,
>
> That from discussion's lip may fall
>   With life, that working strongly, binds,
>   Set in all lights by many minds,
> To close the interests of all.

From 1873 to 1876 he was county school examiner for the county of Edgecombe, (N. C.) certificated 200 teachers during his service as such. He held that the standard of a teacher's grade should be high in order to meet the demand of the times as well as the increased learning of the pupil and parent. In this he enjoyed the approval of all classes of citizens.

In 1872 he was elected by a handsome majority to represent the people of Edgecombe county in the State

Legislature. In which capacity he proved to be "a foeman worthy of his steel." Mr. E. Stamps, (now of Raleigh, N. C.) was his opponent. In 1874 he was elected by a majority of 2350 over H. C. Brown, the "noblest Roman" of all the Democrats of Edgecombe. Was also honored by a seat in the State Constitutional Convention of 1875.

In 1876 he was again elected, by even a larger majority than before, from the Fifth Senatorial District. In the summer of the same year he was chosen as delegate to the Cincinnati Republican National Convention which nominated Hon. R. B. Hayes for President.

Upon the recommendation of the Hon. Orlando Hubbs, then Congressman from the Second Congressional District of North Carolina, Mr. Mabson was appointed United States Ganger and was retained as such by Hon. Elihu White, Collector, as long as the National Administration remained in the hands of the Republican party.

Since his *debut* in public life, wearing well his toga of manhood, he has attended in an official capacity nearly every important convention held in his native State for the advancement of his race or party.

On the 13th of August, 1874 he married Miss Louisa Dudley, of Greenville. N. C. A bright minded son and lovely daughter adorn this propitious wedlock.

In religion Mr. M. is a Methodist. As a speaker he is clear, forcible, eloquent, when he feels the responsibility and importance of the question at issue. In this gift he has few superiors and many inferiors. A characteristic gesture is an impressive, sustained shaking of the forefinger of his right hand in the air above his head when he approaches the climax in one of his powerful appeals to his constituency. Much, indeed, is he like his older brother, Hon. Geo. L. Mabson, of Wilmington, (now no more), a gentleman of gentle birth, noble impulse, lofty bearing and a peerless intellect. This brother was the first colored man to gain admittance to the legal bar of North Carolina. He was also the honorable recipient of battle wounds and a lifelong commission in the civil service of this country. In the State Senate, 1875, March 11th on the consideration of the question of geremandering the town of Tarboro, the Hon. W. P. Mabson evinced a devotion and a statesmanship alike worthy of the man and the occasion, when he uttered the following concluding lines of his great effort in denunciation of the scheme:

"The rights of the citizens of the United States to vote shall not be denied or abridged by the United States, or by any State, on account of race, color or previous condition of servitude."

That this right will be denied if this act passes, is clear to every candid mind.

Will you infringe upon the rights of that citizenship? Will you disregard your constitutional obligations? Will you, my Democratic friends, will you trample under foot the great organic laws of the State and Nation? Will you violate the sacred oaths so solemnly made on this floor to sustain them? Will you not rather do us simple justice and thereby bind the races together in an everlasting harmony alike advantageous to both?

In conclusion. When that noble chieftain Toussiant L'Ouverture was imprisoned in the mountains of Switzerland he wrote the first Consul of France, as follows:—

"I have served my country with fidelity and probity; I have served it with zeal and courage; I have been devoted to the Government under which I was; I have sacrified my blood; I have done my duty. Sire, of your mercy, grant me justice."

So we say. We are citizens of the country; we have sacrificed our blood; we have done our duty; Sires, of your mercy, grant us justice.

Hon. Jacob C. Alman was born in the county of Marlboro, South Carolina, in the month of October, A. D., 1828.

Simon and Hannah Alman were the humble, yet noble souled parents of the subject of this sketch. They were slaves, their son Jacob, as of course, followed the condition of his parents.

Surely "the wisdom of the prudent is to understand his way." 'The good man leaveth an inheritance to his childrens' children." "He that tilleth his land shall be satisfied with his bread." "A man shall be commended according to his wisdom." "In the morning sow thy seed, and in the evening withhold not thy hand: for thou knowest not whether shall prosper, either this or that or whether they both shall be alike good."

The above Scripture appears to apply with peculiar force to Mr. Alman, for he is a large land owner of fertile land, and withal sows and reaps many thousand dollars worth annually. He is an husbandman of great diligence. These gifts and qualities have been a standing recommendation for him to his countrymen for places of honor and trust. And in the enjoyment of this status he lived and moved from the first days of his emancipation to the fall of the Republican party in the South.

In the dark days of slavery, which tried the colored man's soul, Mr. Alman hired his time from his master for $75 per annum. During which time he learned the carpenter's trade, beside the wheelwright trade and was "master mechanic" on the line of boats plying between Cheraw and Charleston. These trades served him to great advantage after freedom.

In 1868 Governor R. K. Scott appointed him County Commissioner, was re-appointed in 1870, holding this position four years. In 1872 he was nominated by the Republicans of his county and elected by the people to the House of Representatives, where he performed his duties so satisfactorily to the people at large, regardless of race or party, that in 1874 his re-nomination by his party was endorsed by the Democratic in convention and was therefore elected without opposition. 1876 found him again before the people, unimpeached, buffeted with no charge of corruption or misconduct or irregularity in office. But he suffered defeat with his party in the whole South at the hands of the Red Shirt and Mob Campaign, which is a lasting disgrace to the Christian civilization of the nineteenth century. This good man and patriot was the victim of sheer fraud and force. Notwithstanding the untimely overthrow of his political friends, he is still an undimmed star among the constellations of his race and a gentleman of parts in the estimation of all the world that knew him. Often did he bring the author into his banqueting house, and as often did his estimable family spread their banner of welcome and comfort over him, and there I "sat under his shadow with great delight and his fruit was sweet to my taste."

In 1874 he was elected by the annual conference of the Methodist Episcopal church, North, to represent the South Carolina Conference in the General Assembly which met in the city of Philadelphia, in which body of great men and measures he stood high. Mr. Alman is a devout Christian gentleman of unbending faith. His whole family are members of the church. If ever a man owed his financial success to moral suavity, piety, intelligence and honesty of purpose, it is Mr. A.

He is worth about $25,000 in money, land and stock. He is of medium size, and brown complexion, quick in movements, interesting in conversation and always pleasand in manners. Thackery says: "A hero, whether he wins or loses, is a hero," still. Such a one as Mr. Alman is the knightliest in "the field of the cloth of gold."

He is the father-head of a large, interesting, intelligent, well favored, pure-minded family of the noblest impulse. Truly "the glory of a man is his offspring," the pride of a child is its parents and "they shall rise up and call thee blessed."

His private life and public administration demonstrate so much fitness and honor, well may he be called "Jacob" being interpreted means: "a supplanter."

Warren Clay Coleman, Concord, N. C.

The sum of a nation's history is the history of the lives of her great men. The characteristic incidents of any age are but accompaniments of the lives and thoughts of the great men of that age. This position could not suggest that men of letters only have been the representatives and reflectors of the things in history that are excellent; on the contrary, we would conclude in the light of our knowledge of what has affected the history and progress of mankind, that this history and progress have been evolved by a "grit and girth" and "pith and worth" without necessarily and parantage in letters, as such.

The conclusions in this connection that are applicable to a nation or age are no less applicable to a race. A study of the progress of the races of the earth from a purely ethnologic standpoint bear abundant proof to the assertion that what men are and what men do make hidtory.

The Negro in America is not an exception to this rule. In neither this servitude nor his freedom has he been an anomaly. Like causes have produced like effects, and what the Negro was in servitude and what he is in freedom are but the natural concomitants of his condition, except that perhaps he has made more out of the circumstances of his freedom than any other people similarly circumstanced. In proof of this last observation the subject of this sketch might be cited. We may not hesitate to go to Concord, North Carolina, to look for a man who illustrates what there is in man and what there is in the Negro.

Mr. Coleman was born a slave in Cabarrus county, N. C., on the 25 of March, 1849. His boyhood was not eventful before emancipation, except it might be noted that he learned the shoemaker's trade and pursued the same to some extent in the interest of the Confederate cause. Being a minor at the emancipation, he was detained as a bound boy and was required to perform drudging work.

This doubtless contributed to arouse his ambition to find a way to better things for himself, or to resolve if he could not find a way he would make one

Mr. Coleman very easily manifested that tact in business which has characterized his success along that line in latter years.

After reaching his majority, for a while he engaged himself variously in trading and peddling and with varying results; all the while evincing an insight into business methods that was sure to gain success by being cherished and pursued.

He concluded to set up a barber shop in connection with a bakery, a somewhat novel combination, but all along the line of Mr. Coleman's nature—that is, his life must be active and reflective of perseverance. Perseverance has been a prominent characteristic of the man, and this coupled with a trustworthy intelligence has brought him the "future good, and future need."

In 1870 he went to Alabama, but returned in 1871, in the meantime receiving instruction in books from his former young master, William M. Coleman. (Name how obtained.)

After returning from Alabama, Mr. Coleman followed farming, but it was apparent his calling lay upon a more select if not a higher plane of activity; and, at the suggestion of his former young master, went in 1873 to Howard University, reaching the University at the close of the session.

The surprise which this last clause must certainly arouse would suggest that up to this time Mr. Coleman had not made sufficient acquaintance with literary affairs to know the order of school terms and sessions.

But nothing daunted, he holds on inspired by his characteristic intelligent perseverence, and enters at the opening of the next session.

His means was not sufficient and he were therefore necessitated to support or aid himself by extra service on the grounds. For this Mr. Coleman was well prepared by temperament and otherwise. He made some money while there also by selling jewelry and articles in kind. It is in the field of barter and trade that the subject of our sketch finds his most attractive and effective school, and his outside efforts were but a practical and captivating complement to the more pretentious school of letters.

To the impressions of the former school mostly by reason of necessity and probably somewhat by inclination, he yielded that he might prosecute its devious courses and attain the varied accomplishments which he now has in its many departments. He therefore returned to Concord late in 1874.

Of course Mr. Coleman found it necessary to do what most successful men have done; viz., to take to himself a helpmeet in the struggle of life, and accordingly married in the fall of 1875, in this he was not mistaken. Mrs. Coleman has been a crowning addition to Mr. Coleman's equipment which has given him the honorable and successful career which has attended him since his marriage.

He at once sought a home, and began purchasing lots and building houses. This he has continued until now Mr. Coleman carries on his regular renting list over one hundred houses. This fact speaks for itself and affords an example that should be a constant reminder and encouragement to the entire colored race. The subject of our sketch has extended his substantial acquisitions to a much wider range. He has purchased and owns excellent farms, and has equipped them with stock and other appurtenances necessary to, and characteristic of progressive agriculture. We would hold all this up to the emulation of our young men and call their attention to the fact which underlies the same, viz., Warren C. Coleman's perseverance, indomitable will and self-reliance.

In 1879 Mr. Coleman entered the field to which he is specially adapted—merchandizing. In this he was very successful; so much so that in 1885, when he was burned out, he was acknowledged to be among the foremost dealers and business men of Concord. In this fire Mr. Coleman lost outright $7,000, and the undiminished firmness with which he sustained this loss is among the historic facts of the race, He had not one cent of insurance, but the rapidity and permanent success with which he re-established himself in the same business place him among our heroes. In these statements there is no exaggeration. Mr. Coleman's steady progress and uniformly increasing popularity justify it all.

In 1881, Mr. Coleman became a stockholder in the N. C. Industrial Association, an organization for stimulating laudable endeavors among the colored people in the State along the lines of agriculture, mechanic arts and general handicap. He became at once an active member of the Association, and a large and varied conttibutor to its annual exhibits. His devotion to the good of the Association has continually promoted him on the roll of officers, filling successively the office of vice president, treasurer and president, which last he now holds with perfect satisfaction to all in any wise interested in the character and aims of the association.

Mr. Coleman's official connection with the association has been a positive gain and constant stimulo s to the organization and his re-election to the presidency bespeaks for it even a more creditable and prosperous future.

Mr. Coleman's interest in education has been no less marked than his push and consecration along other lines. He has always demonstrated a profound interest in all educational endeavors, in school or otherwise, among his people.

As part proof of these assertions the following is noteworthy: Mr. Coleman has carried one student through the full course of Howard University; one through Livingston College, and now has another in the same institution; is supporting two at Shaw University, and two at Oxford, N. C in the Orphans' Home. His contributions are to the educational uplifting of his people are manifold and important.

We have not told the full story of this remarkable man's life. Both time and space forbid. Suffice it to say that Warren C. Coleman has made his way from a very humble beginning to position and fortune. Starting out inexperienced and poorly informed, to-day his experience is by no means limited and his information decidedly above mediocre.

Starting out empty-handed, he to-day controls over one hundred thousand dollars' worth of property.

Before closing this, justice to Mr. Coleman demands that we should mention the fact that he is a man of great urbanity and hospitality, sparing no pains or reasonable expense to make his home a joy to his family and his house a home to his friends. Withal, we point to Mr. Coleman as a Negro Star of the first magnitude.

Who is the Honorable Hiram R. Revels, D. D., of Natchez, Mississippi?

He is a Race Star of the first magnitude, whose reputation and good services are not confined within any specific degree of latitude or territory, but is, rather, national and universal. He was born September 1st, 1822, in Fayetteville, North Carolina. Hedged in darkness by the black laws of his native State, he moved early in life to the State of Indiana for the purpose of improving his education where he attended the Quaker Seminary and graduated from Knox College, Galesburg, Illinois.

In 1847 he donned the habiliments of a gospel minister. After preaching and lecturing for a number of years he settled near Natchez, Miss., continuing his calling in this place until he was entrusted with the duties and responsibilities of Alderman by appointment at the hands of Governor Ames.

In 1869 he was almost unanimously chosen to represent his county in the State Senate. In January, 1870 a new feature pervaded the political atmosphere of this nation when the subject of this sketch was escorted up the aisle of the United States Senate to be sworn in as a National American Senator. This incident recalls the passed into lively remembrance when we see a proud, eagle-eyed Southern slave-holder and himself a United States Senator vacating an exalted seat that he had made obnoxious by treachery. And in order that the sisterhood of his adopted State should be recognised and restored to her place in the grand galaxy of States, a Negro Star in the person of Hiram R. Revels had to be called to give her a new voice, a new life, a new policy. He has filled many honored positions in Church and State with credit to himself, his race and country. Subsequent to the expiration of his term in the Senate he was elected by the trustees of Alcorn University, Rodney, as the president, at an annual salary of $2500.

Later on, Governor Powers appointed him Secretary of State—his service in this capacity was brief. He now rests under the bough of private life near Natchez, Miss., recuperating his health and husbanding his resources.

What can you say of Honorable George H. White, of New Berne, North Carolina?

He is one of the brightest luminaries in the legal fraternity of this, his native State. He is about thirty-seven years of age; and within a few years, comparatively speaking, has succeeded in working and thinking his way up through the environments of poverty and the meshes of ignorance to the honored position of State Solicitor and prosecuting attorney for his native commonwealth. On the criminal side of the docket, he represents the second judicial district, composed of the counties of Warren, Halifax, Bertie, Northampton, Craven and Edgecombe.

He graduated from the Law Department of Howard University in 1877 and was licensed by the Supreme Court of North Carolina in 1879 to practice law in all the courts of the State. For several years thereafter he represented alternately his county in the State Senate and House of Representatives until 1886 when he was elected Solicitor. His influence for good has long been felt and appreciated in North Carolina. As a lawyer he is brilliant, as a debater he is like a sharp cimeter, as a Representative he wears the toga of an Elliott.

Who is Hon. Mifflin Wister Gibbs, of Little Rock, Ark?

He was the first colored man who ever held a Judgeship in the United States or presided over a court of justice in this government. In 1873 he was promoted to high, dignified, judicial honors with all of its grave responsibilities by men and a party who knew of his ability and moral worth.

Born April, 1828, in the city of Philadelphia, and becoming an orphan at an early age, he wisely applied his time and attention to useful books and the great moral code. He is a business man of more than ordinary tact and talent. He is a man of considerable means, enjoying remarkable influence throughout the State.

He is a popular politician and Statesman in every sense of that term. A lover of his race, who is not afraid of lawn sleeves and "lillien skin." Public favors, and he has enjoyed many, set comely upon his brow. Long may his constellation twinkle in the effulgence of its own light, serving as a sentinel to the youth of his aspiring race.

What can you say of Honorable D. Augustus Straker, of Detroit, Michigan?

He is one of our Diamond Stars of Hope. A sparkling orb with a wide radius. Was born 1842 in the Island of Barbadoes. Kept in school after reaching the usual school age on the Islands until he graduated from the Law Department of Howard University.

A profound scholar and an able jurist. He came to America in 1868 at the request of many friends in the States, and engaged in teaching in Louisville, Kentucky. He soon after entered Howard University and graduated there with distinguished honors in 1871 from the Law Department. He has held many places of public confidence. This limited sketch will not permit me to do full justice to the subject.

Mr. Straker is a great criminal lawyer, his mental, discriminating and argumentative powers bring him their reward by crowning his efforts with success. He is an excellent orator and has delivered many lectures for the elevation of his race. He was Dean in the Law Department of Allen University and was also instructor in common law. He was nominated for Lieutenant Governor of South Carolina by the loyal Republicans of that State in the year of 1884, but was of course defeated. He had the title of LL. D. added to the title of LL. B. Columbia, S. C.

Who was Bishop John J. Moore, D. D.?

Bishop Moore was born in Berkley county, West Virginia, of slave parents, about the year 1818. His mother was born free, but at the age of fifteen years was kidnapped in Maryland and sold into slavery in West Virginia, where she married the Bishop's father, a slave. Her maiden name was Biedoubt and her husband's name was Hodge, but a change of owners caused him to adopt the surname of Moore. When the Bishop was six years old his parents by the advice and assistance of friendly Quakers attempted a flight from slavery with their six children, of whom the Bishop was the youngest.

They were recaptured, however, and the four oldest children sold South. A second attempt to gain their liberty was successful, and the Bishop's parents with their remaining two children after many hardships and sufferings reached Bedford county, Pennsylvania. Here a friendly farmer gave them employment and the two boys, William and John, were bound out for a term to his son, also a farmer. Owing to the pursuit of their former owner, the Bishop's parents were obliged to leave the settlement, but the Bishop remained secure on the farm. He was taught to read and write by his employer, and acquired a knowledge of farming. The last of his apprenticeship was served to a brother-in-law of his former master, who exacted six months over the proper time and did not furnish the schooling or clothes and cash provided by law after the expiration of the time. After leaving his ungenerous master, he worked for six months for a farmer in the settlement at six dollars per month. Having saved about fifteen dollars, he concluded to visit Harrisburg, and walked the sixty miles to that place in two days. Harrisburg opened a new world to him, and he regarded the change from his early surroundings with amazement. His small capital becoming exhausted, he sought employment and labored for several months as a hod-carrier. He then worked at hotel waiting and finally became messenger in a bank, where he remained some time, saving his earnings and making some advancement in a common education. In 1833 he became religiously impressed and experienced a spiritual change of heart.

Leaving Harrisburg, he visited his old home in the mountains, where he remained some time, having obtained employment as porter in a store. He became deeply impressed upon the subject of preaching the gospel, in 1834, and after a severe mental struggle, he yielded and returning to Harrisburg, sought and obtained exhorter's license. Nearly a year later he received a license to preach. The greatest obstacle he felt to his acceptance of the call was his illiteracy, he simply being able to read, write and cipher a little. So in 1836 and the following year he employed teachers to instruct him in English grammar, geography, arithmetic and other studies.

From the English branches he engaged in the study of Latin, Greek and Hebrew, in which he acquired some proficiency, and he has continued his earnest efforts at self-culture until the present day.

In 1839 he became connected with a body of itierant ministers composing the Philadelphia Annual Conference of the African Methodist Episcopal Zion Church. Of this conference he continued a member until 1868, when he was elected to the dignity of Bishop. During his connection with that conference he traveled on numerous circuits and filled stations in various parts of Pennsylvania, Maryland and Ohio. Crossing the Allegheny Mountains as a traveling preacher, he proclaimed life and salvation to the fugitive slaves, who had found an asylum in these mountainous regions. Among the coal and iron mines he carried the gospel on foot, walking thirty miles a day and preaching. He left Baltimore in 1852 for California, where he established several churches, one in San Francisco worth $50,-000. The colored people in this country having none which excel it. Returning to the East with his family in 1868, he was made Bishop, in which capacity he has served for fourteen years, having discharged in that office a mission to England and also to British America.

Bishop Moore has always taken an active part in contending for the rights of the oppressed of his race. While in San Francisco, he was engaged five years teaching school, during which time he represented a constituency of that city and county in three State conventions called for the purpose of securing the abolishment of the Black Laws, disqualifying colored persons to bear testimony against whites in criminal cases. He also took part in the agitation for the appropriation of school funds for the colored children. During his busy life of religious labor Bishop Moore has encountered many perils, being three times shipwrecked at sea, and among hostile Indian tribes while the bullets were flying, but he came out of all mercifully preserved for further works of good among his people.

He is author of the "History of the A. M. E. Zion Church," and is also author and editor of the "Sunday School Worker for Parents and Teachers," published and sent quarterly to the Sabbath Schools of his connection.

He speaks with the tongue of fire—a man of great mental force. Whatever of influence Hon. Frederick Douglass exercises over his race in a social and political sphere, the Bishop enjoys the same niche in the Christian church of America. He may be likened to Tycho among our Stellar divines.

Bishop Moore is a proto type of the Christian martyrs during the days of Nero, one of whose amusements was chariot racing by night in his gardens, when he dressed as a common divine. His torches were men and women of the Christian faith, whose clothing was smeared with pitch and then ignited.

At present he resides in Salisbury, N. C., and presides, as the Bishop, over the Third Episcopal District of the A. M. E. Z. branch of the greatest Methodist church in America.

(A part of the above is an extract from a sketch in the History of the Church by the Bishop himself.)

Who is Hon. Blanche K. Bruce?

He was born in old Virginia, March 1st, 1841. By dint of moral courage and native intellectual strength, he acquired character, education, national name and universal fame.

After filling many important and very responsible offices within the gift of the people as well as by executive appointment, in 1874 he was elected to the United States Senate, serving his adopted State "in the highest council of the nation" until 1881, when he was appointed by President Grrfield in 1885 as Register of the United States Treasury. The first and best colored man, so far, to hold his office. As to business qualifications, character and culture and sociability Mr. Bruce is ranked with the best families in Washington, "the city of magnificent distances."

Robert S. Rives.

This attractive generic constellation was born near Carthage, in the county of Moore, North Carolina, June 16th, 1848. At the early age of six he learned the English alphabet within about twenty minutes. He was about the same age when he heard the 23d chapter of Psalms

read, and forming quite a love for it, possessing as he did
then, and does now, a very retentive memory, this then
little sparkling star soon learned to read or repeat this
chapter "by heart." This serving as a substructure for
the form and idea of biblical expressions, his youthful gospel turn of mind soon became attached to the wonderful
teachings found in the 14th Chapter of St. John. His then
owners discovering in him an unusual aptitude for one so
young, gave him a few lessons in Webster's Speller. This
was his first instruction, notwithstanding the fact, he had
been reading quite a while in out of the way places, *sub rosa*.
Just before he was ten years of age he felt the earnest
stirrings of the spirit, whereupon he sought and obtained
pardon for his childish sins.

She who was then called mistress, took him to task
and threatened him, and thereby caused him to stop, for
several years, notwithstanding she was a member of the
Presbyterian church. Early after the surrender he turned
toward the Lord again. He then began feeling his calling
which he very distinctly felt when six years old. He
joined the church at fifteen and fil'ed every office below
the University. He married in 1870, and in 1874 joined
the North Carolina Annual Conference of the A. M. E. Z.
Convention—was sent to a very poor charge two hundred and fifty miles from home, where he received $31.00
for the year. He was therefore necessitated to teach
school, for during this period two full days passed without one morsel being eaten at his humble home (a wife
and two little boys, the eldest now a graduate from the
Normal Department of Livingstone College.

He was ordained Deacon in 1876, and Elder at Salisbury in 1878. In 1879 Bishop J. W. Hood sent him to
the Manchester Station with five other pastoral charges

under his supervision. At the same conference he was honored with the important duty of representing the Central North Carolina Conference in the General Conference which met in Montgomery, Alabama the following year. He also bore the fraternal greetings of his Conference to the S. C. Conference. His next pastoral charge was located at Statesville, N. C., after one year he was sent to Clinton Chapel, Charlotte, N. C., where he held charge for three years, duuring which time he made 3,025 pastoral calls, adding five hundred members to that church.

The church enjoyed the greatest out pouring of God's spirit we ever witnessed. During his pastorate here, he was again honored with the high duty of representing his Conference on the floors of the General Conference which met in the city of New York in 1884. During the sitting of the General Conference in New York, he had the honor of being delegated to the Central Conference which met in Baltimore, Md., in December of the same year, and by substitution had the honor of serving on the Joint Commission which met in the capital city July, 1885; and again he was elected a representative to the General Conference which met in the city of New Berne, N. C., May, 1888. During the three General Conferences of which he was a member, he was on the committee that arranged the Districts and also assigned the Bishops, and at present is a member of the Joint Commission to propose a union of the C. M. E. and the A. M. C. Zion churches.

After discharging the duties of pastor for three years in Clinton Chapel, was elected Presiding Elder and assigned to the Charlotte District of which he is now Presiding Elder.

His advantages for education have been very limited. When but a lad he spent four weeks under the tuition of Mrs. Henrietta McDonald (then Miss Hogans). She gave him $1.00 per month to teach an alphabet class of ten. After entering the ministry he preached and taught for seven years, and often studied on his knees. In 1879 he spent four months in the State Normal School at Fayetteville, N. C., and read physics under Dr. Paul Bearier, of Cabarrus, county, read theology under the instruction of Dr. J. A. Davis, then President of North Carolina College at Mt. Pleasant, N. C., and in 1884 he read Latin under the Rev. Dr Robey, of Charlotte, N. C. Church South.

Rev. R. S. Rives is a devout christian, an intelligent man, a devoted husband, and a kind father, a good provider, a safe yoeman, an energetic reformer, and an eloquent pulpit orator. May his ascending orb ere long reach the destined fullness of light, of usefulness and reward on earth and in heaven.

Nat Turner and Denmark Veazie.

Slavery seemed doomed when the thunders of a volcanic eruption broke forth in the quiet dales where the frolicsome laughter of thoughtless lasses was painfully contrasted with hideous groans of slaves smarting under the driver's whip.

In the early morn of June 16, 1821, in the crescent city of Charleston, S. C. and of August 21, 1831 on the plantations laden with golden grain, in Southampton, Virginia, the reader might have stood aloft and witnessed a second Spartacus, not in Italy, leading the slave element of Rome against the Empress of the world—possibly it would come up to the full measure of your admiration for a deliverer of an oppressed people to see the slave Toussaint l'Ouverture, of St. Domingo, dash upon the tyrant and crush him, and liberate millions of victims—fighting and conquering—almost at the self-same moment, three of the greatest military powers of the world. But it was neither of these, it was Nat Turner claiming the divine right to strike the foe of his race and human liberty. He was born in Southampton Virginia, December 2, 1800 of slave parents. Having a religious cast of mind he could all the more readily discern the sacredness of liberty and the misery of slavery—God in the one, death and hell in the other. In seclusion he sought the will of God, in the battle-ax consolation and freedom He preached and meditated over the deplorable condition of his race until he arrived at the conclusion that "he who would be free must himself strike the first blow." He prepared himself and compatriots as best he could under the circumstances for the event. On the 21st of August, 1831, Nat Turner suddenly appeared like a fiery comet in the Southern sky, shocking the whole slave power in America, slave drivers and masters fell like autumn leaves before his merciless blade. His coadjutors also lay prostrate around him. Finally he was captured and executed. He died as he lived, brave, consciencious, by contending for justice and the unconditional liberty of his people. Turner was 31 years of age when he was hung.

Denmark Veazie was 36 years old when he was exected. Veazie was born on one of the islands, St. Thomas, near Charleston, and who by great frugality, purchased his freedom. To effect the freedom of his race he thought it wisdom to set fire and the sword to do their destructive work on the 16th of June, 1822. He was not successful, however, in keeping his counsel. It was rumored that an insurrection among the slaves was to begin at a certain time, whereupon the whole city, state and nation became aroused. Veazie was executed together with 135 others, unlike l'Ouverture he failed and submitted to fate, as did Spartacus before, and Nat Turner afterwards. These heroes left in their names monumental history and their mission, to free their people, in the hands of posterity and a Christian civilization.

Hon. Frederick Douglass, LL. D.

Mr. Douglass' life career shines like an orb of surpassing brilliancy, ever glowing with the unadulterated lustre of a crystal gem of the first water. All along from his flight from bondage to the end of his eventful life and remarkable services and successes will form one proud "milky way" running through the history of this country.

It is said that no man in France, not even the Cæsars or Napoleons ever did a more daring act than Billand Varennes when he took his life in his hands and marched down the aisle and into the tribune to accuse Robespierre. It was the courage of the gambler, the soldier and the orator united in one man. He won, and the reign of terror ceased from that moment.

Mr. Douglass bearded the lion of slavery in his den—fought the slave power until he agitated the whole North, enlisting in his cause mighty minds, akin to his own. Victory only satisfied his patriotic heart—a victory that set every slave at liberty and inaugurating him into our American citizenship.

As an orator and statesman, he is one of the foremost men in the United States. He was for a number of years the Moses of the colored race of America. Sometime in the year of 1817 Frederick Douglass was born on the eastern shore of Maryland. His mother and grandmother were both slaves, while his father and grandfather were free men. His mother was one of those strong-minded, virtuous, loving women. "All that I am my mother made me" applies to Mr. Douglass as well as to J. Q. Adams, ex-President of the United States. "When God sets out to make a great man He first makes a great woman." It is sufficient to say that Mr. Douglass, rising to the sublime of power and oratorical beauty and strength, is simply the prototype of his mother. In the matter of oratory and eloquence he has no equal, and certainly not a superior in this country.

The author cannot do the subject of this sketch full justice in this small volume; he will, therefore, refer the seeker after truth to larger works on the life and services of Mr. Douglass.

After running away from the shambles of slavery he reached New Bedford, Mass, where he married and entered the Christian ministry in A. M. E. Z. church at that place. He almost instantaneously enlisted in the lecturefield against the institution of slavery. He canvassed the public mind throughout the Northern and New England States. To him more than any other one man, living or dead, is due the war for the freedom of many millions of blacks. For some time he edited a newspaper, "The North Star," in New Bedford and subsequently in Washington City, D. C. During his remarkable career he has been appointed on several commissions of a national character, one of which was the San Domingo commission in 1872.

In 1877, he was appointed Marshal of the District of Columbia by President Hayes, which position he held and honored for four years. Upon the inauguration of President Garfield he was appointed to the office of Recorder of Deeds for the District of Columbia. When Mr. Cleveland was seated as President of the United States Mr. Douglass resigned, whereupon Mr. J. M. Trotter, of Boston, was appointed to succeed him. In 1883 he was elected President of the National Convention held in Louisville by the representative colored men of this country. At the National Republican Convention held in Chicago in 1888 he received, unsolicited, a number of votes for the Presidency of the United States.

The name of Frederick Douglass is sounded in clarion notes on land and sea, far and near. His voice during the ever memorable and exciting days when the abolition of slavery was agitated, was heard, full of majesty and power. It broke flinty prejudices of unwilling minds, just as the mighty winds bend before it the tall cedars of Lebanon, subdued and converted their deep-seated and well fixed convictions as completely as did Paul, when he turned the burning edge of Roman hatred and then converted, by the power of divine speech, the 276 souls on board a ship of Alexandria after the calm of a fourteen days tempest and the Euroclydon of destruction in obedience to his sweet voiced lullaby of prayer had driven its mad, mountain waves to rest, to shame, to hide beneath the bleak shores of Adria.

His eloquence edified friends and admirers—it even divided the wall of fire flames of opposition and in the breach led freedom's hosts through. His intelligent and bold exposition of truth and justice for his race shook formidable arsenals and rallied two continents to his support. His 45 years of great efforts are so many general legacies to his appreciative race. In company with such men as Wendell Phillips, Charles Sumner and others of like mould, he was an intellectual giant among giants. And as Joshua stood at the head of Israel on the plains of Gibeon and pittied his men against the combined armies of five kings, appealing to even sun, moon and stars to help him, so Douglass marshalled the party of liberty and returned with Cæsar's motto wove into his standard, "I came, I saw, I conquered."

To this age and race the Lord gave Douglass. When in the future the dark shadow shall have entered his doorway and undone the silver cord and broken the golden bowl, or the pitcher at the fountain, and the wheel is broken at the cistern, there will be a vaccuum in the galaxy of earth's greatest thinkers, workers and reformers. Who will fill the void?

Who was the Honorable Abraham Hanson?

He was, in May 1862, Commercial Agent of the United States in Monrovia. In December 1863, he was appointed by President Lincoln, as Commissioner and Consul General of the United States to the Republic of Liberia, West Africa. He interested himself in whatever tended to extend and strengthen the commercial and friendly relations between these two countries. Such a negotiation as this is the greatest and most important in national economics. In some respects, it is a Christian movement, establishing humanity, civilization and brotherhood, as well as a commercial union. It often obviates bloody wars between nations, thereby making the consul the most worthy of patriots and living martyrs.

Alexandre Dumas.

A French novelist, was the son of the Republican general. Alexandre Davy Dumas, who was himself the offspring of the marquis Davy de la Pailleterie and a negress. His father died when he was quite a child. He was born at Villers Cotterels, 24th July, 1803. At the age of 20 he went to Paris to seek his fortune, where he received the appointment in the household of the duc d'Orleans, in 1826 he first appeared as an author in a volume of *Nouvelles*, but it was not until 1829 when his historical drama, "Henri III, et sa cour" was brougnt upon the stage that his genius commanded the admiration of the literary world. It would require many pages to enumerate all the productions which have been issued under the name of Alexander Dumas. His best known works are "Les Trois Mousquetaires" (8 vols. 1844) "Le Comte de Monte Cristo" (12 vols. 1841-45) "La Reine Margot" (6 vols. 1845) and "Memoires." He died December 5th, 1870, but his son bearing the same name as his father, was born in Paris, July 28th, 1814, he is a celebrated writer also. Mr. Dumas was installed as a member of the French Acadamy in 1875.

He writes in his shirt sleeves and is said to be the richest author in the world.

> Blest indeed is he who never fell,
> But blest much more, who from the verge of hell,
> Climbs up to Paradise. — *Bayard Taylor.*

Rt. Rev. W. F. Dickerson, D. D.

In writing the life lesson of this Reverend Doctor, the author cannot do better than to adopt the report of the Committee on Obituary, composed of Revs. J. G. Fry, G. W. Hunter, Robt. Lucas, W. H. Bishop and B. W. Morris, at the Annual Conference of the A. M. E. Church held at Company Shops, November 25th, 1885:

To the Bishop and Conference:

Dear Father and Brethren: We, your Committee who were appointed on Obituary, beg leave to report the following:

Bishop William Fisher Dickerson, D. D. departed this life, December 20th, 1884, in the City of Columbia, S. C. He was born in Woodbury, New Jersey, January 15th, 1844. In early manhood he entered the ministry of our church, a member of the New York Conference, in which he rose rapidly to eminence as a preacher. His fame as a preacher spread far and wide, and he was in constant demand on all grand occasions. If I may estimate the intellectual character of Bishop Dickerson, his power of application was enormous. His information was remarkable for its accuracy and the ready command which he had acquired; He weighed the force of words; their origin and meaning was duly considered. His logical power was of the highest order, his grasp like that of a vise. With these transient gifts he combined the natural expression of strong common sense. Many of his social and moral qualities were of the best character. His companionship was gentle, neither stiff nor haughty. He was as humble and simple in his manner as a child His conversation and manners were always characterized by good nature. Candor was one of his characteristic traits. He was unselfish. He lived for others. He was devoted to his wife and children. He was liberal towards his friends. No service was too much for him to perform to render his visitors comfortable. He was loved and reverenced by many of the members of this Conference. We have no doubt his last words, "I want rest, or need rest," was not only rest from his labor which characterized his work as a Bishop in the African Methodist Episcopal Church, but that rest which remains for the people of God, "where the wicked cease from troubling, and the weary are at rest."

Who is Hon. P. S B. Pinchback?

He is a native son of Virginia, manumitted when quite a child by his master-father and sent to Gilmore's High School in Cincinnati. It is foreign to the design of this work to give lengthy biographical sketches of the subjects enumerated in it, therefore, the reader should not look for all that might be said of this distinguished Negro-American.

It is sufficient for the lesson the author desires to teach to say that Hon. P. B. S. Pinchback moved up from the cabin of a slave to the giddy heights of a wealthy gentleman, a lawyer, eminent politician, Governor, Lieutenant Governor and United States Senator from the great State of Louisiana. He was born May 10, 1837. He came up through every official gradation of honor and trust. He is a man of rare mental powers—a born ruler of men and an honor to his race and country.

For several years he was editor of the "Louisianian," a live organ, emitting light, learning to the cosmopolitan class of the readers and infusing and inspiring patriotism into the heads and hearts of enemies as well as friends. He also had the honor of filling many civil stations of life for his State, creditable alike to himself, his race and his adopted commonwealth. Never has his records been blackened with even a charge of corruption, while his private life exhibits the glory of man.

Who is the Hon. Richard H. Gleaves?

From 1872 to 1876 he was Lieutenant Governor of the State of South Carolina. During the Republican regime in that State he was a conferee above reproach and "a foeman worthy of his hire." He went out of office in the great Southern political revolt in 1876. Himself and Governor Chamberlain, the best Governor the State has been blessed with since the war and the last one she has had by the popular vote since 1876, were fraudulently counted out by "Red Shirts and shot-gun aristocracy." President Hayes, administration was the origination and chief impetus to this wholesale fraud and usurpation against lawful authority, peace and dignity of the State. Surely "an honest man is the greatest work of God," is written all through the private and official life of Lieutenant Governor Gleaves.

Francois Dominique Toussaint, surnamed L'Overteur, was born at Buda, in St. Domingo, in 1747. The distinguished Wendell Phillips spoke of him thusly: (which is a sufficient laurel to wreathe his brow as the World's Greatest Liberator and Martyr.)

"Hayti, from the ruins of her colonial dependence, is become a civilized State, the seventh nation in the catalogue of commerce with this country, **inferior in morals** and education to none of the West Indian Isles. Foreign merchants trust her courts as willingly as they do our own. Thus far, she has foiled the ambition of Spain, the greed of England, and the malicious statesmanship of Calhoun. Toussaint made her what she is. In this work there was grouped around him a score of men, mostly of pure negro blood, who ably seconded his efforts. They were able in war and skilful in civil affairs, but not, like him, remarkable for that rare mingling of high qualities, which alone makes true greatness, and insures a man leadership among those otherwise almost his equals. Toussaint was indisputably their chief, courage, purpose, endurance, these are the tests. He did plant a state so deep that all the world has not been able to root it up.

I would call him Napolean, but Napolean made his way to empire over broken oaths and through a sea of blood. This man never broke his word. "No retaliaiation" was his great motto and the rule of his life; and the last words uttered to his son in France were these: "My boy, you will one day go back to St. Domingo; forget that France murdered your father." I would call him Cromwell, but Cromwell was only a soldier, and the state he founded went down with him to his grave. I would call him Washington, but the great Virginian held slaves. This man risked his empire rather than permit the slavetrade in the humblest village of his dominions. You think me a fanatic to-night, for you read history, not with your eyes, but with your prejudices. But fifty years hence, when truth gets a hearing, the muse of history will put Phocion for the Greek, and Brutus for the Roman, Hampden for England, Fayette for France, choose Washington as the bright, consummate flower of our earlier civilization, and John Brown, the ripe fruit of our noon-day, (thunder of applause,) then dipping her pen in the sunlight, will write in the clear blue, above them all, the name of the soldier, the statesman, the martyr, Toussaint L'Overteure."

Who was Zerah ?

He was an Ethopian king and warrior who commanded, at one time, a million men, see Chron. XIV, 9:15. He was the terror of Judah which he invaded, B. . , but was baffled by Asa.

What can you say of Rev. Addison Quick?

While yet he has barely reached the full statue of physical manhood, few abler and more earnest men in the church and race work can be found South of the "Mason and Dixon" line than the Rev. A. E. Quick, pastor of the Wesley, M. E. Church, of Beaufort, South Carolina. The dual essentials of a worthy public man—oratory and capacity for the work assigned or chosen—are not often blended in the person of one individual, but estimated on that basis, Rev. Quick stands out preeminently one of the strong leaders among the disciples of the M. E. Conference, North, and in the recorded deliberations of the body of spiritual and intellectual giants, since his connection therewith, his mind and work are deeply impressed.

He was born of slave parents, December 31, 1857, in Richmond county, N. C. Who Janus-like was born facing the old and the new history of time and men at one and the same moment. His father, John Quick, was a carpenter by trade and hired his time from his master, Benjamin Quick, of Marlboro Co., S. C., giving $300.00 a year for himself. His mother was a seamstress and belonged to Dr. C. C. Covington, near Rockingham, N. C. Elizabeth Quick, his mother, is a noble souled woman, and inspired her offspring by prayers to God and filial devotion, to befit themselves for honorable, happy and useful lives. His father died when the young preacher was three years of age. There was nothing eventful in his career as a boy, but he was always of a religious turn of mind. About the year of 1877 he was converted and joined the A. M. E. Z. Church at his old home at Rockingham. Here he attended the public schools until he entered the State Normal at Fayetteville, N. C., in 1874.

In this institution he was a favorite with both students and teachers; his Chesterfield-like manners, gentlemanly bearing won for him the confidence and good will of all who knew him. In 1884, December 16th, he married Miss L. A. Alman, a lady of high intellectual attainments, and connected himself with the Methodist Episcopal Church, North. After thus preparing himself for the work of life in his Master's vineyard, he entered the Grammar School of Theology at Atlanta, Georgia. He is in no sense inclined to politics save and except wherein the moral and mental development of his race are sought.

He has written and published several sermons by the request of his church, which disquisitions have been commented upon in the most flattering and praiseworthy language by the press and divines. Note the following editorial found in one of the leading white journals of the State:

"Wesley M. E. Church, Beaufort, was filled to overflowing Sunday evening last, it having been previously an-

nounced that the pastor, Rev. A. E. Quick, would at that time preach a sermon to the mechanics of the town. Promptly at half-past eight o'clock the pastor began by selecting for the subject of his discourse the 13th verse of the 44th chapter of Isaiah. To say that the subject was ably handled is but to faintly express it. * * * *
Mr. Quick is but 30 years old, and judging from the progress made by him within the the past two years, he bids fair to become famous both as a logical reasoner and an elegant preacher."—*The Palmetto Post*

On Decoration Day in Beaufort, May 30th 1887, the city was crowded with visitors, military and civil, from all the principal towns and cities of South Carolina and Georgia. After a long and imposing procession the surging mass of grateful citizens came to a quiet around the graves at the National Cemetery. The speaker arose amidst this wealth of heroic hearts and floral offerings and said something that melted the eyes of that vast audience into trickling tears and shouts of joy.

The Sea Island News, published at the same place, speaking of it said:

"Rev. E. A. Quick made a most excellent address that was listened to with the greatest interest. We are sorry we have not space for it but to supply the general demand we give the following extracts:

Mr. President, Ladies, Fellow Citizens and Soldiers :

"Perhaps no one cause of itself could assemble so many of us together as that which now demands the attention of this hour, it is a right or privilege accorded to all men to contribute respect to the dead in some measure. And to-day in obedience to this sacred trust imposed the adjacent cities and towns, the islands and mainland assemble with flowers in hand to wreathe the graves of the past. The highest and most illustrious pride of any Nation or people is its manhood, and especially when this manhood makes life a sacrifice on the bloody altar of the battle in the throwing off the yoke of oppression, tyranny, and despotism. To the brave and noble-hearted, death is always preferable to oppression.

"To-day while this vast multitude of loyal citizens meet to pay their annual homage of respect to the dead heroes of the past, we have met to consecrate ourselves anew to the filial duty. National pride, and common faith that binds 35,000,000 sons of liberty to the altars of the battle-field. We have not met to revive the feelings of the institution of slavery; that institution that covered the pilgrims' land with human carnage; that placed in the hands of Southern Molochs the rod of iniquity polished with stigma and oppression. No, we do not wish to revive these feelings so prevalent in the beginning of this century. No, it shall not go forth that we of this age rejoice in the return of night, but that we rejoice with feelings of a higher pride and better ideas, that characterize an honest and progressive people. Twenty-five years of intellectual growth have narrowed us in our once bitter feeling toward our oppressors. We learned that progress travels not with prejudice. We have grown broader in brotherhood and feelings to the common interest of our countrymen. We would celebrate that faith and courage which made every slave a freeman and citizen, and united a once divided country, with one common interest and feeling.

"Fellow citizens, we are one as American people whatever our feelings of the past have been, we are bound together, white and colored, rich and poor by the blood of these sleeping braves. We are united by one mighty cable of three powerful cords, interest, necessity and common humanity. And so connected by these elements irrespective of color or race that to separate would paralize our country in its development in every possible way and that without remedy. In answer to this broad question a thousand times put, has the colored man any claim on the progress of this country?

"I shall not say his country until his claim is acknowledged. Now, being to the manner born I am free to handle him just as he stands. First, I wish to ask the question, has he contributed anything to the enterprise of this country; if so, in what way? I answer, as a voluntary representative that he has and does contribute alone to the South by his labor in various ways, at least 85 per cent. to her enterprises. He contributes to the material growth of our country through the railroad enterprises, for 85 per cent. of the roads were constructed by him. There is hardly a foundry in the South that has not colored labor in it. Even in the various mines of the South and West, coal, iron and gold are worked by the man of color, perhaps not because they want him to have a place, but because no one can do his work. All of the phosphate mines are run by colored labor; even some of the departments of these mines are controlled by colored men who show considerable skill in the management of the business, and move things with marked facility. The machine shops through the South are partially filled by colored laborers; of course they do the coarser work, but from a cause that presents itself all along the line of color, to allow him a higher place would warrant a strike and clear every shop that has in it a white face. He fires all of the engines of the South, from the stationary to the flying locomotive, and is often the better workman or engineer of the two; but to promote him would be to violate the order of the day, and thus allow the claim of a fairer one. He is certainly the smith and carpenter of the South and West; he is as a manufacturer or producer to the South what the white man is to the North. Masonry, carpentry, and working of iron in ancient times fill quite a page in the history of culture and civilization, the stroke of the painter's brush was among the highest arts in the days of antiquity.

Now, whatever these arts or callings are to the development of this country determines the colored man's contribution to the various enterprises of this country, since he is prime in these departments of work. In these humble, but powerful and indispensible contributions, he is in the interest of his country, in labor, what ancient Greece and Memphis were in literature and art to the world.

The following is an extract from a sermon preached by the subject of this sketch and published afterwards at the urgent request of friends and officials of his church, May, 2d Sunday, 1888. Subject—"The Glorious Ascension of Christ."

The Rev. A. E. Quick took for his text Luke 24—51— "And it came to pass, while he blessed them, he was parted from them and carried up into heaven." * * * * * *

The minister said: This wonderful scene closes the long list of miracles accorded by the Saviour during his visit to the earth, yet no tongue can tell the number of miracles performed by him through all ages, before this his advent, or even after, since every act of grace and conversion is a miracle, as it is not, and never will be, understood by us. Forty days had elapsed since his resurrection, a sufficient time to establish the claim of it. He had appeared at the fisheries, and ate with his disciples, and had appeared in their meeting while they worshipped, and with his own hands and feet, fresh from the print of nails, his pierced side and thorn-pressed brow, dispelled the doubts of Thomas. Having satisfied his disciples as to his claims in every possible respect as their Lord and Master, and having accomplished the great work of redemption, he must return to His Father's Kingdom, and, in accordance with a promise to his disciples to prepare them a place, he had selected as the place of his departure one of prominence and historic fame, Olivet, the pleasure ground of the city populace, that beautiful hill overlooking the city of Jerusalem, a place where afterwards the Roman army encamped, and where the invincible cavalry of Pompey had rested beneath its shades. This was the hill over which the Egyptian infantry swept on their way to the city. The Monarch of Babylon surveyed his legions from this summit as they marched along its base, and over the same paths led captive the three fireproof children with his invincible and prophetic Daniel. Ten thousand Jews had laid down their lives on this ground in defence of their city against Rome. Certainly no spot in Asia is more memorable for events, and certainly not more noticeable when we learn that it was this place the blessed Master chose as the last spot of ground upon which to rest his feet, and from which to show his last form on earth; no more to walk through here with his disciples from Bethany, or to the house of Mary and Martha; no longer the place of agony and prayer for him; but a glorious scene that shall eclipse the past history of Olivet—for the glorious ascension of our Saviour! Here upon this hill Titus delivered his lengthy address to his soldiers for the final struggle and capture of the city. His soldiers thus being animated from here, pressed even to the Temple, and swept the castle. But it is more than historic to us when we think of it, and associate with our memory faith in the event, it becomes life to us. From this hill went forth the irrevocable command to the disciples to go into all the world and preach the gospel to every creature, and to baptize them in the name of the Holy Trinity, and the eternal promise, "I am with you always." The church received its commission from here. Then what a place in our hearts it should fill. France can boast of her Austerlitz, England of her Waterloo, America of her Bunker Hill, and the Union of her Appomattox; but, thank God, the world may boast of her Mount Olivet.

The disciples and friends of Christ had gathered to this place for the final farewell. Anxious spectators moved along and added to the crowd awaiting the satisfaction of some curiosity. The hum of the busy city is lost in anxiety. The crowded streets and thoroughfares of the ancient capital of the religious world did not attract His followers; but, electrified by His counsel and presence, they were absorbed in Him.

While invoking a heavenly benediction upon them, suddenly a supernatural brilliancy enveloped Him; a chariot of celestial cloud swings at His feet and settles in midair, and, enshrined in matchless glory, He mounts the cloud, and upward through the trackless ether he makes his way. Sun, moon and stars are left behind in his flight, till lost to finite eye. Enraptured with his wonderful ascension, his disciples stand gazing upward till an angel returns to satisfy their wonder.

Returning to heaven as the conqueror of death, hell and the grave, he stands at the gate and cries, "Lift up your heads, oh, ye gates, and be ye lifted up, ye everlasting doors, and let the king of glory come in!" The watchman swings wide the gate, and, amid the shout of cherubic legions the God of armies and the King of kings marches in, and upon that undivided, eternal and indescribable throne takes his seat forever.

* * * * * * * * * * * * *

Who was St. John Chrysostom, the Mouth of Gold?

He was a great philosopher and divine, surnamed "Mouth of Gold" from the sublime splendor of his eloquence. He was born at Antioch in 347, (A. D.) His mother, Anthusa, was a pious woman, wholly devoted to her son, who grew up under her loving instruction in an earnest, gentle and serious youth, passing through none of those wild, dark struggles with sinful passions which left an ineffaceable impress on the soul of St. Augustine and gave a sombre coloring to the whole of his theology. He died Sept. 14th, 407 A. D. His works are very numerous. Of these the most valuable as well as the most studied are the Homilies which are held to be superior to every thing of the kind in ancient christian literature.

He was the first christian Bishop under the new gospel dispensation. Poet Edwin Johnson comes from the market-place in a drama between Paulus and Glaucus and converses as follows:

Paulus. Whence is this preacher whom the general voice declares a new Demosthenes?

Glaucus. 'Twas here in Antioch his youthful years were spent; not heedlessly, like our, but hovered o'er with love and counsel, as with angel wings. Like Samuel in the temple, he grew up a priest; the robe his saintly mother wrought of pure example and of precepts wise investing him. Of older men he seemed the natural ruler; but refused to wear the name of bishop, and retired, when death had ended filial duty, to the cell and cave. And now as one who wandered far to rob the hills and strain the streams of gold, returns to spend his princely store, so he comes back to utter words so affluent with wisdom and with grace. The multitude proclaim him Chrysostom, *the Golden Mouth.*

* * * * * * * * * * * *

For my apology hear him thyself. A giant not in statue, if in mind. Nor are his words as blows to break the will. But rather rays that melt the feelings, fire the purpose, and consume the dross of self. But yesterday the great assembly stood responsive to each glance his eye shot forth.

"The changing thoughts that fell, like light and shade,
Upon his lips, or lent his voice its tone."

The celebrated Dr Talmage classed him thus in a sermon on *Christ's Garden*: "There are others planted in Christ's garden who are always ridiant, always impressive—more like the roses of deep hue that we occasionally find, called "giants of battle"—the Martin Luthers, St. Pauls, Chrysostoms, Wickliffs, Latimer's and Samuel Rutherford. What in other men is a spark, in them is a conflagration, when they sweat, they sweat great drops of blood. When they pray, their prayer takes fire. When they preach it is a penticost. When they fight it is a Thermopylæ, and when they die it is a martyrdom."

Who is Joseph C. Price, D. D.?

He is a native North Carolinian and is honored with the presidency of Livingstone College, Salisbury, N. C., which he, in a measure, founded under the auspices of the A. M. E. Zion Church connection. He was born in Elizabeth City, February 10th, 1854. His father was a slave while his mother was free. Early in life he took to books, encouraged by his noble, womanly hearted mother, he advanced to the front rank of scholarship.

After regular attendance upon the Cyprian Episcopal School at New Berne, N. C., under the control of a Boston

Society, to wit: The Lowell Normal School of the first named place. After teaching public schools at various places in this State, he entered Shaw University, Raleigh, N. C., in 1873. Upon being converted to the christian religion he felt to be under some divine impulse to carry the gospel to a wicked world. Following its silent, yet salient behest he returned to his home in New Berne and connected himself with the A. M. E. Z. church. In 1879 he graduated from Lincoln University, delivering the valedictory in the college department. At the annual conference of the A. M. E. Z. church for North Carolina, he was ordained elder and elected as a delegate to the general conference held at Montgomery, Alabama, in 1880.

At the Ecumenical Conference in the city of London, where he had gone as a delegate he made a very fine impression upon the members of that great body of great men and women by his masterful efforts as an orator and debater.

Notwithstanding the length of the following arcicle which we find in a leading Tennessee Journal, (white) the *Cumberland Presbyterian*, we shall append it as a worthy, yet cursory description of his magnetic, intellectual and oratorical powers:

"During the late prohibition campaign in Tennessee the most eloquent and effective address we had the pleasure of hearing was delivered by the Rev. J C. Price, of North Carolina. Mr. Price is a full-blooded negro, whose face is so black that gas will not light it up. He was educated in Lincoln University, Pa., where he spent seven years in the study of literature and theology. He is but thirty-three years of age. He has had the advantage of foreign travel and much observation in his own country. He is a man of noble presence and manly bearing. Every feature of his dark face and every movement of his powerful frame indicate strength of character and force of intellect. His ease and dignity of manner would do honor to any man. Before an audience he is a marvel of eloquence. His voice is as musical as a lute, and his speech as pure as that of the classic Everett. His manly presence, his ease and grace, his keen and pungent wit, his brilliant and glowing sentences, and his intense earnestness place him high among the great orators of the age. All who heard him speak in this State will bear testimony to the truth of what we say of this wonderful man. His appeals to his own people were never surpassed, and we doubt if any man ever made a more powerful appeal to any people than he made to his race in this great struggle. He sees that rum is the especial enemy of the black man, and with the ardor and passion of a strong and powerful nature he pleads with his race to show their manhood and rise above the temptations which threaten to lead the negro to ruin. His arguments are original, his illustrations striking and apt, his diction magnificent and his enthusiasm overpowering. Thousands of the most cultivated and prominent people in Tennessee were thrilled by the great orator, and it was the universal verdict that no man could surpass his efforts to enlighten and influence his race. We have heard nearly all the great temperance orators from John B. Gough down, and we have yet to hear the man who can speak the English language more persuasively or more powerfully than the Rev. J. C. Price. It is simply impossible to give any adequate account of the man's eloquence. Mr. Price is an honor not only to the negro but to the human race. You can count on the fingers of one hand all the orators in the United States who can be ranked in the same class with this sable son of Africa."

 The author of these pages had occasion to write the editor of the *Star of Zion*, August, 1886, concerning Dr.

Prices, speeches in the towns of Wadesboro and Rockingham, N. C. Here is an extract:

The wonderful reports of his oratory—the lively incidents and energy of his personal history—his being entirely negro, too, taken together with the further fact that he is a native of North Carolina—all conspired to produce a stronger desire to hear him.

An aggregate of about six hundred upturned faces, dumbfounded, awe-struck, captivated, beaming forth with manifestations of approval, was a sight not often seen hereabouts. Prof. Price is most assuredly an able man, and without offense to any one, he is *sui generis*. In his work and speeches with the people he is achieving a higher, grander state-craft of national benefit than the whole army of average coffee-house politicians could or would in a decade of centuries (who as a rule, seek office merely for the dear people's sake).

He towers high among the champion orators of this or any other age of American history. Indeed he is our orator. I admire him for his sterling ability and indomitable moral courage. I honor him for historical truths and race pride, and I love him for what he is and for all that he has done and is now doing for our race and the whole Southland in general. As Mr. Price descended from the rostrum a noted white lawyer of this place stepped forward and grasped his hand and said: "Mr. Price when I had listened, enraptured two or more hours, I expected to see you fag or exhaust, but at that moment and to the close, you rose higher, like the mounting lark wafted in the wealth of her own music, turning ever and anon on wings of fresh delight." On Thursday night he spoke in Rockingham to an unusually large, appreciative audience, including some of the profoundest jurists and ablest divines in the State. Here he was particularly happy in his masterly effort, vanquishing every fear and every power rousing into life and action. His was in the highest degree instructive, beautiful, and impressive—*tres atque rotundas*—like all the productions of that finished orator, which can best be comprehended, for there is no truer or worthier description than to call it "Websterian." "His manner of speech," as Lord Bacon said of the king, "was indeed prince-like, flowing as from a fountain, and yet streaming and branching into nature's order, full of facility and felicity, imitating none and inimitable by any. 'Tis idle for me to add that his style is charming, elocution perfect, and his voice delightfully musical, his argument overwhelmingly established the claims advanced for his race.

CHAPTER XII.

LEGAL FRATERNITY.

"We have turned our backs upon the past;
We stand in the present and look to the future.
The past is lost to us, the future is ours,
Let us make it a glorous one!"

"May we discern, unseen before
A path to higher destinies."

Who was General Robert Brown Elliott?

He was a colored Statesman, born in Boston, Massachusetts, August 11th, 1842. He received his primary education at private schools. In 1852 he entered High Holborn Academy in London, England. In 1855 he entered Eton College, England and graduated in 1859, studied law and practiced his profession until his untimely death. He was a member of the State Constitutional Convention of South Carolina in 1868. He held a seat in the House of Representatives of the same State from July 6th, 1868 to October 23d, 1870, and was appointed March 25th, 1869 Assistant Adjutant General, which position he filled until he was elected to the 42d Congress, and was again elected to the 43d Congress by a large majority. He died in New Orleans August 9th 1884, where he was in the service of the Treasury Department of the government.

It was a vigorous application of the "eternal fitness of things" that prepared General Elliott for the higher destinies of life. He leaped forward and "bearded the lion in his den." He chose the bar with the view of standing, like an armed knight, between his oppressed people and the cupidity of the courts. The law furnishes an arena for the pyrotecnic pisplay of one's talents. As a lawyer he was true, faithful, constant, honorable in the discharge of duty—a typical lawyer. He was the first colored Attorney General in the United States, to which position he was elected in 1876 in and for the State of South Carolina. His comely form and genteel manners won for him pleasant allusions, his wise conclusions on questions of law and State economy challenged the admiration of the forum as well as the National Congress. As a lawyer he was without a superior in the Southland.

Well might Shakespeare write of such a genius:

"His life was gentle and the elements
So mixed in him that nature might stand up
And say to all the world,
This is a man."

In the case of the impeachment of Judge Montgomery Moses, Gen. E. said: "The law-abiding sentiment of the people is the vital force of the body-politic. Among all civilized nations, and in every age, the purity of the Judicial tribunal has been an object of profound solicitude, and has been invested with the most carefully considered safeguards, and the one without which all others are as "sounding bras and tinkling symbols" is found in the spotless purity of the Judge.

On January 6th, 1874, when the House of Representatives had under consideration the Civil Rights Bill, he rose to the full heighth of manhood as he proclaimed amidst a large, intelligent body of European and American Diplomats and Congressmen, while the world gazed upon him as the ablest negro defender in a legislative capacity: "I regret, sir, that the dark hue of my skin may lend a color to the imputation that I am controlled by motives personal to myself in the advocacy of this great national justice. Sir, the motive that impels me is restricted by no such narrow boundary, but is as broad as your constitution. I advocate it, sir, because it is right. The bill, however, appeals not only to your justice, but it demands a response from your gratitude." In this new position he very early gave evidence of his ability as a skilful parliamentarian, and a ready debater as well as a legislator. Mr. D. A. Straker says of him: "In his speeches his logic was forcible, his propositions sound and his arguments conclusive; and when it was necessary to stir the ire of his opponent by satire he made him feel as if in a hornet's nest."

Elliott, like all other great men, was *sui generis*, and a man of rare powers. He was a perfect intellectual acrobat. Like the surges of the Mississippi, when aroused he moved all abreast before him, concentrating and turning all lesser streams and rivers into his sweeping channel.

He was not afraid to meet the stoutest Democrat and measure arms with him in a political discussion, nor was he ever known to leave the arena without the discomfiture of his opponent."

Who is John Francis Quarles?

He was a distinguished Negro lawer of the State and City of New York. The most reliable test within the realm of thought by which to estimate the mental capacity of any race is the judicial discernment as seen in the career of some of its legal minds. It is by the urging of different analogies: the masterful contention at the Bar; the comparison, adjustment and reconciliation of one point with another that the sagacity and legal acumen of contending counsel as well as the wisdom of the Court is seen and exercised.

Indeed, when a lawyer is perplexed with a case that falls not fairly within the provisions of any existing statute or approved decision and for which his file of degests affords no precedent, it is then that the powers of the mind bristling vividly with legal learning dives into the intricate beauties of analogy, discovers and proves the correspondence between his own and other cases.

It was this energetic research—this love of discriminate investigation—this insatiate restiveness to illustrate and demonstrate fundamental truths in connection with the conventional and national rights of men that entitle the Honorable John Francis Quarles of New York to rank high among the proudest judicial minds who did battle before the able bench and bar of the cosmopolitan city.

He was an able expounder of the law—highly educated In private life at home he was "the prince of good fellows"—and all through his eventful life, from childhood in knee-pants sporting in gay summer on Georgia's balmy plains or in the International Courts, in Washington or Europe, he was the same staunch and sturdy craft, heart of oak from keel to taffrail—a paragon of purity.

John Francis Quarles, a colored lawyer whose office was at 318 Broadway, New York City, died at his home in Flushing, Wednesday, January 28th, of an acute attact of pneumonia. Mr. Quarles had been ill for sometime from an irritable stomach, but he left his sick bed to go to Albany to help secure the election of William M. Evarts to the United States Senate. He returned a week ago, and was compelled to take his bed again. It was not until Tuesday afternoon, however, that he displayed symptoms of pneumonia.

He was born in slavery at Atlanta, Ga., thirty-eight years ago. His father was a preacher of distinction. The son was bright, and was made a pet in his master's family. After the war, through the influence of Charles Sumner, he was entered at Westminister College, Pennsylvania, where it is said, he graduted at the head of his class. He studied law under the direction of Charles Sumner in Washington. It is said he was the first colored man that was ever admitted to the bar as far South as the Capital. In 1870 President Grant appointed him Consul to Port Mahon, the capital of Minorca, one of the Baleraic Islands. He served during Grant's term, and, at his own request, he was transferred by President Hayes to Malaga, a more important and profitable post. While at Port Mahon he married Marie Jacqueminot, a daughter of the French Consul at that port, and a granddaughter of Napoleon's Marshal of the same name.

He resigned and returned to this country in the spring of 1880, just in time to participate in the Garfield campaign. He opposed the nomination of Garfield, and used his influence among the colored delegates from the South for Blaine. In 1882 Secretary of the Treasury Sherman appointed him special Commisioner to visit the United States Consuls on the Spanish coast. In the recent campaign he was an active supporter of Mr. Blaine. He felt very much depressed when Mr. Blaine was defeated.

Among the criminals that he defeated were Wliam Leighton, a mulatto, who killed his mistress in Twenty-seventh street, about two years ago, and Charles H.

Rugg, the murderer of Mrs. Maybee and her daughter in Oyster Bay, L. I., about a year ago. He had just taken Rugg's case to the Court of Appeals where he was to argue it next week. He also made himself a warm friend of Cadet Whittaker, who, after his trial at West Point and his court martial in New York City, made his home at Mr. Quarles's house. He was a member of the Queen County Bar Association.

Mrs. Quarles was so overcome by grief that no arrangements were made for his funeral, but it is likely that his remains will be sent to Atlanta. He left no children. It is supposed he was worth about $5,000. He leaves a large law library. Mrs. Quarles has a brother who is a Colonel in the French army, and is at present in China, and another brother a real estate broker in Paris.

> "If thou saidst I am not peer,
> To lord in Scotland here,
> Lowland or highland, far or near,
> Lord Angus, thou hast lied."

Judge Jonathan J. Wright, of the Supreme Court S. C.

Ex-Associate Justice Wright, of the Supreme Court of South Carolina, died at his home in this city on Wednesday night Feb. 18, 1885. He had been suffering for several years from consumption, and for the past two months had been in an extremely critical condition. In his death there has passed from the stage another of the most conspicuous figures in the Revolution of 1876. In view of the prominent part he took in the events preceding the downfall of the Chamberlain Government, a review of some of the incidents of his career will be interesting.

Judge Wright was born in Luzerne County, Pennsylvania, February 11, 1840. He was the son of a farmer who removed to Susquehanna County, Pennsylvania, when the subject of this sketh was quite young. He was industrious and ambitious, and saved up enough money to attend the Lancasterian University at Ithaca, New York, for which he had prepared himself in the district schools in Pennsylvania. After returning home he read law in the office of Bently, Fitch & Bentley at Montrose, meanwhile teaching school upon a first-class certificate which had been granted to him by the county board of examiners. He read law in the office of Judge O. Collins, at Wilkesbarre, Pa., where he also taught school.

In 1865 he was sent to South Carolina by the American Missionary Association to organize schools. He landed in Beaufort and after remaining there a year returned to Pennsylvania, where he was admitted to the Bar in August 1866, being up to that time the first and only colored man ever admitted to practice law in that State. He returned to South Carolina in the same year with an appointment from Gen. O. O. Howard as legal adviser of refugees and freedmen. He established his headquarters at Beaufort and continued to act in that capacity until his election to the Constitutional Convention of 1868, when he resigned. Soon after the adjournment of the convention, in the proceedings of which he took an important part, he was elected to the State Senate from Beaufort county.

Col. A. K. McClure, in writing some sketches of the members of the Legislature for the New York *Tribune*, said: "The most notable negro in the Legislature is Senator Wright. He is a full-blooded negro, of medium size, with a finely chiseled face and handsomely developed head." The New York *Nation* in speaking of him, said: "He is said to be the best educated negro in the State, and enjoys the reputation of being the ablest man of his race. He stands nearly six feet in height and has a head singularly thin and very high in the region of benevolence and self-esteem."

In February, 1870, Wright was elected Associate Justice of the State Supreme Court to fill the unexpired term of Solomon L. Hoge, who has been elected to Congress.

After his election to the Supreme Bench the Union League of Charleston, of which Tom Mackey was president, passed resolutinos congratulating the General Assembly upon its wise choice and pronouncing it as the judgment of the League that he was "the (W)right man in the (W)right place." The Charleston *News*, commenting upon his election said: "As Senator Wright was industrious. He spoke more, perhaps, than any of the other Senators and generally very clearly. He now holds the highest position held by a colored man in the United States."

The honorary degree of L L. D, was conferred upon Judge Wright by the Avery College at Allegheny City, Pennsylvania.

Upon the expiration of his first term he was re-elected to the Supreme Bench for the full term of six years and qualified December, 15, 1871.

In connection with his resignation from the Supreme Bench, the following letter from Governor Hampton to Judge Wright is now published for the first time:

COLUMBIA, S. C., August 6, 1877.

To J. J. Wright, Judge, &c.—Dear Sir: Your favor of this date, covering your resignation of the office of Associate Justice of the Supreme Court of this State, is at hand and contents noted.

I accept the same as a tribute on your part to the quietude of the State, and as in no sense an acknowledgement or in truth of the charges which have been made against you.

Respectfully yours,

WADE HAMPTON, Governor.

The Court of Sessions Adjourns in Honor of his Memory.

In the Court of General Sessions yesterday W. J. Bowen, Esq., announced to the Court the death of Judge Wright, and moved that the Court stand adjourned as a tribute to the memory of the deceased. In making the motion Mr. Bowen took occasion to pay an eloquent and feeling tribute to the life and services of the dead Judge. Although not associated with him to any great extent at the Bar, yet from his friendly and social relations with the deceased he could bear high testimony to his domestic virtues, which could scarcely be said to be marred by his few human frailties. Mr. Bowen's eulogy was short, but was delivered with earnest impressiveness.

The motion was seconded by J. W. Polite, Esq., who alluded to that particular trait of character of the deceased which always induced him to devote so much of his time to the elevation and amelioration of the condition of the younger generation of his race. He also touched upon the notable virtue of charity which characterized the relations of Judge Wright to his fellow men.

S. J. Lee, Esq., also warmly seconded Mr. Bowen's motion. His long acquaintance with the deceased, both in public and private life he said, enabled him to speak more familiarly of his personal history, and he was fortunate in the respect that he could heartily endorse the sentiments uttered by the preceding speakers. He laid much stress on the services of Judge Wright to the people of this State in 1876-77, and spoke of such services as sufficient to entitle the deceased to the grateful memory of the citizens of the State. Mr. Lee then in an elaborate eulogy vindicated the title of Judge Wright to be called a Christian and a man of eminent ability, and a true and constant friend to his people.

Upon the hearning of these remarks Judge Aldrich, in compliance with the terms of the motion, adjourned the Court until this morning.

Who is A. C. J. Taylor, of Topeka, Kan?

He is a practicing lawyer in Topeka. He was born in Macon, Ga., 1856 of slave parents. For a few years after attaining ability to "tote his own skillet," he rambled off to Indiana, seeking the knowledge that afterwards made him a man, where he attended school, and finally entered Princeton University where he completed his studies. He thereupon went to Kansas, opened an office in Topeka—after filling several importand puplic stations he was elected by a very flattering majority as Corporation Attorney for the City aboved named. His practice is large and profitable.

Upon the death of Hon. Moses A. Hopkins, in 1886, President Cleveland appointed Mr. Taylor as Minister resident and Consul General to the government of Liberia, West Africa, which position he held until the last of the winter season of 1888, when he voluntarily resigned, ostensibly to meet the urgent demands for his legal services in this country. He enjoys to-day a lucrative practice before the City, State and United States Courts, including the Supreme tribunal of the nation.

In politics he is conservative, Supporting the Democratic nominee for the presidency.

Who is Hon. Geo. H. White, of New Berne, N. C?

He is one of the Solicitors, or State's Attorney, of the State of North Carolina. He was elected to this very responsible position by a large majority vote in the 2nd. Judicial district, comprising some of the wealthiest and most intelligent counties in the State. He was the regular Republican nominee, but a so-called Independent Republican and an uncompromising Democrat ran against him. The returns showed that his majority was larger than the entire vote received by both of the other two gentlemen.

He is about 35 years of age, was educated at the Whitin Normal Institue, Lumberton, N. C., Prof. D. P. Allen, Principal. He was admmitted after a thorough examination by the Supreme Court to practice law in all the Courts of the State. He has been honored more than once to a seat in the State Senate. At present he is the only colored Solicitor, or States prosecuting attorney in the United States of America.

In complexion he is brown. In statue he is at medium, moderate in dress and respected by all who have the pleasure of his acquaintance.

Who John H. Collins, of Halifax, N. C?

He is a successful lawyer in Eastern North Carolina. lives in Halifax Co., and preceded Mr. White as Solicitor for eight years in succession.

Colored Men as Jurors, by William Hannibal Thomas.

Trial by jury is one of the primary and sovereign rights of American citizenship; the bulwark of personal liberty, the medium of justice between man and man, and the foundation of judicial procedure in all civilized nations. The statements embraced in this article apply to the jury system of the South in answer to some recent criticisms on negro juries, that appeared in the *North American Review*, which affirmed that negroes made incompetent jurors, and should be set aside; that they possessed no judicial disernment, and in the trial of cases, are chiefly the tool of demagogue attorneys. These are grave accusations, which, if true, justly render negro juries censurable and unworthy to exercise such functions. As a matter of fact, colored men represent but a small percentage of the whole number of jurors impaneled; a venire composed exclusively of colored persons would be a phenomenon in a Southern court. The ratio of actual jurors bears no appreciable proportion to the colored population eligible for such service; under these circumstances, conceding the truth of these criticisms, the influence of colored jurors in the practical administration of law would not effect the final determination of causes.

But are these things so? Are colored men morally and intellectually incapable of exercising the duties of jurors? It is admitted that there is a radical difference between the jury verdicts of the two races. Many white men, when engaged in such service, are governed by race prejudice, and biased by partisan motives. In the determination of issues between colored and white suitors, such juries invariably find in favor of white persons without reference to the merits of the case. The unsupported statement of a white witness will carry more weight with an average jury than the sworn testimony of a score of credible negroes. A white man's word is infallible, and is not to be controverted by a negro's. So reasons court and jury. The spirit of caste dominates all judicial procedure in presentment, trial and sentence.

* * * * * * * * * * * *

In contrast, colored men are painstaking, conscientious and reliable in jury service. They are not purchasable factors, and in making up their verdicts are not actuated by a spirit of revenge or ignorant bigotry, but rather an instinctive sense of the equities of a case. Colored jurors sometimes exercise those prerogatives inherent in such functions, and discredit testimony offered by white men when it is known that the evidence submitted is untrue. It is then that manly independence involves censure, while servile acquiescence wins commendation. Colored jurors are frequently coerced, by methods of intimidation, in conclusions at variance with their honest convictions. Such methods are reprehensible; the negro should always vindicate his manhood by sturdy independence, uninfluenced by cajolery or animadversion.

Some instances of the efficiency and honesty of negro jurors are herewith submitted. The recent case of Murphy vs. Ford, and others, in New Orleans, La., is fresh in the public mind. The deceased, Murphy, was shot, without warning or provication, in cold blood. The testimony adduced was conclusive as to the gilt of Ford and his accomplices. The jury stood eleven for acquittal and one for conviction, the latter a colored man. Eleven white men are eager to condone a brutal murder; the negro alone was brave enough to insist upon a vindication of justice. Comment on the integrity of the white jurors is unnecessary. A recent trial involving a similar homicide has just been terminated in Abbeville, S. C. I am advised that the case was devoid of mitigating circumstances, and when it was given to the jury ten white men promptly voted for acquittal, while two colored jurors stood out for conviction. Of ourse a mistrial was the result, as in the previous case; but the vote of the colored jurors was a rare act of courage in a lawless community. I note a third case. During the trial of a civil suit in West Virginia, in which the plaintiff was a wealthy white man, he petitioned the court for a colored jury, alleging that it was impossible to obtain justice at the hands of a white jury. The negro is a law-abiding citizen who may prove as a conservator of law, the source of inspiration and the agency of judicial reform in the South. My own experience as a lawyer justifies the statement that colored men as jurors are as reliable as white men in reaching sound legal conclusions; that life and property are equally as safe in their hands, while their verdicts are freer from race prejudice and rarely influenced by mercenary considerations. I should be pleased if the facts warranted a similar conclusion in favor of the white jurors of the South, but I fear another generation will arise before such testimony can be truthfully recorded.

Who was George Lewis Ruffin, LL.B.?

He was one of the ablest jurists in the State of Massachusetts; rising as he did from the onerous duties of a barber in Boston to high judicial honors by dint of study, moral courage, a mother's influence and a restless docile mind.

The subject of this sketch was born of a free parentage, G. W. and N. L. Ruffin, in Richmond, Va., December 16, 1834. By force of our "peculiar" Southern "institution," he was carried by his affectionate mother, to Boston where he might be enabled to acquire the highest moral and intellectual development. The barber shop was both a living and a schooling for him. Here between the click of his scissors and the rustling pages of his book he eked out a competency for himself and his mother's family and at the same time built up a scholarship broad and brilliant in all its parts.

In the office of Jewell & Gaston he read law and finished his course in Howard University, Washington, D. C.

From his resident ward, Mr. R. was elected in 1869 and '70 by the popular vote to the Legislature of his adopted State in which capacity he reflected credit upon himself, his constituency and his race. From that time he held many positions of honor and trust.

When General B. F. Butler become governor of the State, he nomsnated the honorable Mr. R. as judge of the District Court of Charleston. This was November 7, 1883. Three other eminent gentlemen were seeking the place, but lawyer Ruffin moved ahead and was sworn in by Governor Butler himself. He married a Boston lady of culture and character. Four living children testifies to the fitting marrital relation, devotion and affection of their departed father. He was a member of the twelth Baptist church of Boston.

He was an earnest christian and died, November 19, 1886, triumphant in christian hope.

WEALTH AND BUSINESS.

Can you instance a few names of individuals and firms showing the wealth, business tact and success of the negro in the U. S. Yes. From the corupiled exhibit of Mr. J. W. Cromwell, editor of the *Peoples' Advocate,* Washington, D. C., I will note the following:

The Carolinas take the lead in the number of well-to do negroes. North Carolina has twenty who are worth from $10,000 to $30,000 each. In South Carolina the negroes own $10,000,000 worth of property. In Charleston fourteen men represent $200,000. Thomas R. Smalls is worth $18,000, and Charles C. Leslie is worth $12,000. The family of Noisettes, truck farmers, are worth $150,-000. In the city savings bank the negroes have $124,-936.35 on deposit. One man has over $5,000. He recently bought a $10,000 plantation and paid $7,000 in cash.

In Philadelphia John McKee is worth half a million. He owns 400 houses. Several are worth $100,000 each.

The negroes of New York own from five to six million dollars' worth of real estate. P. A. White, a wholesale druggist, is worth a quarter of a million, and has an annual business of $200,000. Catherine Black is worth $150,000.

In New Jersey the negroes own $2,000,000 worth of real estate. Baltimore has more negro home-owners than any other large city. Nineteen men are worth a total of $800,000. John Thomas, the wealthiest, is worth about $150,000. Less than one hundred negroes in Washington are worth a total of $1,000,000.

In Louisiana the negroes pay taxes on $15,000,000; in New Orleans and $30,000,000 in the State. Ioure Lafon, a French quadroon, is worth $1,000,000. The Mercer Bros., clothiers, carry a stock of $300,000. Missouri has twenty-seven negroes worth $1,000,000, in amounts ranging from $20,000 to $25,000.

The richest colored woman in the South, Amanda Eubanks, made so by the will of her white father, is worth $400,000 and lives near Augusta, Ga. Chicago, the home of eighteen thousand colored people, has three firms in business whose proprietors represent $20,000 each, one $15,000, and nine $10,000. The Eastlake Furniture Company is worth $20,000. A. J. Scott has $35,000 invested in the livery business, and is worth $100,000, including a well-stocked farm in Michigan. Mrs. John Jones and Richard Grant are worth $70,000 each. A. G. White of St. Louis, formerly purveyor of the Anchor Line of steamers after financial reverses, has, since the age of 45 retrieved his fortunes and accumulated $30,000. Mrs. M. Carpenter, a San Francisco colored woman, had a bank account of $5,000, and Mrs. Mary Pleasants has an income from eight houses in San Francisco, a ranch near San Mateo, and $100,000 in government bonds. In Marysville, Cal., twelve individuals are the owners of ranches valued in the aggregate from $150,000 to $180,000. One of them, Mrs. Peggy Bredan, has besides a bank account of $40,000.

These statistics show that the brother in black is making some headway in the world. He is learning to "tote his own skillet."

The following is culled from Mr. John K. Hawkins, work: "Africans in America, &c."

"One of the best evidences of progress of the colored people of this city is their rapid accumulation of wealth. It would be difficult to say just how much property is owned by them, or how much they pay in taxes into the city treasury, but the amount is known to be large.

"The well-to-do portion of the colored people take very little interest in politics, preferring to attend strictly to their business, and lay up something for a rainy day.

"The richest colored man in the city, John McKee, is not known to be colored except by his neighbors and relatives. He is said to be the owner of more than two hundred houses in this city, and is worth between $200,000 and $300,000.

"Mr. McKee is a real estate dealer, and lives in a modest little three-story house at 1030 Lombard street. He has a small office in the basement of his house, around which are placed rows of shelves. Upon these, methodically arranged, are little paste-board boxes, numbered and labeled, containing the deeds to his property and other valuable papers. He makes a specialty of improving and building up the lower part of the first ward. He has put up in that portion of the ward, known as the "Neck," more than twenty houses, within the last two years.

"The principal street in this newly built up settlement is name McKee street, after him. McKee Avenue, in the fifth ward, and McKee's court, near Broad street, in the seventh ward, also take their names from him.

"While Mr. McKee is a man of very little education, he does not employ a clerk, and when asked how he managed to attend to his enormous business, he replied: 'I keep it all in my head.' Mr. McKee is not known to be a man who gives liberally to charitable purposes, but he sometimes opens his purse to benevolence, first exacting, however, a promise that nothing shall be said about it A few years ago he was elected Colonel of a colored regiment, and out of consideration of this compliment he uniformed and equipped the eight hundred men. When the regiment was disbanded a few months afterwards, he lost all interest in military matters, but he still carries his title as Colonel, with pride. Mr. McKee is an inveterate smoker.

"William Still, who resides in the large and handsome residence 244 south Twelfth street, is another rich colored man. His wealth is estimated at \$200,000, and there are those claiming to know, who say that this figure is too small by \$50,000. Mr Still is a coal dealer, and owns a yard on Washington Avenue, where he keeps several men employed. In the busy season he runs as many as a dozen carts. Mr. Still made his first money as a sutler, at Camp William Penn, during the war, when he is said to have realized quite a fortune. His position as Secretary of the Underground Railroad before the war gave him the opportunity to become acquainted with persons of prominence and influence, who afterwards secured for him the appointment as sutler. When the war closed, he embarked in his present business, and his fortune has steadily increased. Mr. Still is a man of much more than ordinary ability and a few years ago published a history of the Underground Railroad. The maintenance of the 'Home for Aged and Infirm Colored Persons in West Philadelphia, is largely due to his efforts. While Mr. Still is not known as a politician, he has been active in more than one campaign, generally acting with the Independents.

"Robert Purvis' wealth is variously estimated to be between $100,000 and $150,000. He lives in a four-story residence at the northwest corner of Sixteenth and Mount Vernon streets. Mr. Purvis is one of the few colored men of the country who have never known what poverty is. He has always been surrounded by luxury and refinement. He at one time tried the expensive experiment of running a model farm a few miles out of the city, but was wise enough to give up before the fortune was gone. Having neither taste nor inclination for a business life, he has contented himself with a life of ease. Mr. Purvis enjoys a high social position among white people.

"Isaiah C. Wears, who only a few years ago was a poor barber, has taken such wise advantage of his opportunities that he is now worth $50,000. He is a real estate broker and politician.

"Mr. Wears was a nephew of Joshua P. Eddy, who died about two years ago, leaving property valued at about $100,000. For several years before the old man died, he was unable to attend to his business, and Mr. Wears acted as his agent. At the death of Mr. Eddy, Mr.

Wears came into the possession of the larger part of the property, through a bequest, and he is now adding to his fortune by very shrewd speculations. Mr. Wears had very few school advantages in his younger days, but of late years he has applied himself to study, and is known as a man of wide information. He is one of the most forcible campaign speakers that the colored race has yet produced, and his services are in constant demand during political contests.

"Of the rich colored women in this city, Mrs. Jones, widow of the late well known caterer, Henry Jones, on Twelfth street, below Walnut, stands first. Her wealth was left to her by her husband, and she is known to be worth more than sixty thousand dollars. She carries on the business of catering, still serving the families her husband served in his day, and it is supposed that she is yearly adding to her fortune.

"Jno. D. Lewis, the only colored lawyer in the city, and a practitioner in all the courts, is a man of wealth, and were it not for his expensive tastes, he could easily live without his practice at the bar. He is the owner of property to the value of forty thousand dollars, all paying investments. Mr. Lewis made his money as a tobacco manufacturer, in Toronto, Canada. He afterward studied law in Boston, came on here, and was admitted to the bar. He has been successful in building up a handsome legal business, and is said to be making money.

"Of the colored caterers, who have made money in their line, Chas. Franklin has perhaps been the most successful. He lives in good style on Lombard street, above Broad. Mr. Franklin owns several valuable houses, and his wealth is computed at forty thousand dollars. He is taking life easy, and he seldom serves a party unless it is given by some one of his old established customers.

"Thos. J. Bowers, living on Tenth street, below Lombard, is another colored man of means. Just what he is worth is not known, even by his most intimate friends. He was left money and property by his father. By selling coal and speculating in real estate, he is thought to be worth from twenty-five to thirty thousand dollars at the present time. He goes to Saratoga every season for his health.

"Of the younger colored men who are making money by strict attention to business, Thomas Boling, a flour merchant, on Lombard Street, above Ninth, is probably the most successful. The business which he established a few years ago in a small way has grown until Mr. Boling is enabled to make a handsome bank deposit every month. He is worth not less than twenty thousand dollars.

"W. G. Harvey is another colored man who pays taxes on a large amount of real estate. He is worth more than fifty thousand dollars. He is a shoemaker, and still follows his trade. His reputation as one of the finest workers on ladies' shoes in the city, has kept him constantly employed in this paying line of business, and he is still making money at it. He lives in a neat little house at 1124 Carpenter Street, which he owns, and he seldom leaves his store except to collect his rents from his other properties, or make a deal in real estate.

At the celebration of the twentieth anniversary of the organization of the colored schools of Lexington, Ky., a few days ago, Col. John O. Hodges, superintendent of the public schools, among other things, said: "In 1865 there were 3,956,000 colored people in the South, without a single school; now there are 7,000,000 people with 12,-

000 schools, 16,000 teachers with 1,000,000 pupils—an average of 60 pupils to each teacher—and 15,000 pupils in the colored high schools. The colored people in the South now have 80 newspapers, 2,000,000 church members, donate annually $3,700,000 for church purposes, own 5,000,000 acres of land, produce annually 1,000,000 bales of cotton more than they did before the war, have an average deposit of $55,000,000 in the bank, and own taxable property assessed at $100,000.

A Prosperous Colored Planter.

When the war was over Barney Houston, colored, who lives in Centreville township, near Anderson, did not have a copper. He was over 50 years old, but his age had not subdued his enterprising and industrious habits. After renting land for a few seasons his partner, Henry McGowan, colored, and himself determined to buy the 140 acre farm which the were cultivating. The owner asked $1,900 for it. These two colored men had two horses, and after making the first payment they worked steadily and persistently season after season until they owned the property. Finally a division of the land was made. "Uncle" Barney, as he was called, taking fifty acres. He has a nice house upon his little farm now, and is only a short distance from Anderson. He has just been offered four thousand dollars for his property, which he refused, as he values it at five thousand dollars. He does not owe a dollar now, and can get all the credit he wants.

We will venture the assertion that this colored man didn't fool away much of his time over politics.—Charleston *News and Courier*.

"Besides these few mentioned, there are more than a dozen other colored men and women in the city who are worth upwards of twenty thousand dollars, and this number is constantly increasing."

Hon J. C. Alman of Bennettsville. S. C., is listed at twenty thousand dollars in real-estate. Was 6 years State Represenatative in his native State of South Carolina. Is a middle aged christian gentleman. No one more than he understands the beauty of the daily courtesies and little kindnesses which go so far toward pleasant living. The Lincoln heirs of Dallas are said to have become the owners of $14,000,000 recently by bequest. Mr. W. C. Coleman, of Concord, N. C. is a gentleman of means and intelligence. He is a successful merchant, is also proprietor of a feed and sale stables and is reputed to own the finest horses in the State.

There are in many Southern cities many handsome residences owned by colored men, and many of them exhibit a tact for business and accumulating wealth not found in thousands of whites whose education is far superior, and whose experience in business extends far back beyond the time when these colored men were released from servitude.

By THE REV. DR. B. T. TANNER.

Read in "the National Conference of Colored Men of the United States," at Nashville, Tenn., May 6th 1879, by Mrs. Dr. Wylie, of Philadelphia.

Christianity is the religion of the Lord Jesus Christ. American Christianity is that phase of it found in America, meaning by America the United States; for it is a significant fact that this heterogeneous nation has audaciously possessed itself of the continental appellation. Before, however, we address ourselves directly to the subject presented, it is in place to recognize the fact that American christianity in many of its phases is largely a thing of America, therefore measureably distinct from European christianity and measurably distinct from the christianity of Asia or of Africa, in so far forth as the Divine faith may be said to have taken foot-hold upon either of these two great divisions of the earth. A continent eventually gives individuality to the religious faith of the people who eat its bread and drink its waters and regulate their lives in accordance with its political and social institutions. Therefore it is perfectly legitimate to speak of a continental christianity; or, as in the case in hand, of American christianity as contradistinguished from the christianty of other continents, perfectly legitimate to inquire as to its theory and practice The question, therefore, in place to ask is: What has been the phase of individuality given the American theory of christianity by the agencies, physical, political and social, recognized above; and to what extent have they affected its practic?

The theory of American Christianity, what is it?

At this moment we deem it in place to say that the theory of christianity in general is one thing, the theory of the multiplied forms of ecclesiasticism, or what might be called churchianity, is quite another. Christianity is of God, ecclesiasticism is of men; this of earth, that of heaven Christianity draws on our faith; ecclesiasticism on our judgment; this suffers change, that endures forever.

And yet nothing is more common than to hear men speaking of them as one and the same. We are quite ready to confess that they should be one and the same, at least mankind thinks so; quite ready to confess that the followers of each of the various systems claim that they are. But in view of the fact that these systems vary greatly from each other, it is very certain that each of them cannot be the exact counterpart of christianity unless we credit it with chameleon-like properties. Nothing can be truer than the axiom: If the Roman theory of ecclesiasticism be christianity, then the Greek theory and the Protestant theory cannot be accepted as christianity, but only as approaches to it. And so of each and all the systems which are equally the glory and shame of christendom. If one of these systems be exactly true, the others, to the extent that they differ, are exactly false. But we comfort ourselves with the fact, as we have said, ecclesiasticism—Roman, Greek or Protestant—is one theory; christianity is another; and so of their respective theories. That we may the more readily comprehend the theory of christianity let us for a moment look at those forms of ecclesiasticism which govern christendom, for it should be remembered that the agencies heretofore recognized are even more prolific in producing the one than in giving individuality to the other.

As we have intimated, christendom may be said to have three leading ecclesiastical theories.

The first of them is, possibly, the Roman theory. We say possibly, for we prefer not to touch the question of priority as respectively urged by the Latins of the West and the Greeks. But it could not be expected that we should present here the hundred and one shades of belief which go to make up this theory, a theory which claims to be the exact and only counterpart of christianity. It is sufficient to say that it is roundly autocratic; that it finds the Word of God, not only in the written word, as received by the ancient christians and the more ancient Jews, but supplemented by the apocryphal books, lifted by the Tridentine council to the level of the canonical. These, with the traditions of the early church, and the decisions of the councils as held from time to time, constitute the sources of its authority. That, however, which distinguishes this theory of Roman ecclesiasticism from the ecclesiasticisms of the world is the recognition of the Bishop of Rome as Christ's vicegerent, and consequently clothed with the largest possible plenipotentiary powers.

Quite similar to the theory of the Latins is the theory of the Greeks; so similar indeed, that to characterize it, it is only necessary to show wherein it differs from the Roman or the Latin. All that Rome accepts in the shape of scriptures and traditions, rites and ceremonies, with the Apocrypha and slight differences in the service, Constantinople—the recognized head of Greek ecclesiasticism—accepts, rejecting only the claims of the Pope to universal primacy. This they stoutly deny, and when called upon to submit, curiously enough make answer in the words of the great

Gregory, (himself one of the Popes,) that the title of "universal Bishop, by whomsoever assumed, is profane, antichristian and infernal."

The third and last of the ecclesiastical theories is Protestantism.

Whatever else Protestantism may or may not be, it certainly is not what the Pontiff, the venerable Leo XII declares it to be. Says he, in his famous Encyclical of 18th December, 1878: "You, reverend brethren, very well know that the object of the war which ever since the sixteenth century has been waged by the innovators against the Catholic faith, and which has every day increased in intensity down to the present time, has been that, by the setting aside of all revelation and the subversion of every kind of supernatural order, an entrance might be cleared for the discoveries, or rather, the delirious imaginations of mere reason."

With due deference to the saintly character of the Pontiff, it is only necessary to say that, as a Roman is justly supposed to know more of the Roman theory of ecclesiasticism than any one else, and the Greek of the Greek theory, even so ought Protestants to be credited with a more exact knowledge of the theory they accept than any one else. Protestantism, as its name indicates, is indeed a *protest* against what its early founders regarded as abuses in the two theories named above. But while it is thus largely negative, there is a still larger vein of the positive in it, in that it exalts the written word of God to a supremacy never before given. The Protestant theory of ecclesiasticism may be defined as the theory that accepts the Bible as the one rule, and the only authoritative rule for life and practice. What it commands is to be done; what it forbids is to be let alone.

We have given here, briefly, the theories of the three leading ecclesiastical organizations of the world—theories, as we have said, largely distinct from the theory of christianity. And yet, according to the world's *usus loquendi*, they are often regarded as one and the same, while this is the very gravest necessity for recognizing the distinction. And therein, white men in Europe have voted, in so far as they were able, both out of existence. Failing therein, both white men and black men in America, while they have not gone to the mad length of those in Europe, have stumbled as upon a rock. Referring to this sad subject as it relates to white men, the *Independent*, (N. Y.,) has said:

"Among all the earnset-minded young men who are at this moment leading in thought and action in America we venture to say that four-fifths are skeptical of the great historic facts of christianity. What is taught as christian doctrine by the churches claims none of their consideration, and there is among them a general distrust of the clergy, as a class, and an utter disgust with the very aspect of modern christianity and of church worship."

Referring to this subject as it relates to black men, Bisop Payne writes:

"REV. B. T. TANNER:

"*Dear Doctor:* In answer to your query as to my personal knowledge of the effect of American caste upon the most thoughtful of our race, time will only allow me to mention two examples: Mr. R. F., one the most gifted young men of the city of P., born and reared in it—born and reared in the bosom of the P. E. church, had prepared himself for confirmation. But within a week or ten days of the Sabbath when that rite was to be performed by Bishop Onderdonk, he (the Bishop) made a speech in favor of African colonization, in which he uttered sentiments so adverse to the interests of the colored American that Mr. R. F., said: 'No such bishop will I allow to put his hands on my head.' Then he gradually drifted into such bitterness against the 'church' that he subsequently said to me: 'I will just as soon go to a brothel to be taught morality as to go to any of your churches.'

"Another member of the same family, who, like her gifted brother, was born and reared in the bosom of the Protestant Episcopal church, and lived in it till she was the mother of a half dozen children, in reply to my exhortations for self-consecration to Christ, said to me: 'Show me the black man's God, and I will serve him; he is not the black man's God, he is the white man's God.'

"This lady belonged, like her brother, not to the ignorant classes of colored people, but to the highly intelligent and wealthy class. She was independent in her circumstances; kept her servants and a white governess in her homestead.

"Fraternally,

D. A. PAYNE."

In what consists the mistake of these chivalrous souls? Verily it is that they failed to recognize the fact that churchianity is a thing as distinct from christianity as the servant is from the master, as the dry tree is from the tree that is green, as the light of the moon is from the light of the sun, as man is from God.

We have seen the theories of the church, let us see what is the theory of christianity, especially the theory of American christianity.

And here we dare not touch upon any disputed dogmas; for the moment dispute occurs, necessity for belief ceases, and the matter passes over from the realm of christianity to the realm of ecclesiasticism. In the christian realm men see eye to eye: "Thy watchmen shall lift up the voice; with the voice together shall they sing; for they shall see eye to eye when the Lord shall bring again Zion."

What is the theory of christianity, that theory in regard to which men, indeed, see eye to eye, and because they do, gives us the plain guarantee of its divinity? Brief, indeed, is this divine theory; so brief that it may be given in less than a dozen words. It is with the sequence which logically follows—God your Father, Christ your Saviour, Man your Brother. More than this is ecclesiasticism: nothing less than this is christianity. Wherein is that theory about which there is not, as there must not be, any contradiction. With it upon their lips, the Latins and the Greeks, with upturned eyes, repeat together the glorious "Pater Noster;" with it upon their lips both Greek and Latin cry out: "All hail, Luther! All hail, Calvin!"

How eminently worthy is such a theory as this to be called christian, after the glorious Christ. Until the Christ revealed it the world was all astray. None could tell the relation man bore to the God whom even the heathen recognized; none could tell the relation man bore to his neighbor. Nor was any found to point unerringly to a Saviour sufficiently potent to take away the sin of the world. But the Christ broke the silence of the ages, and symphonies of music were heard all around. The Christ dispelled the clouds, and floods of light poured down from the upper realm. The problem was solved—the enigma made plain. God is Father, Jesus is Saviour, man is brother. In this consists the soul, body and divinity of the theory of christianity in general, and of American christianity in particular; for it is to be asserted without fear of contradiction, that in no portion of christendom has louder and longer paeans of praise been sung to this revelation that in America. And so great has been the influence of the agencies recognized, we might say that God as **Father**, Christ as Saviour, and man as brother, are the **very** bulwarks of our American theory of religion. Upon **these** have been built that spiritual temple which to-day is the glory of the Republic.

Leaving this, therefore, we approach the subject of the Practice of American christianity, and we could but wish its treatment afforded the same high pressure as did the treatment of its theory. But alas, alas, a defection, as it relates to the four millions of Africo-Americans in the land, greater than that the world ever before witnessed, with brazen eyes, is seen to stare truth in the face, and with a spirit akin to that of the Malachian age, asks: "Wherein have we dispised Thy name? Wherein have we polluted Thee?"

The tameness with which we spoke of the nation's enthusiasm for that theory of christianity which presents not only God to us as Father, and Christ as Saviour, but man especially as brother, was doubtless observable; and yet abundant room was given us for exhibiting what the Bohemians of to-day call "gush," but we did not. We failed to enter into particulars; failed to tell how the fathers engrafted it into the very constitution itself; aye, made it the corner-stone of the political structure they built; failed to tell how it was the inspiration of the days that tried men's souls; failed to tell how our poets have so attuned their harps to its music that it is the one key recognised by the world. Especially did we fail to tell how the agencies of the continent, physical, political and social, ministered to it, as did angels minister to him who was tempted in the wilderness. But in the practice of all this they have fallen infinitely lower than man has ever fallen from so high and glorious an ideal; lower than did the

Jews fall in the wilderness; lower than they fell in the days of the judges, and lower than they fell in the days of their last prophet. Circumcision has been neglected, even the circumcision of the heart. Human sacrifice has been practiced—the human sacrifice of slavery—which God, who cast jewels of truth to the nation, has been turned upon and not rent, (for divinity is insecable,) but impudently questioned.

The practice of American christianity, what has it been in the past? What is it in the preasent? As we approach the subject, aptly may we quote Scripture, "How art thou fallen from heaven, O Lucifer, son of the morning! How art thou cast down to the ground, which didst weaken the nation!"

The practice of American christianity, politically and ecclesiastically, has been, and morally is, such as to make the world hold up its hands in horror. Politically, how have they framed mischief by a law ecclesiastically? How have they gone with the multitude to do evil?

We speak of the practice of American christianity politically. What was it? Let the slave enactments of the several State Legislatures show. In his work, "Sketch of the Laws Relating to Slavery," Judge Stroud lays down twelve propositions, in which is seen the burden of the outrage imposed upon the christian bondmen of America by the christian slaveholders of America. They are as follows:

Proposition 1. The master may determine the kind and degree, and time of labor to which the slave shall be subjected.

Proposition 2. The master may supply the slave with such food and clothing only, both as to quantity and quality, as he may think proper.

Prososition 3. The master may, at his discretion, inflict any punishment upon the person of his slave.

Proposition 4. All the power of the master over his slave may be exercised, not by himself only in person, but by any one whom he may delegate as his agent.

Proposition 5. Slaves have no legal right of property or things, real or personal; but whatever they may acquire belongs in point of law to their masters.

Proposition 6. The slave, being a personal chattel, is at all times liable to be sold absolutely, or motgaged or leased, at the will of his master.

Proposition 7. He may also be sold by process of law for the satisfaction of the debts of a living, or the debts and bequests of a deceased, master, at the suit of creditors or legatees.

Proposition 8. A slave cannot be a party before a judicial tribunal in any species of action against his master, no matter how atrocious may have been the injury received from him.

Proposition 9. Slaves cannot redeem themselves nor obtain a change of masters, though cruel treatment may have rendered such a change necessary for their personal safety.

Proposition 10. Slaves being objects of property, if usurped by third persons, their owners may bring suit and recover damages for the injury.

Proposition 11. Slaves can make no contracts.

Proposition 12. Slavery is hereditary and perpetual.

When it is remembered that Judge Stroud builds these propositions upon foundations of laws as they existed in the Southern States in *ante-bellum* days, the terribleness of this practice of American christians will be made to appear. We could almost wish for time to refer to these enactments themselves, but owing to the ground that it would be necessary for us to travel over, it is impossible. Sufficient is it to say that in the certification of his dozen propositions, instead of painting too deeply the facts, as might rationally be supposed from the darkness of the picture presented, the Judge may justly be charged with a somewhat miserly use of his abundant materials.

As stated above, these propositions rest upon the action of the States in their semi-sovereign capacity. But let us glance at the action of the States, as a whole, in the capacity of their full nationality. What has been the practice of the nation? In the Constitution, section 2, article 4, we find these words:

"No person held to service or labor in one State, under the law thereof, escaping into another, shall, in consequence of any law or regulation therein, be discharged from such service or labor, but shall be delivered up on claim of the party to whom such service or labor may be due."

According to the decision of the Supreme Court, this constitutional provision is only to be exercised by the Federal Government. In the exercise of that unhappy interrogative, Congress, in the year 1793 and in the year 1850, ordered the rendition of bondmen who had the pluck and fortune to escape from the slave States into the States nominally free. Of the inhumanity, to say nothing of the non-christianity of the act of 1793, the men of this generation know nothing, save as they may glean from the provisions of the act itself, and from cotemporaneous history. Not so, however, with the act of 1850; for of its unnatural, unchristian and ungodly provisions, the men of to-day know only too much. Concerning these provisions we will be personally silent, confessing to what

Scripture says, without, of course, appropriating to ourself the wisdom: "Surely oppression maketh the wise man mad."—Eccles. vii, 7.

The just Judge, however, whom we have had occasion already to mention, referring to the shameful fact that both these acts of Congress intrusted the awful power of rendition into slavery to the judgment of a single person, and utterly regardless, too, of his capacity, moral or otherwise, says:

"But the strong objection to the tribunal is that question affecting human liberty, not for a day or year, but for a lifetime, is committed to one person, and that person chosen by the very men who would take away the inestimable gift of the Great Author of our being."

There will be found those ready to say that such proceedings as we have been describing were the work of men who can only be called christians in the most far-fetched sense. We would only be too glad to recognize the strength of the point taken, were there any weight in it, but no feather was ever more imponderable. Is it not a fact that not a few of them stood high in the church, and prided themselves on being called reverend? And, lastly, is it not a fact that when these very enactments were not officially indorsed by the leading church organization of the country, they were passed over in sphinx-like silence, and the man of their number who dare lift up his voice against the great iniquity was pronounced an innovator, a disturber of the peace; aye, in the majority of cases he was pronounced an infidel.

We could wish that some pen would do for the churches of the country what Judge Stroud has done for the State Legislatures and for Congress, put them on record. Not for purposes of revenge would we have this done, but rather as a warning to future generations. Wherefore does God, in his Word, record the defection of his people, individually and collectively, but that his people in all after time might be warned? Even so would we have recorded the defection of the American church and people from the high christian ideal marked out in the divine Word, and which they profess to embrace in all its height, depth, length and breadth, embrace, even with enthusiasm. Especially would we have this done for the additional reason that they have never repented of their past recognition of, and affiliation with slaveholders; at least, they have never repented in the eyes of men, and are still largely, both in the North and in the South, in the practice of the slave-holding spirit.

But what have we to say directly upon the practice of American christianity, by professed christians? In answer to the query, let us give the action of a few of the leading church bodies. We begin with the Friends, or Quakers. These pride themselves, and are prided upon in the record they present. When compared with the record of others, they possibly have occasion to congratulate themselves, as has undoubtedly the man with one eye occasion to congratulate himself upon his seeing capacity, who finds himself numbered with men having no eyes. And yet even in regard to the Qurkers, we can hear the great Evangel of time say: "Nevertheless, I have found somewhat against thee." What is it? Let history tell, and in its own words. We quote from "Stroud's History and Genealogy of the French Colony:"

"A short time after Francis Daniel Pastorious arrived in Pennsylvania, he became a member of the Society of Friends. He married about that time, Anna, the daughter of Dr. Klosterman, of Muhlheim. He was one of the first who had any misgivings about the institution of slavery, and in 1688 he wrote a memorial against slave-holding, which was submitted to the meeting of Germantown Friends, and by them approved of, and Pastorious was appointed to lay the memorial before the yearly meeting held in Philadelphia the same year. It was the first protest against Negro slavery submitted to a religious society in the world. Whittier, the poet, who had an opportunity of seeing the original manuscript, says it was a bold and direct appeal to the human heart. The memorial found but little favor with the yearly meeting, and it was said that Pastorious returned to his home at Germantown with sadness depicted on his countenance."

Westcott, the historian, says the first person who wrote a book showing the evils of slavery was Ralph Sandeford, a young merchant on Market street, Philadelphia. He had resided for some time in one of the West India Islands, and had witnessed the cruelties inflicted upon his fellow-man, and in the year 1728 his book was published, showing the evils of the system, and for so doing he was disowned by the Society of Friends.

Upon this action of the Quakers we have only to say, when it is remembered that precedents are portentous either for weal or woe, it assumes gigantic proportions. A different action at such an early period, followed up with that audacity which christian faith inspires, as reckless as the assertion may seem, might have saved the nation from centuries of guilt and suffering.

From the Quakers we turn to the Baptists, concerning whom it is only necessary to make a single historical quotation. Says Daniel Benedict in his "General History of the Baptist Denomination in America," 1813, vol. 2, page—:

"The Baptists are by no means uniform in their opinion of slavery. Many let it alone altogether; some remonstrate against it in gentle terms; others oppose it vehemently; while far the greater part of them hold slaves and justify themselves the best way they can."

From the Baptists we come to the Presbyterians. We mention the action of two members of the great Presbyterian family; the one with possibly the cleanest record; the other with the same regard to that, that is possibly the worst. In 1832 the united Presbyteries in the Western Synod passed the following resolution: "That the religion of our Lord Jesus Christ called upon christians to renounce the evil (slavery) as soon as it can be done without worse consequences to society and the slaves themselves." Just as if either society or the slaves themselves could suffer worse consequences. But how they improved on this empty statement, let Mr. L. Boyd (Springfield, Ohio,) tell us:

" We were present," says he, " at the meeting of the general Synod of the West, held at New Concord, Ohio, in 1841, and remained during all their sessions, and had an inhabitant of another planet, or person from a distant part of our globe been there, and heard all their deliberations as I did, he could not have known, either from their prayers, sermons, or any discussions on the floor of the Synod, that human slavery existed in the country."

Of the Old School Presbyterians it is sufficient to say that in the general assembly of 1845 they passed a resolution that "slave-holding as it exists in the United States is no bar to christian fellowship."

Passing over the practice of Roman Catholics and Protestant Episcopalian christians, whose icy conservatism is well known, we conclude with the Methodist Episcopal church South, and the Methodist Episcopal church.

When we say that the churchmen of the Methodist Episcopal church South believed in slavery and Negro subordination, and followed up that belief with a consistency absolutely admirable, in that seven hundred of them absolutely laid down their lives for it in the late war between the States, we can with mutual satisfaction say "good day."

Had the christians of the Methodist Episcopal church followed up their belief with the consistency of their Southern brethren, then indeed would we have had presented the most beautiful picture of the age. But, alas, with steps growing weaker day by day they pursued the tenor of their way, and thereby justify the remark of a historian: "The Methodists in some places set out on this principle: Their ministers preached against slavery; many set them at liberty; but I believe at present (1813) their scruples are nearly laid aside."

Admire the certain sound of 1784:

"Question 12. What shall we do with our friends that *will* buy and sell slaves? Answer. If they buy with no other design than to hold them as slaves, and have been previously warned, they shall be expelled and permitted to sell on *no* consideration."

But mark the change twelve years wrought: "And if any member of our society purchase a slave, the ensuing quarterly meeting shall determine on the number of years in which the slave so purchased shall work out the price of his freedom."

The sound of 1824 is completely changed, and slaveholding is recognized in the church of Wesley, who pronounced slavery "the sum of all villainies."

"Our preachers," says the general conference of 1824, "shall prudently enforce upon our members the necessity of teaching their slaves to read the word of God, and to allow them time to attend upon the public worship of God on our regular days of divine service."

But perfectly distressing to the ear is the sound sent out by the Methodist conference, annual and general, in the years that followed.

Take the following, for instance, as passed by the general conference of 1840, in the city of Baltimore. It was offered by the Rev. A. G. Ferr, of Georgia: "*Resolved*, That it is inexpedient and unjustifiable for any preacher to permit colored persons to give testimony against white persons in any State where they are denied that privilege by law."

The Ohio annual conference, after they indorsed the above, passed the following: "*Resolved*, That those brethren of the North who resist the abolition movements with firmness and moderation are the true friends of the church, the slaves of the South, and to the Constitution of our common country."

New York, following in the wake, passed the following: "First, That this conference fully concur in the advice of the late general conference (1840) as expressed in their pastoric address. Second. That we disapprove of the members of this conference patronizing, or in any way giving countenance to a paper called *Zion's Watchman*, because, in our opinion, it tends to disturb the peace and harmony of the body by sowing dissension in the church."

But it may be argued that this gradual defection of the Methodist Episcopal church from the truth was owing to its connection with the South. It would be unjust not to recognize some force in these remarks. Exactly how much, however, may be seen when we inquire as to their action after the great session of 1845.

Notwithstanding the rule of 1784 had long been inoperative, yet was it allowed to recur in the Book of

Discipline. But, in 1860, sixteen years after their severance from the South, in that darkness which immediately preceded the light, the laws of 1784 declaring slave-holding sufficient cause of expulsion, was made to give way to the following harmless expression of *opinion:* " We believe that the buying or selling of human beings, to be used as chattels, is contrary to the laws of God and nature, and inconsistent with the Golden Rule, and with the rule of our discipline, which requires us 'to do no harm,' and 'to avoid evil of every kind.' We therefore affectionately admonish all our preachers and people to keep themselves pure from this great evil, and to seek its extirpation by all lawful and christian means."

So much for the Practice of American christianity in the past. But what of its practice in the present?

We confess that this is far the greater question of the two. The gauge of man's conduct that tells is not the gauge of yesterday, but of to-day. With this measuring-rod in hand let us proceed to measure the present practice of American christians. Already do we hear expressions of deepest satisfaction at the suppressed symmetry and beauty presented. And we admit that to the superficial eye there is occasion for satisfaction. What is more beautiful than the action, say, of the bishops of the Methodist Episcopal church South laying their holy hands on the heads of their late bondsmen and exalting them to the lofty work, not of the ministry in general, but that of the Episcopacy itself; nor stopping here, but preparing for them a most excellent discipline, and publishing and editing for them a most creditable paper?

And so likewise the Southern Presbyterian church. What right is more delectable to the average vision than seeing them lay off a Presbytery for their colored brethren, and give it the sanction and influence of their great names?

Remembering that these are the days of Southern men and Southern territory, we are ready to grant them a phase of beauty most attractive to a phase of vision not uncommon to human eye. But if these be satisfying, how infinitely more so is the practice of the christians of the North, especially such christians as operate with the American Missionary Association, and the Methodist Episcopal church; nor will we be invidious in distinction, but say of all the christian denominations of the mighty North, Protestants and Catholic. How grand is the work of the American Missionary Association! How christian is its practice! Behold the schools and the churches it sustains in the land of the freedmen. Its last report presents the following statistics:

Missionaries at the South, 69. Teachers at the South. 150. Churches at the South, 64. Church members at the South, 4,180. Total number of Sabbath-school scholars. 7,436. Schools at the South, 37. Pupils at the South. 7,229.

Quite similar is the doing of the Methodist Episcopal church, at the following summation of its work shows:

Chartered institutions, 5. Theological schools, 3. Medical colleges, 2. Institutions not chartered, 10.

In these institutions the number of pupils taught during the year is classified as follows: Biblical, 400; law. 25; medical, 30; collegiate, 75; academic, 275; normal, 1,000; intermediate, 510; primary, 605. Total, 2,940.

But sad to tell, there is a fly in all the precious ointment of American christians, the fly of caste. There is a fly in the matter of that Southern ordination; for why leave out these faithful children of the church, and tell them henceforth, act for yourself? There is a fly in the matter of colored Presbyteries, for why draw the line at all? There is, in short, a fly in all the Godlike christians of the great North, in that they are endeavoring to keep up the middle wall of the partition between the two classes, if not at the South, certainly at the North. All through the South, as at the North, the great M. E. church says to her black children, "go there," and to her white children, "come here." Separate schools, separate churches, and separate conferences is the order of the day. And as with this great church to-day, so with the other churches of the land. Everywhere in the North and in the South caste prevails, differing only in degree; the churchmen of the North reprimanding the churchmen of the South. You can ostracise the Negro to the extent of keeping him out of your parlor, but don't kill him, especially, don't keep him from voting the Republican ticket. And where is the difference between this reprimand and the reprimand an intemperate father gives to his sons? "My son," said he, "you can drink two glasses of rum, but don't drink three." The spirit that practices moral ostracism upon a man solely on account of his color, is twin to the spirit that practices political ostracism for the same reason.

To the colored American both are equally hateful and hated. He wars upon both, having vowed a vow like to that of Hannibal of old; that he will never sheathe his sword till both lie bleeding and dead at his feet. Nor has he any respect for the men that practise either. It is a trial to him that he must at times listen to their soft talk. His soul rankles to say, "they are a trouble unto me; I am weary to bear them."

And yet, brethren, the morning cometh. Caste is doomed, its death is simply a question of time. The *Chang* of slavery is already dead. The *Eng* of caste must follow. America will not fail of her destiny. Her theory of christianity is to be her practice. Called of God to solve the highest political and social problem, its perpetuity is assured till the work has been done, to the furtherance of which I invoke the blessing of Almighty God.

THE ROMANCE OF THE NEGRO.

This article appeared, 1871, in the November number, volume XV, of the *American Missionary Journal*, which I re-produce in this little book as being worthy of considerate reflection, and which will, doubtless, prove a stimulus to race pride in the reader:

There has been a Lost Theory as well as a "Lost Cause" for the South in the late war. Before the great modern event and its consequences, the popular and almost universally received theory in the South was that the negro, if ever freed, was bound to retrograde, and that, after having proved a misery to himself and a nuisance to others, he would by providential interposition be extinguished, doomed to altogether disappear: as Carlyle, "maker of books," hath it, "to roam aimless, wasting the seed-fields of the world, and be hunted home to Chaos by the due watch-dogs and due hell-dogs, with such horrors of forsaken wretchedness as never were seen before!" This theory was generally accepted in the South, *nem. con.*; it not only involved the present writer—he was even its zealous advocate. "Lo, the poor negro," was the common *decantatum*, whenever anything had to be said in deprecation of the cruel abolitionists. Since the war there have been persons in the South, not to be entirely classed as ignoramuses, who have looked from day to day for the gradual extinction of the negro, for the stages of his disappearance from sublunary affairs in this hemisphere. It is not unusual in Southern companies to hear such snatches of conversation as follows: "The niggers are dying out. Dr. Asinine tells us that in the circuit of his practice they are dying like rotten sheep. Maybe they have diseases which are not incident to the whites, and that they are thus doomed to perish. . . . . "Then you know, there is infanticide, their common crime. When, I am told that in the ditches and sloughs back of Crowtown, it is common to see little dead niggers lying like drowned puppies. Did you hear what a Louisiana gentleman told at the Virginia Springs last summer? He wanted a cook, and a negro woman applied to him for the place, with strong recommendations. But she had incumbrances, children, and on this account alone he told her she wouldn't suit, and rejected her. The next morning he was surprised to find her returned with a very cheerful and animated face, when she said : "I'se all right now, sah got no 'cumbrances no more, I'se put dem out de way; de picaninnies done dead!'"

Those who have been looking for the providential riddance of the negro, and have been constructing mortality tables to suit themselves, must have been rather surprised, waking up some morning not long since, to read in the newspapers and outgiving from the United States Census, our *ne plus ultra* of statistical information. We are there given to know that since 1860 the negroes of the South, despite the experiences of the war, have increased nearly ten per cent. (or more exactly speaking, 9.7 per cent.) and that in the United States of to-day there are not less than five millions of black people! We can no longer shut our eyes to what we may be unwilling to believe. The day for prophesying for the black man of America a fate similar to that of its red man is past. The fact, welcome or unwelcome, must be accepted, that this race, in numbers already a considerable nation, of characteristics different from the white man's, is being mixed into the society and political system of America, and is working out there an experiment attended by the circumstances of a peculiar romance. A comparatively small number of Africans, brought across seas from their native wilds, grown up into a people of millions, trained in the harsh school of slavery, but a school whose benefits are that the negro is brought to his present capacity for an experiment more hopeful than has ever yet been made for his true civilization, are to be displayed to the world not only as a new test of the social and political system of America, but as a last supreme effort to take off a reproach that has lain for ages on the African, and to meet the prejudices against him in a new arena, and under auspices that have never been offered before. It is the apparition of a new figure and actor in the civilized world; a great historical and ethnological problem to be solved anew; a condition of things sprung out of the dramatic circumstances of a great war; a sudden transformation that exceeds the surprise of fiction; a new prospect dawned on what had been before supposed the most hopeless and melancholy outlook of history—the regeneration of the African; an intense study already commenced of this hitherto hopeless race; the *discovery*, so to speak, of the negro as a unique, poetical character, issued out of circumstances the most unpromising, yet already displaying capacities and virtues that have captured the observation and interest of the world. In this romance the writer desires a share, as in a great event of history that has happily occured in his times and generation, a crisis and a scene with which Providence has allowed him to be contemporary, and of which he is scarcely content to be an idle spectator.

It is astonishing how little the slave-holders of the South, despite their supposed knowledge of the negro, really knew of what was in him; what little idea or anticipation they had of capacities he is now exhibiting. The difficulty was that slavery was a perpetual barrier to an intimate acquaintance with the negro; it regarded him as a *thing*, and was never concerned to know what was in the sodden and concealed mind of a creature that represented only so much of productive force, and was estimated, body and soul, in dollars and cents. If one, even of Southern gentlemen, with the best intentions, sought knowledge of the negro, and made opportunities to converse with him, he ran the danger of being suspected as an abolitionist in disguise, or at least of being condemned as a "low person." Yet, despite the difficulties of the subject, this writer had in the period of slavery commenced the study of the negro *as a man*; he was already persuaded that there might be found in him virtues very peculiar, and even greater than what Northern authors, who had written novels and romances in his behalf, had ascribed to him; and his discoveries he had entitled "Black Diamonds." The negro had suddenly become as a new book to one who had been many years a slave-holder, and, as such, profoundly ignorant of the barbarian who did his pleasure.

The tenderness of the negro was a beautiful virtue of character; there was not a more affectionate nature in the world. His humor (he has no wit) was a study of itself; a rich and genial humor in which there was, remarkably, never a trace of vulgarity, and coupled with which was the apparently opposite tendency to a tender and poetical melancholy. His religious hymns offered a unique literary collection that has not yet been made. Here was a creature wholly uncultivated, his ignorance guarded in slavery (it being a misdemeanor in many of the Southern States to teach him to read or write), yet, after all deliberate efforts to crush out of him the character of man, and make him a mere laboring animal, exhibiting traits of character to reward the scholar, and virtues to assign him a high place on the roll of humanity. Slavery did not even deprive him of the virtue of courage; having somehow not proved in his case what it has so often been in the history of the world, an emasculator, to the degree that *slave* has stood as the synonyme for *coward*.

Let no one doubt the courage of the negro, although he wore the badge of an ownership on his body and his life was one long submission. There are even black heroes and martyrs in the unknown graves of Virginia. An incident of the war was related the other day by a friend, Dr. White, of the Alleghany Springs; and none of his hearers ventured to reflect upon his manhood, or to joke upon his sensibility, when they saw his eyes fill with generous tears as he related the simple story. He had served as a major in the Confederate army, and was attended there by a favorite slave. On the eve of one of the great battles of Virginia he called the slave to him and said, "George, there's to be a battle to-morrow. You having nothing to do with the fighting, and you can keep out of the way during the day." "No, sir," replied the boy, speaking slowly and thoughtfully; "I'll go with you. Ole misses made me promise before I left the home place that I would stay with you all the time, and bring back her chile 'live or dead. I must be by you to-morrow; don't ask me not to, Mas'r Isaac." "But George," remonstrated his master, "you can't shoot." "You gi' me a gun, sir," was the reply, "and (argumentatively,) I reckon I can kill as many of them as they can of me!" The next day the poor fellow fell, shot through the head, and died instantly at the feet of his master. His body sleeps in a grave which the affection of that master has adorned, and where his memory has often kept vigil as over one who had " laid down his life for his friend."

No candid person in the South will deny that the general experience of the negro since emancipation has been progress; that in nearly every respect of his life he exhibits some improvement from that date. Southern men are not very ready to advertise this to the world; they would probably confess it with reluctance to a Northern commission of inquiry; but in private conversations among themselves, where no pride of controversy interposes, they freely admit it and wonder as it. The negro moves. He is showing the greatest eargerness for knowledge and education; attested by the fact, for which examination is challenged, that in the free schools of the South, where he has equal admission, there are more black children than white ones in proportion to the population of each race in the given community. So far from becoming the idle vagabond that the pressimist theorizers would have him after enmancipation, he is exemplarily industrious; attested by the fact that to-day the negro represents nearly all the labor of the South, and admitting this test, that of persons in equal condition of poverty and of necessity of work, there are far more poor whites than negroes who are idle in the South. Of the vices that were to assail and destroy the negro in his new estate of freedom there are no proofs; quite the contrary. The terrible vice of intemperance, which has been the usual scourge of weak races, and the almost unfailing incident of a precocious civilization, is comparatively unknown among the Southern freedmen. So far from being improvident, the wonder is how the negro economizes, gets so many good clothes and real comforts out of his very scanty wages. As a voter he has shown a discretion and independence that have nonplussed the wisest of our politicians. There were white wiseacres who, some time ago, supposed that the negro's vote might be procured by the merest solicitation, a mere wink from his employer; and a common joke in the South on the Fifteenth Amendment was that the disfranchised white man might buy some cheap old negro to do his voting for him. Never was such disappointment. The spectacle has not been uncommon in the South of a negro who paid a deference to the white man scarcely less than he had shown in the days of slavery, who possibly yet said "Mas'r" who did his work in all humility and with all subjection, yet going openly to the polls and casting his vote there against the party of his employer. Such an instance of self-respect and moral courage is to be admired even by those against whom it acts. A distinguished Virginia politician recently assured the writer that he had not known of one single instances in the State, of a negro selling his vote for money; and yet the same gentleman remembered, in the days of the old hustings, not unfrequently seeing a white man approach a knot of politicians, saying with the greatest composure, "Gem'men what'll you give me for my vote?"—and a half dollar or a pint of whiskey generally concluded the bargain. In the jury-box the virtue and fidelity of the negro are remarkable, to the extent that it has already been observed that the worst negro criminals prefer to be tried by white juries rather than by peers of their own color. In fine, in most of the conduct of the negro is to be preceived the evidence of his deep sense of being on probation, a condition in which much will be exacted of him by either the hostility or the incredulity of criticism, and in which he can justify himself only by the most undoubted proofs of his worthiness; and indeed it is this visible impression upon the negro, as of one watched, that affords the best assurance of his continued improvement and progress.

Of the many interesting points of the negro, it is proposed here to select one especially for examination, and to make it the particular text of some reflections. It is a subject that will repay investigation. It is the Eloquence of the Negro. Here is a kind of genius that has often been found in uncultivated races, and the peculiarity of which is that it is not an affair of learning, not a creature of books, and, though the highest and dearest form of art, yet one in which the artist is least indebted to education or to professional training. It is of the phenomenon of such a genius that the negro has already aroused expectations. His universally admitted gifts of imagination, his extraordinary faculty of language, his delight in rhetorical exercise, afford reason to believe that there may yet be in reserve a development of negro character to astonish the world, and to confer upon him an interest new and altogether romantic.

The command of language which even the uneducated negro shows is singular; almost marvelous when we consider that, unable to write, he has only had the means of acquiring words by the ear, and that in a limited intercourse with the white man such as was allowed him in slavery. A language obtained without the assistance of books, picked up by the sense of hearing, is ordinarily a villanous compound (witness the "pigeon English" of the Chinaman); the vocabulary acquired is small; and there is a characteristic absence of selection, a habitual use of the first words that occur to the memory. What is remarkable of the negro's acquisition is the extent of his vocabulary; the fewness of his solecisms, his strong aversion to slang, and, on the whole, the purity with which he speaks a tongue that he has obtained only by the ear, and in a very limited practice. The abominable lingo ascribed to him by novel-writers and paragraphists in the newspapers is often an absurd caricature, a mode of speech that is heard neither in Virginia nor in Demerara. His faculty of selection in the use of words is his most remarkable gift; he has an ambition for polysylables; and even in the former days of slavery there was not a negro who had ever the advantage of listening to educated white persons but might command on occasion not a few words of "learned length."

Of course, some ludicrous mistakes are the consequences of his ambition; the wonder is that they are so few, and that the negro speaks an English so pure and ample. It will be found on studious examination that most of these mistakes are incident to the negro's method of acquiring language by the ear, that he has been betrayed by some likeness of sound, a phonetic imitation. Jack Averett, the negro orator of Virginia, had doubtless heard from the pulpit the story of Esau's silly bargain for "a mess of pottage." So the next time he mounted the rostrum, he was heard to declare that he "would never—no never—sell his birthright" (*i. e.*, the new vote Jack has) "for a nest of partridges." (And yet, by the way, the figure, as of a trifling consideration, was not alltogether unapt; the practice having been in the harvest fields of Virginia, that if a slave in reaping was so fortunate as to discover a partridge's nest, he carried it and its contents to his young master or mistress, who usually rewarded him with fourpence 'apenny, or some equivalent dole of sugar or molasses.)

But eloquence does not depend upon the extent of a vocabulary, nor is it wholly, nor even principally, we dare to say, an affair of words. Even with his necessarily limited mastery of language, the negro sometimes speaks with a power that astonishes the best educated of his white listeners; and it is not unfrequent that the black preacher in his log meeting-house finds among white auditors or intruders that those " who came to scoff, remain to pray."

In the pulpit the negro is in his best element. Here he is a born orator, and without those embarrassing necessities which want of education imposes upon him in other callings. Wherever the address is to the passions, where it is not incumbered by reasoning or calculation, the negro speaks with most freedom and effect; illustrating the cardinal rule of eloquence, that the orator himself must feel to make others feel, and that, no matter how imperfect the language, yet, if spoken out of the consciousness, it has a power which no rules can explain, which no art can approach, and for which nothing will account but that sympathy of souls which is the unsolvable mystery of our common humanity.

Bishop Doggett of the Methodist Episcopal Church South, who lately presided over a colored Conference in Tennessee, was struck by the eloquence displayed in this body, as well as by the fact that more than half of them had since the war taught themselves to read, and were able to refer to the Bible and to the discipline book with all the readiness of their white brethren. The good Bishop tells of the occasion a pleasant incident. "There were several remarkable characters," he writes, " among the members of Conference. One was named Willis. He was a presiding elder, as rotund as a hogshead, and somewhat resembling one. He was advanced in years, of deep piety, without education, of decided ability, and perfectly black. He arose on my left, and said, " Bishop, may I speak?" knowing the prevalent penchant for speaking, I replied. "That depends upon the nature of the subject." He replied, " It is in order." I added," Proceed, then." He commenced by saying, "I want to open a daguerreotype." I was equally amazed and amused. It was a most indefinite and enigmatical exordium. As ludicrous as it appeared, it was really well conceived. His meaning was that he wished to present an affecting picture to the contemplating of the audience. That picture was the relation in which the Rev. Thomas Taylor had stood to them for the last three years. He delineated his them, with force and beauty, melting into tenderness as he proceeded, great pearly tears rolled down his dusky cheeks. His tribute was positively eloquent. He concluded by offering a resolution that Brother Taylor be requested not to dissolve his relation with this colored Conference. I forgot and forgave what I thought the ignorant blunder of his first sentence. He did "open a daguerreotype" most effectually and maintained his credit as an original orator."

In political discussions the negro, as has been intimated, is not so happy or forcible as in the religious meeting-house, partly from the want of knowledge to furnish him with illustrations. Yet in legislative assemblies and on political occasions, despite his necessary ignorance in such arenas, the black man is sometimes found astonishing his auditors and putting to confusion the scoffers. There is a cheap school of humor become fashionable in Southern newspapers, which consists of fictitious reports of negro speeches made after some grotesque inventions in grammar and rhetoric. The caricature has been overdone; it wounds the negro, is a perpetual thorn in his side, a source of bad blood; and it disgusts those educated readers who can see nothing but a wanton pleasantry of self-conceit in this stupid persecution of the negro by reporters and would-be wits of rural newspapers, and but little real humor in easy accumulations of bad spelling and the invention of a senseless jargon. Such charcoal sketches have had their day, and can no longer be practised upon the credulity of readers. The black man has had an opportunity to speak in Cangress, to command audiences too large and notorious to admit the facility of misrepresentation. It was testified by the late Reconstruction Committee of Congress that the best speech made before them in behalf of the admission of Virginia was that of a young negro named Bland, who until the date of emancipation had been a slave; and it is remarkable that on this occasion Bland spoke in behalf of what was then called "the white man's party" in Virginia, and stood in company with some the most distinguished old politicians of that State, whose oratorical efforts he surpassed. He was only twenty-five years old, and the promise of his genius was cut short by his untimely death in the Capitol disaster at Richmond.

The writer had the fortune to hear this sable orator but a little while before his death. He was a brown-colored negro, slightly formed, dressed with scrupulous neatness, and had an ease and modesty of behavior that made a graceful combination, and at once conciliated his audience. The occasion was a political convention at Lynchburg, in which it was stated that a certain white man had obtained a *quasi* independant nomination for Congress, and threatened to divide the Radical vote with the regular nominee. Bland expostulated, to no purpose; the white candidate had evidently made up his mind to follow Mr. Sumner's advice to Secretary Stanton in the matter of office-holding, and to "stick." Bland at last had recourse to denunciation. It was a spectacle not to be forgotten, one indeed that epitomized a great social revolution, and was worthy of historical distinction. A negro, elate with passion, pointing the finger of scorn and of command at a white man, who a few years ago might have bought him as cattle in the shambles, and held a lash over his body; abashing one of his former masters or drivers by a superiour virtue, and presuming to rebuke him in the name of a great political party! He spoke for twenty or thirty minutes, sometimes in really choice language, and with a fluency in which there was not a single break. No report of the exact words can be attempted from memory; but the substance of the speech was well defined and connected. He said that office-seeking had been alleged as a reproach of his race; it was an honorable ambition to serve the public (and here he quoted a sentiment from Daniel Webster's funeral oration on Calhoun); "but" (and here he is reported literally) "it need not Holy Writ to enforce the lesson that the last should be first, and that he only was fit to govern who was able to obey." He concluded eloquently; but the negro's characteristic fondness for big words stuck in at the last. He would fasten upon the refractory white candidate " the worst name that the great Republican party had for its worst enemies, those who were enemies in disguise; a name that would follow him to his political grave—the name *dis-organ-izer!*" The weight of the last word, with the emphasis and deliberation bestowed upon it, was crushing. The best test of eloquence is its effect; and the conclusion was that the white aspirant got up, and said in a very whining, mendicant tone that he " begged leave to say, after the address of Mister Bland, that he begged leave to withdraw his name as that of a candidate for Congress."

It is worth while to attempt to determine what are the characteristics of the negro's eloquence, and to investigate its effects. There is a common popular notion that the black orator is disposed to *rant*, that he has great physical energy of delivery, and that his discourse is loud and colicky. This is a mistake. The forte of the negro orator is decidedly the pathetic; he is most effective in the low tones. In his melancholic cast of speech, he has the habit of sometimes changing or half-singing his words—what his race very characteristically knows as "moaning"; and it has occasionally the most weird and touching effects.

Another common imputation on the negro's oratory is that he is excessively fond of tropes; hence a suspicion of tawdriness of rhetoric. Now, although the imagination of the negro leads him into figurative language, it is remarkable that his favorite, almost exclusive figure is the simplest one in the rhetorician's repretoire—allegory; and so fond is he of this figure that often his whole speech on a given occasion is nothing more than one extended allegory. "Speaking in parables," as he calls it, is his favorite rhetorical pastime. There is a great fondness for Biblical illustrations. But few instances of abstract ideas occur to the negro's discourse. His strong imagination leads him to personify nearly every object of his discourse, and this produces a vividness and reality that are his peculiar virtues as an orator.

Indeed, regarding eloquence as a very profound problem of the conciousness, instead of an art to be objectively taught, the unlearned negro may claim an eminence past dispute. The intense realization of what he says is the peculiarity of the negro's speech, rather than any number or mode of figures of speech; and in this respect it must be insisted that his eloquence is of the purest and severest school. His faculty of illusion is what strikes one most in observing the negro speaker. He seems able to transport himself into the scene he describes, or into the emotion he has summoned; and it is this faculty which which, beyond all accomplishments of language and structures of art, is simply and surpassingly the thing called eloquence. The starting eyes, looking over and beyond his audience; the unheeded perspiration of the brow; the large, clumsy hands, trembling with emotion, and raining down from the air, in which they are raised, an impalpable influence, attest that the negro speaker is *feeling* what he says, when he is in the full tide of exhortation, when, perchance, he sees his favorite religious phantasm, "the old ship of Zion," far away on the stormy waves, or sings, as of a longing spectator, the hymn of "Swing low, Chariot," one of his favorite visions of the sky. Art might take its lessons from many of the rude, but impassioned scenes that are to be found in a negro meeting-house; and to study the black man as an orator is an employment that remains to reward the adventure of the scholar in a new and unbeaten path of discovery.

The subject is one to be investigated, and worth investigation. Surely not the least of the romances attaching to the negro in his recent introduction to the interest and curiosity of the world is that in what has heretofore been considered the unsightly and unpromising son of Africa, may yet be found the type of a being long lost in æsthetic history—a true orator. Who knows, indeed, but that the "forest-born Demosthenes" may yet prove to be a black man? EDWARD A. POLLARD.

It affords the writer pleasure to note the fact that he relies largely upon the "Black Phalanx," by Colonel J. T. Wilson, who was chosen by his comrades in the G. A. R., to be the historian of the Negro soldiers, for military data.

From a beautiful source comes the idea, and there is no less truth than poetry in it:

"We have gathered posies from other men's flowers;
Nothing but the thread that binds them is ours."

The several causes which led to the war of American independence, 1775, are too well known by the reader to need further explanation or comment; therefore it is sufficient to remark that our intelligent and fair-minded orators, historians and poets all give the sable patriots credit for having been instrumental in checking the British advance and saving the day to the American arms.

When, where, and by whom was the first blow struck for American independence?

By Crispus Attucks, a runaway slave, who led a crowd of white and colored against the soldiers, "with brave words of encouragement." By the shot of the enemy Attucks, the gallant leader, and first martyr to the cause of American liberty, was the first to fall. He, and Samuel Gray and Jonas Caldwell were killed on the spot. Samuel Maverick and Patrick Carr were mortally wounded.

The four hearses formed a junction in King street and then the procession marched in columns six deep, with a long file of coaches belonging to the most distinguished citizens, to the Middle Burying Ground, where the four victims were deposited in one and the same grave, over which a stone was placed with the inscription:

"Long as in Freedom's cause the wise contend,
Dear to your country shall your fame extend;
While to the world the lettered stone shall tell
Where Caldwell, Attucks, Gray, and Maverick fell."

In this we see the first blood which was shed in the colonies for national independence, was by a Negro.

As with Crispus Attucks, so it was with many thousands of others in the protracted struggle against the Lion, in which the oppressed Negro readily enlisted in the ranks, and marched, and fought, and bled, and died, side by side with the white patriot, for freedom, which, after it was gained, was denied him.

The action of Attucks on this ever memorable occasion electrified the whole sweep of the colonies, and put a new phase upon their grievances. This engagement took place on the 5th of March, 1770, in the city of Boston.

Who was Peter Salem?

He was undoubtedly one of the chief heroes on the battle-field of Bunker Hill, June 17th, 1775.

When the British Major, Pitcairn, mounted the redoubt in this great battle, shouting "The day is ours!" this hero, Peter Salem, fired the contents of his rifle into this distinguished officer's body, killing him instanly and checking for a time the advance of the British charge. Six months and four days after the battle at Bunker Hill, namely, December 21st, a petition was prepared and presented to the General Court of Massachusetts Bay for a proper and substantial recognition of the great and distinguished services of Peter Salem. His bravery, patriotism and unquestionable thirst for liberty was tested also on the battle-fields of Concord and Saratoga.

It would prove an Hurculean task, and a fruitless attempt were we to assay to chronicle the names of the many eminent colored soldiers, and leaders in heroic deeds, predicating inborn valor, equaled only by Napoleon's Old Guard at the battle of Austerlitz, or Hannibals Invincibles at Trebia.

In this war there were 5,000 colored braves who enlisted for American Independence, while about 40,000 were rolling around his Majestys Standard under Generals Clinton, Dunmore and Cornwallis—Both belligerents pledging themselves, by Resolutions, Declarations and Proclamations to share with "Gods image cut ebon"— their colored comrade, the reward their contentious.

Mr. Wilson, is his "Black Phalanx" writes: "To speak of the gallantry of the Negro soldiers recalls the recollection of some of their daring deeds at Red Bank, where four (400) hundred men met and repulsed, after a terrible, sanguinary struggle, fifteen (1,500) hundred Hessian troops (whites) led by Count Donop."

This is one instance indexing many thousands of others equally conspicuous and equally happy in results for the American cause.

When the true light of this great war, which tried men's souls, shall illuminate the historic page, the names of Major Jeffrey, Jordan Freeman, Samuel Lee, Quack Matrick, Jonas Armistead, Jonathan Overton, Sambo Latham, Samuel Charlton, James Easton, Ebenezer Hill, Prince Whipple, Jonas Caldwell, Samuel Maverick, Salem Poor, Samuel Gray, Simon Lee, Crispus Attucks, and others, shall shine forth clad in bright and heavy coats of mail forever, their watching spirits keeping abreast of time will, ever and anon, be found rejoicing in the results of their devotion and sacrifice—universal suffrage and the equality of all men before the law.

> Flung to the viewless winds
> Or on the waters cast,
> Their ashes shall watched
> And gathered at the last,
> Around us and abroad
> Shall spring a precious seed
> Of witneses to God.

Their returning dust kissed, with a war-like shout, the horrifying fields of gore until victory was sealed with blood in the battles of Lexington, April 19th, 1775, Bunker Hill, June 17th, 1775, Fort Moultrie, June 28th, 1776, Long Island, Aug. 27th, 76. Here the British had in line of battle 30,000 trained men of war under the command of Generals Howe and Clinton, while the Americans had only 9,000 soldiers under Gen. Putnam. This was a signal victory for American arms.

Trenton, 1776, Princeton, Jan. 2nd, 1777, Brandywine, September 11th '77, Germantown, October 4th, '77,

Saratoga, September 19th, and October 7th, 1777. This engagement came off between the American Gen. Gates and the British Burgoyne.

Monmouth, June 28th, 1778, Camden, August, 17th, 1781, Eutaw Springs, September 8th, '81, Fort Griswold Springfield, Guilford Court House, Bennigton—Point Bridge, Concord, Stillwater and Yorktown, September 28th, 1781.

But alas! the sad fate of Major Jeffrey was the reward of a large majority of these trusting, sable sons of war.

How was he treated by his white Comrades after undergoing so much endurance and sacrifice for what he was led to believe was intended for a blessing on all Americans regardless of color or former condition?

He was a brave commander of both white and colored troops at the battle before Mobile, during the campaign of Major-General Jackson. He was a Tennesseean. In this battle the charge made by Major Stump was a failure. Stump retired in disorder—his troops confused. At this juncture Major Jeffrey (colored) being at the time a private, seeing the miserable retreat of the white Major and his command, and comprehending the disastrous result which was about to befall his countrymen, rushed forward, mounted a horse, took command of the troops and by heroic effort, rallied them to renew the charge, completely routing the British and leaving the Americans masters of the field.

He was highly respected and revered by both races in the army as well as in Nashville, where he resided. For his soldierly qualities and knightly courage and bearing he was christened in the name of " Major," by General Jackson. Soon after this he was forced to resent an indgnity imposed upon him by an incorrigible non-descript and for thus defending himself against an unprovoked attack, he was led into a public place and whipped with a raw hide by those whose hearth-stones, property, lives and liberty he had so nobly defended in the thickest of many bloody battles. He was now seventy (70) years of age and died almost immediately after this ungrateful, miserably humiliating castigation. He fought for the independence of his country, and died heart-broken because of the ill treatment received at the hands of his comrades, to indulge the whim and passion of a ruffian who, in all probability, never fired a gun nor spent a dollar for his country's independence. Many others were re-enslaved.

In these few lines we discover a struggle unexampled, a race of heroes, a devotion unparalleled in ancient or modern history. 'Tis sad to reflect that for all this gallantry he enjoyed none of the blessings he acheived, through blood and prayer for his so-called country.

More than 15,000 colored soldiers fightihg the Lion of the world, nearly eight years of devastation, in more than twenty-five pitched battles, but all of this sacrifice failed, under the power of Slaveocracy, to sever the tie that bound them to an unhappy existence. The Negro, however, made a record which in itself is a lasting legacy to the millions now reading his efforts and the millions yet unborn, as reflected from the light of honest history.

CHAPTER XIII.

WAR OF 1812.

In this war the Negro in arms only sustained the enviable reputation he had won for his race thirty-seven years earlier. The cause of this war grew out some Naval restrictions on the part of England, relative to the management of her sailors, prejudicial to the American Navy. Several sailors escaped from an English vessel and found lodgment in an American ship—the Chesapeake. The names of the seamen deserting the English ship Melampus, then lying in Hampton Roads, were William Ware, Daniel Martin, John Strachan, John Little and Ambrose Watts. After some consular correspondence, a demand was made by letter addressed to the Commander of the Chesapeake, Commodore James Barron, to deliver up the so-called deserters. The demand was refused and a broadside was opened upon the Chseapeake by the English frigate Leopard.

Hard upon four years elapsed before the assault upon the American vessel was settled. Still, however, the cause of the belligerent attitude of these two great powers remained. War was promptly declared June 17th, 1812. It was carried on principally upon the water between the armed vessels of the two nations, therefore no great forces were called into active service upon the field. The colored men entered the service with alacrity; in the naval department of this war we swelled the number of those who manned the nation's guns upon the rivers, lakes, bays and oceans, in defense of Free Trade, Sailors Rights and Independence, on the seas as well as on the land. We cannot put in figures anything like the accurate number of colored men who stood by the paraphernalia that brought to the arms of the States such a just recognition as fairly eclipsed the admiration of the world, and quit the engagement with banners shouting to every man and gun, "with lightning rolled in every fold, and flashing victory."

It is recorded in history that the battle of Lake Erie was the most memorable naval encounter with the British; of it Rossiter Johnson in his discription of the engagement, says:

"As the question of the fighting qualities of the black man has since been considerably discussed, it is worth noting that in this bloody and brilliant battle a *Large* number of Commodore Perry's men were Negroes."

More by the love and hope of freedom, which ever animated them, they responded to the call of General Jackson, "with a zeal and energy," says Mr. Wilson in his "Black Phalanx," "characteristic only of a brave and patriotic people." They entered the ranks of their country's defenders whenever that realm has been assailed by foes without or traitors within. He deems it very fitting that he close this chapter in the language of the profound thinker and historian above referred to: "As in the dark days of the Revolution, so now in another period of national danger, the Negroes proved their courage and patriotism by service in the field. However, the lamentable treatment of Major Jeffrey is evidence that these services were not regarded as a protection against outrage. In the two wars in which the history of the Negroes has been traced in these pages there is nothing that militates against his manhood, though his condition, either bond or free, was lowly. But, on the contrary, the honor of the race has been maintained under every circumstance in which it has been placed."

Of their struggle, wearied and despondent, as had been their career for nearly 200 years at that time, they caught the inspiration by the hope of impartial liberty, and rallied to the strong support of Jackson's banner, since under it they were promised all the blessings of a free people.

As to their mark on history's wall,

> "Time cannot wither it
> Nor custom sale
> Its infinite variety and beauty."

REV. A. M. BARRETT.

Rev. A. M. Barrett, of Raleigh, N. C., was born Feby. the 7th 1844, near the little town of Carthage, Moore County, N. C. He and his ancestry were the chattel property of Rev. R. G. Barrett.

Edward and Catherine Barrett were the respected parents of this distinguished divine.

His father, a consistent christian, died at his old home near Carthage, 1878. But his mother died much earlier. She however, lived to the ripe age of sixty-five and died 1863. She bore the cross of Christ, for thirty-five years, with patience and pleasure, though life with the poor slave was one long, cold and dreary night of suffering and often for whom death was the only relief obtainable.

From the early age of nine to nineteen this bright star was a waiting man, or livery boy, for his master on his circuit and pastoral visits (for he was a Presiding Elder in the M. E. Church, South).

During these days of bondage and travel, our subject enjoyed the confidence of his owner. His master and mistress taught him to read and write, notwithstanding this was "contrary to the (Black code) statutes, in such cases, made and provided." After his master moved down to the city of Goldsboro, (N. C.,) our divine's task was comparatively light, for his master sold his livery. This afforded Rev. A. M. B., a better opportunity to study. He taught Sunday-school, lectured and preached to his people. While in this place he was employed at a good salary, as sexton in the white church.

At Beaufort, (N. C.,) July the 16th, 1861 he was licensed or allowed to preach to his comrades in bondage. Then he was only seventeen years old: He professed religion at the age of fifteen and cultivated the spirit of true piety as he advanced in years. The great kindness shown him by his master and mistress was quite unusual, and grew out of the aptitude and purity of character as exhibited by young Barrett. He possessed a wonderful talent for discoursing upon topics of faith and duty to God and man, and evinced such a wonderful knowledge of the Bible that he was not only respected by both races but was also granted privileges which were denied others of his race.

This anti-bellum, but clandestine preparation, served him a great purpose and enabled him to enter at once, when white winged peace and freedom flashed over the dark horizon of the South, upon a career of usefulness, that redounds alike to his individual credit, and an honor to the race he represents.

He was the first colored man in the county of Moore to obtain a public school teacher's certificate by an examination at the hands of the county examiner who was then Lawyer A. R. McDonald. This was in the fall of 1865. He got a good grade.

In 1866 he married Miss C. J. Kelly, of Carthage, and in the same year joined the A. M. E. Z. Church under Elder (now Bishop) J. W. Hood. He went forth organizing churches and schools, and of course met with great and deserved success.

At the North Carolina Annual Conference held in Lincolnton, he was elected Recording Secretary and was at the same time ordained Deacon, November 27th 1867, by Rt. Rev. J. J. Clinton, presiding Bishop, and was appointed to the Haywood charge, where he had been laboring for some considerable length of time. He was ever zealous of his engagements and never lost an appointment by reason of service as teacher in the public schools. On one occasion the water courses were all swollen high, and to his discomfiture, impeded travel by buggy or horseback. He was, in consequence of this fact, advised by friends not to venture or hazard the risk of getting drowned, but nothing would satisfy his mind but the fulfillment of his appointment; so he "spread his sails," as it were, to the breeze, with Bible and hymn-book in hand, "feet shod," so to speak, "with the gospel preparation," and walked in the cold through mud and rain to his church, where he found his flock anxiously awaiting his arrival. It was indeed, a severe ordeal, but all enjoyed the task. This shows the moral heroism in the man and accounts for his wonderful achievements. His first text, preached in the light of freedom, was from Psalm ix:17. "The wicked shall be turned into hell and all the nations that forget God."

In 1868, at the regular fall election, he was elected as Magistrate for his township and with the view of the better understanding his duties as such, he read both statute and common law. His rulings in his judicial capacity reflected credit upon his constituency and race.

While pushing the arts of peace, he has taught school every year since Emancipation, and served as Secretary for a number of years, the annual Conferences which he attended.

Again in 1871 he was promoted. This time to the eldership by Rt. Rev. Bishop Logan. He has always endeavored to advance the cause of temperance among all the people with whom he mingled.

He was a delegate to the General Conferences of his connection which met at the following places:

At Charlotte, (N. C.,) in 1872, which elected Elder J. W. Hood, D. D., as one of the Bishops, and also promoted him (Elder Barrett) to the presiding Eldership. At Louisville, (July 22nd,) 1876—at Montgomery, Ala., in 1880 and also attended as a spectator to the General Conferences held in New York, 1884 and at New Berne, (N. C.,) 1888.

In 1876 he visited the Centennial Grounds at Philadelphia. Here he saw in one hour the work of a century of National life.

After his return home from the Louisville Conference he entered the St. Augustine Normal School in Raleigh. From this institution he graduated in due course of time. His children have made quite a reputation in this school.

During his labor on the Wadesboro District, (1881 and '84, and again 1888) the District proved itself equal in good works to any in the Conference circuit, both financially and spiritually. Greater harmony never prevailed. "Behold, how good and how pleasant it is for brethren to dwell together in unity: It is like the precious ointment upon the head, that ran down upon the beard, even Aaron's beard; that went down to the skirts of his garments; as the dew of Hermon, and as the dew that descended upon the Mountains of Zion." " No good thing will he withhold from them that walk uprightly." Such has been, and is to-day, the propitious manifestation of God's approval of Rev. Barrett's faith and good works. He has been instrumental in bringing many thousands of souls to Christ. He has preached one hundred and fifty funerals. Secured scores of lots for churches and saw that they were paid for and the deeds given for the same, and a good building reared on each. His habits of temperance and economy are indeed, exemplary. He neither smokes, chews nor drink intoxicants. In the fall of 1872 he coveted the pleasures of a home, so he negotiated with one B. E. Webster for the purchase of one hundred acres of land in Moore county, for which he paid $500—$250. cash, balance in a short time afterwards. In 1776 he bought two city lots in the city of Raleigh, he erected a dwelling house on each with other neccessary out-buildings—his dwelling costing near $1000. The property here costing $1,310.

Since then he has acquired possession of a good lot in the town of Sandford. He owns also two lots in Pee Dee, (a R. R. Station). This is a few miles South of Lilesville, N. C. Besides these he owns another tract of land in Moore county. On this place he erected a grist and saw mill.

Another friend was a partner with Rev. B., and owned an interest in the mill. Brother B.. sold his interest to his partner and bought another place. This was in 1876.

He managed in this wise to acquire an education of a higher order. That is to say, he would remain in St. Augustine during the week and on Friday evening would leave about 4 o'clock p. m., to go to his Circuit many miles away, but would be on hand Monday morning to take his place in his class. This he did for two years and six months. Of course he traveled to and from his ministerial appointments by railway.

Several of his children, the oldest ones have been engaged teaching—sometimes assisting their father, but were frequently principals of their own schools.

He lost two children by diptheria—namely, James W. Hood, aged five years—Edward Jas. Bailey, aged three years—both were corpses at the same time and both were buried in the same grave, they were funeralized by Rev. J. Alston, taking his text from Job i, 21.

In June 1880 his nine months old daughter, J. M. C., was called hence away, to bathe in that celestial joy, to join in that rapturous melody, "hard by the throne of God"

"Where saints immortal reign;
Where infinite day excludes the night,
And pleasures banish pain."

She was his pet, but God needed her.

Never has Rev. B. been arraigned before the ecclesiastical court, Conference, or any other court, nor any other body, for moral imbecility or unchristian conduct, in deed or action; neither for the commission of improprieties or the omission of domestic or ministerial duties.

These lines of poetic beauty seem, like a golden strand, to run all through the life lessons of the individual sketched in this narrative:

"Honor and fame from no condition rise;
Act well your part; *there* all the honor lies."

CHAPTER XIV.

WAR BETWEEN THE STATES, 1861-5.

What was the cause of this war?

The northern cause was preeminently the national unity of states, with freedom as a basis, while that of the southern cause was for slavery and disunion. Slavery was the chief aggravation of this war.

What effective steps were taken by the South to dissolve this Union?

In 1861 the Southern National Convention, held in Montgomery, Alabama, passed resolutions dissolving its connection with the United States, and styling itself the Southern Confederacy of America.

NEGROES AS SOLDIERS.

LETTER OF GEN. LEE ADVISING THEIR USE IN THE CONFEDERATE ARMY.

In a speech delivered in the Confederate House of Representatives, in February, 1865, by Mr. E. Barksdale, of Mississippi, on the bill to authorize the employment of negro troops by voluntary enlistment, he quoted a letter of Gen. Lee, which, it is said, has not been generally published. Mr. Barksdale, who is a member-elect of the 49th

Congress, furnished a copy of the letter from his musty files. It is as follows:

Hd'qrs Confederate States Armies,
February 18, 1865.

E. Barksdale, House of Representatives, Richmond:
Sir—I have the honor to acknowledge the receipt of your letter of the 12th inst., with reference to the employment of negroes as soldiers. I think the measure not only expedient but necessary. The enemy will certainly use them against us if he can get possession of them, and as his present numerical superiority will enable him to penetrate many parts of the country, I cannot see the wisdom of the policy of holding them to await his arrival, when we may by timely action and judicious management, use them to arrest his progress. I do not think that our white population can supply the necessities of a long war without overtaxing its capacity and imposing great suffering upon our people; and I believe we should provide resources for a protracted struggle, not merely for a battle or a campaign.

In answer to your second question, I can only say that in my opinion, the negro, under proper circumstances, will make an efficient soldier. I think we could do as well with them as the enemy, and he attaches great importance to their assistance. Under good officers and good instruction, I do not see why they should not become soldiers. They possess all the physical qualifications, and their habits of obedience constitute a good foundation for discipline. They furnish a more promising material than many armies of which we read in history, which owed their efficiency to discipline alone. I think those who are employed should be freed. It would be neither just nor wise, in my opinion, to require them to serve as slaves. The best course to pursue, it seems to me, would be to call for such as are willing to come, with the consent of their owners. An impressment or draft would not be likely to bring out the best class, and the use of coercion would make the measure distasteful to them and to their owners.

I have no doubt that if Congress would authorize their reception into service, and empower the President to call upon individuals or states for such as they are willing to contribute, with the condition of emancipation to all enrolled, a sufficient number would be forthcoming to enable us to try the experiment. If it proves successful, most of the objections to the measure would disappear, and if individuals still remained unwilling to send their negroes to the army, the force of public opinion in the states would soon bring about such legislation as would remove all obstacles. I think the matter should be left, as far as possible, to the people and to the states, which alone can legislate as the necessities of this particular service may require. As to the mode of organizing them, it should be left as free from restraint as possible. Experience will suggest the best course, and it would be inexpedient to trammel the subject with provisions that might in the end prevent the adoption of reforms suggested by actual trial.

With great respect, your obedient servant,

R. E. LEE, General.

Who was elected as Cheif Executive of this new Empire of Slavery?

Upon its organization Jefferson Davis was chosen President, and A. H. Stephens, of Georgia, as Vice President, with its capital at Richmond, Virginia.

The question of freedom and slavery had been under discussion for more than a quarter of a century, and when the humane sun of liberty began to pearce every community, and to find, and formulate, and develop a healthy sentiment for freedom, the slave-god began to put on the war-paint and challenge the North for a test at arms.

When and where was the first gun fired in this war?

At Fort Sumter, South Carolina, April 12th, 1861, at 4 o'clock, a. m.

What was the condition of the Union Army after the first year's progress of the war?

It was found to be inadequate to contend with a million and a-half trained white soldiers on the battle-field, and four and a-half millions of colored men supporting them from the cornfields by forced labor. It was this condition of affairs that led to President Lincoln's celebrated Emancipation Proclamation in 1863, and the call for colored volunteers.

How was the call for colored troops appreciated by colored people?

The privilege of fighting for their own freedom and the union of their country was regarded by them as being the Olympian archway to the universal suffrage of their race.

Enlistment commenced promptly, and ere long, the following summer (1863), had passed into sombre autumn 150,000 colored men were fighting like Spartan braves for a free, united government.

What was the number of colored soldiers who served in the army?

The rolls show 180,000; but Mr. Wilson, in his "*Black Phalanx*" claims 220,000 who enlisted in the ranks of the army.

It is well known that the first systematic attempt to organize colored troops during the war of the rebellion was the so-called "Hunter regiment." The officer originally detailed to recruit for this purpose was Sergeant C. T. Trowbridge, of the New York Volunteer Engineers (Col. Serell). His detail was dated May 7, 1862, S. O: 84, Dpt.

South. The second regiment in order of muster was the First Kansas, colored, dating from January 13, 1863. The first enlistment in the Kansas regiment goes back to August 6, 1862, while the earliest technical date of enlistment in any regiment was October 19, 1863, although, as was stated above, one company dated its organization back to May, 1862. My muster as Colonel dates back to November 10, 1862, several months earlier than any other of which I am aware, among colored regiments, except that of Col. Stafford (First Louisiana National Guard), Sept. 27, 1862. Col. Williams, of the Frst Kansas colored, was mustered as Lt. Col., on Jan., 13, 1863; as Col., March 8, 1863. These dates I have (with the other facts relating to the regiment), from Col R. J. Hinton, the first officer detailed to recruit it.

The first detachment of the Second South Carolina Volunteers (Col. Montgomery), went into camp at Port Royal Island February 23, 1863, numbering one hundred and twenty men. I do not know the date of his muster; it was somewhat delayed, but was probably dated back to about that time. Recruiting for the Fifty-fourth Massachusetts (colored) began on February 9, 1863, and the first squad went into camp at Readville, Massachusetts, on February 21, 1863, numbering twenty-five men. Col. Shaw's commission, and probably his muster, was dated April 17, 1863 (Report of Adjt. Gen. of Massachusetts for 1863, pp. 896-99). These were the enlisted colored regiments so far as I know.

What Generals commanded the colored soldiers in this civil war?

Generals Hunter, Butler, Thomas, Grant, Mead, Burnside, Gillmore, Rousseau, Granger, T. J. Morgan, Vail, Curtin, Phelps, Weitzel, Stoneman, Gilliam, Burbridge, Wade, Brisbin, G. L. Stearns, Freemont, Banks, Wilde,

Ferrero, Sedgwick, Binney, Paine, Dwight, Ullman and Steadman.

What can you say of the Black Phalanx as to bravery and discipline?

Mr. Wilson says: "As a phalanx they were invaluable in crushing the rebellion. Let their acts of heroism tell. In the light of history and of their own deeds, it can be said that in courage, patriotism and dash, they were second to no troops of either ancient or modern armies."

Name some of the chief battles in which the colored soldiers won fame.

Port Hudson, Fort Wagner, Milliken's Bend, New Market Heights, Petersburg, Olustee, Bull Run, Ball's Bluff, Roanoke, New Berne, Gaines' Mill, Mechanicsville, Seven Pines, Savage Station, Glendale, Malvern Hill, Fredericksburg, Chancellorsville, Antietam, South Mountain, Knoxville, Vicksburg, Gettysburg. These battlefields are as many stars, reflecting ever, in brilliant rays, amidst the gloom and partiality of general history, the black man's military valor and sacrifice.

OFFICERS.

"They were officered by the elite, such as Col. R. G. Shaw, of the 54th Massachusetts, a former member of the 7th New York regiment, and upon whose battle monument his name is carved; Cols. James C. Beecher, Wm. Brinly, and a host of others, whose names can now be found on the army rolls, with the prefix, General, commanded these regiments. Of those who commanded southern regiments this is equally true, especially of those who served in the 9th, 10th, 18th, and 19th corps. Col. Godfred Weitzel, who, in March, 1855, had been promoted to Major General of Volunteers, commanded the 25th corps of 30,000 negro soldiers!"—*From the "Black Phalanx."*

The following is an extract from an oration of Wendell Phillips, in Boston, December, 1861, relative to the possible service of the colored man, who, at that time ought to have been carrying a musket instead of a hoe:

"All I know is that the Port Royal expedition proved one thing—it laid forever that ghost of an argument, that the blacks loved their masters—it settled forever the question whether the blacks were with us or with the South. My opinion is that the blacks are the key of our position. He that gets them wins, and he that loses them goes to the wall. Port Royal settled one thing—the blacks are with us, and not with the South. At present they are the only unionists. I know nothing more touching in history, nothing that art will immortalize and poetry dwell upon more fondly—I know no tribute to the Stars and Stripes more impressive than that incident of the blacks coming to the water-side with their little bundles, in that simple faith which had endured through the long night of so many bitter years. They preferred to be shot rather than driven from the sight of that banner they had so long prayed to see. And if such was the result when nothing but General Sherman's equivocal proclamation was landed on the Carolinas, what should we have seen if there had been eighteen thousand veterans, with Fremont, the statesman-soldier of this war, at their head, and over them the Stars and Stripes, gorgeous with the motto, 'Freedom for all! Freedom forever!' If that had gone before them, in my opinion they would have marched across the Carolinas and joined Brownlow in East Tennessee, the bulwark on each side of them would have been one hundred thousand grateful blacks; they would have cut this rebellion in halves, and while our fleets fired salutes across New Orleans, Beauregard would have been ground to powder between the upper millstone of McClellan and the lower of a quarter million of blacks rising to greet the Stars and Stripes. McClellan may drill a better army—more perfect soldiers. He will never marshal a stronger force than those grateful thousands."

Describe the battles of New Market Heights and Milliken's Bend.

On the 29th of September, 1864, Gen. Grant ordered Gen. Butler to cross the James river at two points and attack the enemy's line of works. The enemy's position laid on the top of a hill, from this redoubt led a steep incline into a marsh where the union soldiers were gathered.

Of it Gen. Butler has this to say:

"On that plain where the flash of dawn was breaking, Butler placed a column of the Black Phalanx [which consisted of the 5th, 36th, 38th, and 2d Cavalry reg'ts], numbering three thousand, in close column, by division, right in front, with guns at right shoulder shift. The center of the line was given to the 18th corps, composed of white troops under Gen. Ord, and they drove the enemy from a very strong work, capturing several pieces of cannon. Gen. Butler had been severely criticised by officers of the regular army for organizing twenty-five regiments of negroes. "Why," said they, "they will not fight." In contradiction of this assertion Butler made up his mind to prove the worth and value of the Black Phalanx. Notwithstanding their gallantry at Petersburg, and on the Fredericksburg road, the metal of the 25th corps of the Army of the James was to be tried; so Butler took command of the Phalanx himself, with a determination to set at rest forever the fighting capacity of a portion of his command. Addressing the Phalanx, he said, pointing to the works on the enemy's flanks: "Those works must be taken by the weight of your column; not a shot must be fired." In order to prevent them from firing, he had the caps taken from the nipples of their guns. "When you charge," said he, "your cry will be 'Remember Fort Pillow.'" 'Twas in the early gray of the morning, ere the sun had risen, the order "Forward!" had set the column in motion, and it went forward as if on parade—down the hill, across the marsh, and as the column got into the brook they came within range of the enemy's fire, which was vigorously opened upon them. The column broke a little. As it forded the brook it wavered! What a moment of intense anxierty! But they forward again. As they reached the firm ground, marching on steadily with close ranks, under the enemy's fire, until the head of the column reached the first line of abatis, some one hundred and fifty yards from the enemy's works, then the axemen ran to the front to cut away the heavy obstacles of defence, while one thousand men of the enemy, with their artillery concentrated, poured from the redoubt a heavy fire upon the head of the column of fours. The axemen went down under that murderous fire. Other strong black hands grasped the axes in their stead. The abatis was cut away. Again, at double-quick, the column went forward to within fifty yards of the fort, to meet another line of abatis. The column halted, and there a very fire of hell was poured upon them. The abatis resisted and held the head of the column which literally melted away under the rain of shot and shell; the flags of the leading regiments went down, but a brave black hand seized the colors. They were soon up again and waved their starry light over the storm of battle. Again the axemen fell; but strong hands and willing hearts seized the heavy sharpened trees and dragged them away, and the column rushed forward, and with a shout that rung out above the roar of artillery, went over the redoubt like a flash, and the enemy did not stop running within four miles, leaving the Phalanx in possession of their deemed impregnable work, cannon and small arms. The autocrats of the regular army could croak no longer about the negro soldiers not fighting. This gallantry of the Phalanx won for them and the negro race the admiration of the men who supported Jeff. Davis and the slave power in the Charleston Convention in 1860. Ten years after this splendid victory of the Phalanx, in support of their civil rights General Butler, then a member of Congress, made an eloquent appeal in behalf of the equal civil rights of the negro race. In it he referred to the gallant charge of the Phalanx. He said: "It became my painful duty to follow in the track of that charging column, and there, in a space not wider than the clerk's desk, and three hundred yards long, lay the dead bodies of five hundred and forty-three of my colored comrades, fallen in defence of their country, who had offered up their lives to uphold its flag and its honor, as a willing sacrifice; and as I rode along among them, guiding my horse this way and that way, lest he should profane with his hoofs what seemed to me the sacred dead, and as I looked on their bronzed faces, upturned in the shining sun, as if in mute appeal against the wrongs of the country for which they had given their lives, whose flag had only been to them a flag of stripes, on which no star of glory had ever shone for them—feeling I had wronged them in the past, and believing what was the future of my country to them—among my dead comrades there, I swore to myself a solemn oath—may my right hand forget its cunning and my tongue cleave to the roof of my mouth, if I ever fail to defend the rights of those men who have given their blood for me and my country that day, and for their race forever. And God helping me, I will keep that oath."

Special correspondent N. Y. Tribune.

MILLIKEN'S BEND.

The following account of the battle of Milliken's Bend is given by Captain Miller, an eye-witness and participant in the same—it therefore deserves full credence:

"We were attacked here on June 7, about 3 o'clock in the morning, by a brigade of Texas troops, about two thousand five hundred in number. We had about six hundred men to withstand them, five hundred of them negroes. I commanded Company I, 9th Louisiana. We went into the fight with thirty-three men. I had sixteen killed, eleven badly wounded, and four slightly. I was wounded slightly on the head, near the right eye, with a bayonet, and had a bayonet run through my right hand, near the forefinger; that will account for this miserable style of penmanship. Our regiments had about three hundred men in the fight. We had one Colonel wounded, four Captains wounded, two 1st, and two 2d Lieutenants killed, five Lieutenants wounded, and three white orderlies killed, and one wounded in the hand, and two fingers taken off. The list of killed and wounded officers comprised nearly all the officers present with the regiment, a majority of the rest being absent recruiting. We had about fifty men killed in the regiment, and eighty wounded; so you can judge of what part of the fight my company sustained. I never felt more grieved and sick at heart than when I saw how my brave soldiers had been slaughtered—one with six wounds, all the rest with two or three, none less than two wounds. Two of my colored sergeants were killed; both brave, noble men, always prompt, vigilant and ready for the fray. I never more wish to hear the expression "the niggers won't fight." Come with me a hundred yards from where I sit, and I can show you the mounds that cover the bodies of sixteen as brave, loyal, and patriotic soldiers as ever drew bead on a rebel. The enemy charged us so close that we fought with our bayonets, hand-to-hand. I have six broken bayonets to show how bravely my men fought. The Twenty-third Iowa joined my company on the right, and I declare truthfully, that they had all fled before our regiment fell back, as we were all compelled to do. Under the command of Col. Page, I led the Ninth and Eleventh Louisiana, when the rifle-pits were retaken and held by our troops. I narrowly escaped death once. A rebel took deliberate aim at me with both barrels of his gun, and the bullets passed so close to me that the powder that remained on them burnt my cheek. Three of my men who saw him aim and fire thought he wounded me each fire. One of them was killed by my side, and he fell on me, covering my clothes with his blood; and before the rebel could fire again, I blew his brains out with my gun. It was a horrible fight, the worst I ever engaged in, not even excepting Shiloh. The enemy cried 'No quarter!' but some of them were very glad to take it when made prisoners.

"Col. Allen, of the Sixteenth Texas, was killed in front of our regiment, and Brig. Gen. Walker was wounded. We killed about one hundred and eighty of the enemy. The gunboat 'Choctaw' did good work shelling them. I stood on the breastworks after we took them and gave the elevations and direction for the gunboat with my sword, and they sent a shell right into their midst, which sent them in all directions. Three shells fell there, and sixty-two rebels lay there when the fight was over.

* * * * * * * * * * *

"This battle satisfied the slave masters of the South that their charm was gone; and the negro, as a slave was lost forever. Yet there was one fact connected with the battle of Milliken's Bend which will descend to posterity as testimony against the humanity of slave holders, and that is that no negro was ever found alive that was taken prisoner by the rebels in this fight."

The eminent Dr. John Ashhurst, Jr., M. D., Professor of Clinical Surgery in the University of Pennsylvania, has the following to say in his work on the Principles and Practice of Surgery: "The behavior of men when shot in battle is influenced by a variety of circumstances, thus, marked differences have been observed in accordance with the race of the person wounded. The Anglo-Saxon is usually calm and philosophical; the Celt is sometimes gay and merry, and at other times depressed and gloomy; the Teuton phlegmatic. The negro soldiers, during our late war, were, according to the testimony of Dr. Brinton and other army surgeons, the most patient and enduring of all our wounded. Another peculiarity was, that while the white troops of all races almost invariably threw away their muskets, the negro as regularly brought his into the hospital with him, and was not satisfied to have it taken from his sight."

CHAPTER XV.

CAPABILITIES AND OPPORTUNITIES OF THE NEGROES OF TO-DAY.

The article given below was prepared and read before the National Conference of Colored Men of the United States, held in the capitol at Nashville, Tenn., May 6, 7, 8 and 9, 1879. Mr. Still is a gentleman of means and culture, and is thoroughly identified with every interest of his race. For the richness of thought, statistical information &c., contained in the deduction, I assume to append it for the benefit of all concerned:

OPPORTUNITIES AND CAPABILITIES OF EDUCATED NEGROES.

BY WILLIAM STILL.

According to the programme, I am to present for the consideration of this conference some thoughts upon the "Opportunities and capabilities of educated Negroes."

Long before the advent of emancipation, and ever since the attitude of our people in this country has absorbed no small share of my study, I have looked upon their condition with intense interest, feeling to be fully identified with them, however regarded. However, in the discussion of the subject, I take it for granted that I shall best meet the required demands by confining myself chiefly to the momentous problem involved in the Negro's status since emancipation.

To say that the dawn of freedom fifteen years ago found him other than very poor, without land, without education, without homes, without protection, universally proscribed, and wholly dependent, would be to deny facts with which all are familiar.

Thus opening his eyes in freedom, and taking his first trembling steps in pursuit of his manhood, he is at once made to realize the great change in his existence.

Although without a penny in his pocket, the gnawings of hunger soon admonish him that he must have something wherewith to satisfy this demand of nature. He is without a roof over his head. In this condition he is not safe either in sunshine or storm. Those who procured his freedom, save the army, are in distant parts of the country, far from being accessible to his immediate pressing appeals. But not so with those whom he had so recently been compelled to serve. They are all around him. In needing shelter, or employment, or a piece of land to till or purchase, or a store where to buy his provisions, clothing, medicine, or what not; a physician to attend him when sick, a lawyer to defend him when in trouble, a scribbler to write him a receipt or an agreement, or a conveyancer to draw him up a deed, the only sources to apply to in ninety-nine cases out of a hundred were those from under whose yoke he had been delivered.

Viewed in this light, what possible reason was there for supposing ehat millions of people thus situated would have other than severe and sore trials to encounter for at least a score of years before he could reap largely the fruits of freedom. Common sense alone would abundantly prove that without education, however industrious, he would be but poorly qualified to protect and economize his hard earnings. And without being thus prepared to protect himself, how is he to get property? How is he to become a thrifty farmer or planter? How is he to get a footing as a storekeeper or tradesman? How is he to advance and become a skilled mechanic, an able attorney, a good physician, or a man capable of properly divining the word of truth in espousing the teachings of the Bible?

So long as the masses are found in this uneducated attitude the day is not yet when their peculiar troubles will cease. The fact that there was a universal hungering and thirsting among the freedmen, when freedom had come, and, at the same time a goodly number of noble-hearted, liberty-loving men and women in the North who were ready and willing to brave the perils of the South to help sdtisfy this thirst and hunger, is abundant cause for trusting that the race will in due time be uplifted.

Surely there never was a people more needy and deserving of education. And it hardly can be too much to add that this generation will find it difficult, in surveying the various fields of Christian missions and philanthropic works, to find any laborers who have more nearly emulated the example of Him who said, "For I was hungered and ye gave me meat; I was thirsty and ye gave me drink," &c., than some of the teachers among the freedmen of the South, as I shall endeavor more fully to indicate in another part of this paper.

This silent, potent force, this labor of love to God and good will to man has kept in a great measure the heads of the freedmen above the waves and billows. In the earlier dark days of his struggles, seeing his unprotected and wretched condition, the government instituted the Freedmen's Bureau with a view of meeting his immediate pressing wants in various ways. Through this agency a great deal was accomplished for a short time, but through the politicians and bad management, its usefulness was soon brought to naught.

At this grave juncture not a few adherents of the doctrine of emancipation felt well satisfied that if the ballot could only be given to the freedman, he would be well able to take care of himself against all odds. Accordingly the fifteenth amendment was passed, and the ballot came.

This boon was regarded as the top stone to the fabric and a complete solving of the Negro problem.

He is henceforth expected naturally to vote in a body for the party who conferred this boon upon him, notwithstanding his want of knowledge and his peculiar surroundings.

In the midst of this unsettled attitude, in order to encourage his aspirations and incite in him habits of economy, with a view of enabling him to buy property and to begin the world more independently, the Freedman's Savings and Trust Company was organized. Doubtless this enterprise had its origin in the minds of men with the best intentions. And at first some men widely known for their worth and devotion to the cause of freedom were among its patrons and managers. But soon afterward unscrupulous men, under fair and insidious professions, by scheming, effected a radical change in the charter, and thus got the control out of the original hands into their own, when they had matters much as they desired them. How very sadly the freedmen had to pay for this operation is too well known.

However, in this bold undertaking the most signal fact verified was to the effect that even under very great poverty and ignorance more than 70,000 freedmen could be found ready and willing, on simple faith, to intrust their hard earnings to the amount of some $57,000,000 to the custody of this concern, under the delusion that the government was fully obligated for every dollar of its liabilities, when, in fact, the government was not liable for a single dollar.

In recalling the fiery trials and great hardships which the freedmen have had to undergo from without and within, my sole motive is only to intensify the fact which has unwaveringly been paramount in my mind, namely: under any circumstances, even the most favorable that could be expected, there are great suffering and very hard work for the Negro to undergo, in whatever light his condition may be regarded. But under no circumstances is his elevation to be accomplished and his rights respected, except through the medium of education.

And now I will endeavor to show how the Negro's opportunities and capabilities may be made available in remedying his own ills, and in bringing deliverance, not only to himself, but in largely adding his quota toward helping to bring about peace, order and prosperity to the entire South:

1. He is about the only laborer in the South; he has been fully inured to hardships all his life; he need apprehend no greater danger of having to compete with any other class of laborers. In a sense, therefore, he is in an attitude, with the aid of some book knowledge, to understand the value of his labor—capital. With education, when he works he will know how much he earns. Many ignorant laborers cannot tell. When he spends he will know how much he spends; an ignorant man cannot keep his account. When he buys a piece of land or undertakes to build, he will first sit down and count the cost, to see

if he is able to finish; or whether some one is going to palm off on him a bogus deed or a fraudulent agreement. When he works on shares, or deals at stores on credit until the crop is harvested, he will know how to keep his store book, and the importance of having his agreement and receipts, &c., carefully witnessed and preserved against the time of settlement. In thousands of instances an ignorant man is imposed upon simply because he can be imposed upon with impunity, by men who would not fancy being caught acting thus toward an intelligent one. In ninety-nine cases out of a hundred this rule would be likely to hold good.

An intelligent man would not feel bound to work under or rent under a man whom he would have every reason to believe would beat him when the settling day arrived. On the contrary, he would not only shun such an employer himself, but he would advise his friends to do likewise.

This management, athough silent, would be very potent in effecting a remedy. The better class of Southerners would have no fault to find with this course, and the high-handed and outrageous element would have but little sympathy from any source, and very hard work to manage their operations.

2. With some book knowledge, a man in finding himself badly located could readily perceive how a change might better his condition. Through the aid of his geography, maps, books and papers, and his ability to hold correspondence with other localities, the way of getting out of his present thraldom would not be far to seek.

Every citizen, white or black is free to exercise this privilege in this respect, no one will deny. If one place does not suit him he can go to another of his own choosing.

Here I am reminded that emigration is exciting a good deal of attention at the present day.

Never were men more in need of intelligence. in order that they might judge wisely concerning the present exciting crisis. If not wide awake, they are likely to jump out of the frying-pan into the fire.

But if he can read he may study and learn what practical emigration has done for millions on this continent. The great Western States, for instance, afford an opportunity for a good illustration. Emigration certainly has been the making of all the Western States, if not of this entire country. It was never conducted, however, under any *en masse* system, but generally on individual account, or under the auspices of voluntary small companies.

While the great majority of these emigrants at first went poor, they carried with them a thorough knowledge of husbandry, mechanism, storekeeping, trading, and all kinds of industrial labor; besides very many had been inured to hardships, and were quite willing to rough it in the woods, in log-cabins—to begin labor by cutting down and clearing up the forest under great difficulties. Among those thus emigrating were skilled laborers—men who could make axes, plows, cultivators and implements of husbandry of every description—men who could not only do the most ordinary manual labor, but could build great bridges, railroads, steamboats; who had a knowledge of printing; could publish papers and books, could teach schools of learning, from the lower rudiments up to the higher mathematics—men who could construct factories, build foundries, organize banking institutions, &c. Besides, in adjacent parts of the country capitalists were ready, whenever signs indicated successful investments, to furnish all necessary means if on no other grounds than simply personal interest.

Now, I am compelled to say, with deep regret, that our poor people are not prepared to emigrate under any such encouraging aspects. They have been too long shut out from the light of knowledge to be ready for any *en masse* emigration movement. In going, with very few exceptions, they could only hope to find employment as hewers of wood and drawers of water, in fields where laborers might be sufficiently numerous to meet all demands either in rural districts or in the towns. Thus with apparently continued hard struggles only, to combat, the road to success would still be dark and discouraging.

The Great teacher said on one occasion:

"For which of you intending to build a tower, sitteth not down first and counteth the cost, whether he have sufficient to finish it? Lest haply, after he has laid the foundation, and is not able to finish it, all that behold him begin to mock him, saying, this man began to build and was not able to finish."

How applicable this lesson is to everyday life, and if heeded how often men would be prevented from butting their heads against a stone. With the "army of ten thousand to meet him that cometh with twenty thousand," the "sitting down and counting the cost" might be of the greatest consequence.

A hint to the wise is sufficient.

3. Equality in business. This is a question that should interest every intelligent colored man.

More or less from a boy I have studied this question, and since emancipation I have weighed the situation of our people, uneducated and almost universally filling the lower callings as laborers, with intense interest. Scarcely have I ever met an intelligent colored man from the South but that I am sure to ply him with a number of questions after this order: "How are the freedmen getting on? Are they getting education and into more comfortable houses? Are they getting into business; and if so, what? Is the marriage relation being more firmly cemented?" Generally the answers have indicated much improvement, in some in some instances very marked, notwithstanding the outrages neighborhoods. In order that I may the more forcibly bring out the idea that I wish to convey, I will here quote an extract from an old letter written by the poetess and lecturer, Mrs. Harper, directly from the old mansion of the late ex-President of the Confederacy, which reads thus:

"My Dear Friend: It is said that truth is stranger than fiction; and if ten years since some one had said that in less than ten years you will be in the lecture field; you will be a welcome guest under the roof of the President of the Confederacy, though not by special invitation from him, that you will see his brother's former slave a man of business and influence; that hundreds of colored men will congregate on the old baronial possessions; that a school will spring up there like a well in the desert dust; that his former slave will be a magistrate upon that plantation: that labor will be organized upon a new basis; and that under the sole auspices of the moulding hands of this man and his sons will be developed a business whose transactions will be numbered in hundreds of thousands of dollars, would you not have smiled incredulously? And I have lived to see the day when the plantation has passed into new hands, and these hands once wore the fetters of slavery. Mr. Montgomery, the present proprietor, by contract, of between five and six thousand acres of land, has one of the most interesting families that I have ever seen in the South. They are building up a future which, if exceptional now, I hope will become more general hereafter. Every hand of his family is adding its quota to the success of this experiment of a colored man both trading and farming on an extensive scale. Last year his wife took on her hands about 130 acres of land, and with her force she raised about 107 bales of cotton. One daughter, an intelligent young lady, is postmistress, and I believe assistant bookkeeper. One son attends to the planting interest, and another daughter to one of the stores. The business of this firm of Montgomery & Sons has amounted, I understand, to between three and four hundred thousand dollars a year."

This was very refreshing news to me when it was first received; so much so that I put it into the hands of Col. J. W. Forney, and he published it in the Press with a fitting editorial. One more incident worthy of note, namely, for several seasons, I have been informed, this enterprising firm has competed with the leading cotton planters of the South, at the annual fairs held at St. Louis, and two seasons at least has carried off the premiums.

Here, too, are other notable cases, both male and female, who have achieved wonders, considering their opportunities, which might be named, but I cannot take the time now to particularize them. However, it is with especial satisfaction that we can point so definitely to a family who have accomplished so much in so short a period of time. Indeed this is precisely the kind of power we want to see growing among us. True, it makes but little noise. but it is very potent in dealing deadly blows against prejudice and in favor of our common manhood.

I apprehend but few comparatively realize how greatly our cause would be strengthened by even a very moderate number of substantial business men in the various branches of productive industry—conducting farms, stores, trades, and engaged in literary pursuits that require brains. These matters should deeply concern us, especially those of us who are educating our sons and daughters. Only as we are showing signs of improvement and determination in these respects shall we be able to retain the sympathy and cooperation of our old friends, and enlist the interest and agency of new ones. So long, or whenever we are not found advancing under freedom, and with the opportunity of education, we shall do little toward breaking down the color line or toward conquering the prejudices which now proscribe our sons and daughters who are fitted by education and character to fill stations in life other than menial ones.

I am aware that I am now treading on tender ground, and would fain forego doing so, if I could be just to my subject and my unfortunate race by shunning this unsavory truth, upon which I think we need have our minds stirred about as much as any other that I know of—of a temporal nature at least; for I feel quite convinced when looking at the attitude of our people, and the work before them, that there is but one way out of the old ruts into the liberty and prosperity that we feel naturally and legally entitled to, namely, simply 'redeeming the time,' by intense earnestness, by rigid economy, by encouraging one another in every honorable and commendable undertaking, by acquainting ourselves with the lives and labors of good men and women who have labored successfully to bring about great reforms; and have had overwhelming difficulties to overcome. Also by studying the lives of individuals who have had great poverty to begin with and no friends to aid them; but with undaunted courage, perseverance, and a firm faith, have removed the mountain, and established themselves among the foremost men of their day. Our country is full of characters of this description, both of native and foreign birth, and, I am glad to say, some among our people not excepted.

"Knowledge is power," is one among the books we ought to study well, after acquainting ourselves with the Book of Proverbs. Also, we should not forget to make ourselves familiar with another work of great value, namely, a volume called "Pursuit of knowledge under difficulties."

The lives of self-made men are readily obtainable for a mere trifle, and contain generally very profitable and instructive reading, when well selected. By reading such instructive works, and by ignoring all light and trashy literature of a yellow-cover grade, we could summon to our aid the well-digested thoughts of men of character and great success, which would doubtless inspire us greatly in struggling through our difficulties.

The truth is, good books of all kinds are so cheap and common, on every vital subject, that no man who can read is excusable if he is not well informed generally. Indeed, we must make hay while the sun shines.

For it must be admitted that the public attention is in a peculiar sense turned toward us, and in a measure, whether we understand it or not, we are held responsible to demonstrate by unmistakable signals that we are advancing morally, mentally, and financially.

Now, it will not do for us to cry, there is a lion in the way all the time, but we must move the lions out of the way ourselves, occasionally.

Many of the hardships which daily beset us on every hand would soon vanish under intelligent business enterprises and energy.

In the days of slavery, when many believed and advocated the doctrine that the Negro had no brains or mental capacity for business, oratory, or science, our good old abolition friends wanted no better combatants to refute this fallacy than the fugitive slave, matchless orator, and able editor, Frederick Douglas, now the honored Marshal of Washington. The giant intellect and powerful eloquence of Rev. Samuel R. Ward proved effective on one occasion in quelling a New York mob (black as night, he was), when the police force seemed utterly powerless with that mob. It seemed almost providential to have such men as Henry Bibb, William Wells Brown, J. W. Loguen, and many others (who had all worn the yoke, and had only released themselves by escaping on the underground railroad) demonstrate by their rapidly acquired intelligence and education that it took but a very few years for a fugitive to render himself capable of writing an interesting narrative, or filling an editorial chair, or of instructing and entertaining large audiences either in America or on the other side of the ocean.

The freedmen have only to seek to emulate the example of these men in order to make their mark in business, letters, art, or any of the advanced callings among educated men. Indeed, only as desert can be proved by the acquisition of knowledge and the exhibition of high moral character in examples of economy and a disposition to encourage industrial enterprises, conducted by men of our own ranks, will it be possible to make political progress in the face of the present public sentiment.

Being far behind in the race, our people must not deem it too great a requirement to be obliged to put forth double exertions to catch up. If they undertake farming, they must try not only to have their lands well cultivated, but they must have their houses, barns, fences, stock, &c., all up to the times. Again, if we turn our attention to mechanism, we must have our eyes single to one paramount aim, namely, to let our work prove that there is no color line in mechanism or art. If we should choose to fill a sphere of a professional character, as a physician or attorney, we must not imagine that our patients or clients are ignorant, and will be satisfied with mere pretension or ordinary attainment; and, if we fail of success, that we can be excused simply by pleading prejudice. If we venture to open a shop or store, let us not forget that we must not only sell as cheap as anybody else, but we must sell equally as good goods, and at the same time be a little more accommodating to every body, without regard to race, color or politics. If we would avail ourselves of credit, we must learn to practice by the rule—our word is our bond. By such a single eye to success, however unfair or over-exacting such demands might seem in the eyes of some, our advancement would be steady and sure, and the results in every way sufficiently gratifying to make up for whatever self-denial and extra pains or labor required.

One fact all must agree upon, namely: Our condition is very lowly, and in many respects sad. And there are no signs discernible to my mind that we are likely to have our status improved very soon, either through politics or the liberal bestowal of land, money or the preferments of any positions by the Government. Hence, we have nowhere else to look but to self-reliance and to God.

4. True, we are not friendless. We are not without wise and faithful counselors and instructors. We are not without sympathizers who pity us and wish us well, if nothing more. We are not without a Government that acknowledges us as citizens and equals before the law. We are not debarred from emigrating to the North if we cannot live in peace at the South. We can go to any foreign land if we cannot endure our lot in the land of our nativity. We are largely accessible to churches, and some very good schools have been provided for us. And now I

wish briefly to consider our opportunity with regard to the educational work existing for our special benefit. This is an agreeable task, although it would be very hard to portray, or even feebly indicate, the labors and achievements of the noble-hearted and self-sacrificing men and women who have been diffusing education among the freedmen in various Southern States during the last decade.

Before me I have the annual report of the American Missionary Association for 1888, and find that the society have 37 schools, colleges and universities in the South, 7 of which are regularly chartered, and are located as follows:

HAMPTON NORMAL AND AGRICULTURAL INSTITUTE, HAMPTON, VA.

Number of pupils, 332. The course of instruction embraces three years. During this period the pupils are made as proficient as possible in reading, penmanship, arithmetic, United States history, grammar, physiology, moral science, natural philosophy, vocal training, Bible lessons; likewise instruction in agriculture, &c., General S. C. Armstrong being principal.

BEREA COLLEGE, BEREA, KY.

In this institution, under the presidency of Rev. John G. Fee, the peculiarity of the color line is not known. Here the higher branches, embracing the classics, are taught, and its success has been highly gratifying.

FISK UNIVERSITY, NASHVILLE, TENN.

This widely-known and justly famed university is represented by an able faculty and the popular Jubilee Singers, and, without a doubt, is destined to accomplish a marvelous work for freedom, and to live long in history. Rev. E. M. Cravath is its president; number of pupils,

338. The instructions embrace mental and moral science, Greek, Latin, French, Mathematics, Music, &c.

ATLANTA UNIVERSITY, ATLANTA, GA.

Rev. E. A. Ware is president. English branches and the higher mathematics are here taught also. Number of pupils, 244.

TALLADEGA COLLEGE, TALLADEGA, ALA.

Chartered in 1869. Rev. E. P. Lord, principal. Number of pupils, 272. English branches, with higher grades, are also taught in this institution.

TOUGALOO UNIVERSITY, TOUGALOO, MISS.

There are 190 pupils in the various departments of this institution, with the regular higher branches taught, under the presidency of Rev. G. Stanly Pope.

STRAIGHT UNIVERSITY, NEW ORLANS, LA.

Here a thorough corps of able professors and teachers is found, and the pupils number 287. President, Rev. W. S. Alexander.

My allusion to the work of the American Missionary Association must suffer single with these 7 institutions. Of course, this only simply indicates the great work that is being carried forward in this single direction. The remaining 29 schools in the South supported by this organization, although deserving the highest commendation, cannot be characterized here, simply for want of time and room. Indeed, I regret having to treat in the same manner some fifty or more like institutions, under the auspices of Methodist, Presbyterian, Protestant, Episcopal friends, &c., who have been quietly though earnestly pushing the cause of education effectively among the freedmen. Add to this list some seventeen theological schools, under the auspices of various denominations, namely: Congregational, Methodist, Presbyterian and Baptist, and a faint idea, at least, may be gathered respecting the opportunity of the Negro to-day over his opportunity fifteen years ago, or before freedom was proclaimed.

Material might here be found for a large volume of rare interest and great value, and I trust the day is not far distant when a colored man of ability will engage in the work of diligently gathering these rich materials, and will bring forth in a manner not only creditable to himself and race, but will also do equal credit to the scores of worthy and faithful teachers.

Doubtless the time will come when an enterprising historian will take advantage of the opportunity to honor the heroic and brave Christian men and women who have faithfully labored in this mission.

Of two other universities not to allude to would be to leave my task very incomplete. I wish now to speak of Wilberforce University, at Xenia, O., and Lincoln University, Oxford, Chester county, Pa. Wilberforce is under the general conference of the African Methodist Episcopal Church, and chiefly since its organization has been presided over by the senior Bishop of that denomination, Rev. D. A. Payne, D. D., in the success of which his whole being has been deeply interested, and to make this institution an honor and a powerful agency to the negro of this country, especially that it might appear that a university could be conducted under the supervision of colored professors, and well-taught students graduated there, who need not be ashamed of their *Alma Mater;* and the success has been highly gratifying in this respect. The classics are taught, also algebra, arithmetic, geometry, grammar, geography, composition, music, &c. While it must be admitted that it has had many head winds to encounter, it has steadily been growing in interest and popularity, and is wielding a commendable influence. Professor B. F. Lee, one of its graduates, has been president ever since the resignation of Bishop Payne.

Lastly, I must conclude my notice of the opportunity offered our people, by various fountains of learning, sustained by philanthropic benevolence, by a brief description of that unrivaled school, Lincoln University. Having been more or less acquainted with its workings for the last twenty years, I can speak unhesitatingly. My oldest son graduated there; also two of my nephews graduated in the collegiate course and likewise in the theological. I have been personally acquainted with most, if not all, of the professors, and have had great opportunity of becoming informed about them indirectly through many of the students and graduates, and all I need say, is, I have the very highest esteem for Lincoln University.

The following extract of a letter from the president, Rev. J. N. Rendall, D. D., received only a few days before I left Philadelphia, will indicate precisely what ideas are held by the president and faculty with regard to educating colored students, and to my mind the argument is unanswerable:

"Our desire and aim is to give to the colored youth who come to us every advantage in education which we ourselves possess. Whatever is good for our minds is good for them. If it quickens, if it sharpens, if it refines, if it enlarges the view, they need these benefits, and have an immediate use for them. It is a great mistake to imagine that the leaders in thought and society among the colored people only need to know a little of arithmetic and of the other common branches. These are essential, but they are not all. Society is to be organized; churches are to be established and administered; the principles of domestic economy are to be applied, and industry encouraged. It will not answer to make the foundations of these widest interests narrow. These precious interests must be intrusted to the hands of men who have the advantage of a liberal culture in the world's experience, as it is given in history and in scientific discovery. Above all, they ought to be imbued with the principles of Christian morality.

"There is no special morality or gospel for colored men. They must have what the world has gained by its long experience, add what God has given in his bounty. This effort is not premature, so far as it respects the ability of the colored youth to profit by it. We have found our students able to learn all that we can teach. There is the same diversity of talent among them as in others. We say this from an experience with both classes.

Now, I ask, in conclusion, that you will compare the opportunities which I have presented with those of fifteen or twenty years ago, and see if there is no room for thankfulness and encouragement; see if there has not been very decided improvement, and see if there is not good reason for every one of us to renew our efforts to advance education and true and undefiled religion; to promote more economy, more union, more regard for morality, more willingness to seek out and extend a helping hand to the "million" who are of the most lowly and degraded. In this wide field, oh, what a strong and clear voice comes to us all, heed it not as we may: "He that reapeth receiveth the wages!" ' In the morning sow thy seed, and in the evening withhold not thine hand!" "The race is not to the swift, nor the battle to the strong, but to them that endure to the end!"

I fear, my friends, that we have hardly waked up to behold what opportunities and capabilities there are all around us, by which we might elevate our manhood, and forever settle the question of our equality before all mankind.

The author will add that the Shaw University, at Raleigh, N. C., Dr. H. M. Tupper, president, and the Livingston College, at Salisbury, N. C., Dr. J. C. Price, president, are equal in facilities and influence to any like institutions South of Washington.

APPENDIX.

ON THE SUBJECT OF INDUSTRY; ON EMANCIPATION DAY. JANUARY 1st. 1883.

As to the dark pages of the past, we should shut our eyes, (I mean both white and colored), wheel in line and press forward on the king's highway to life and the pursuits of happiness, "for the times are changed, and we are changed with them." I am anxious to witness the rapid removal of the evil results of that system of wrong—human slavery—that the last ear-mark of oppression may vanish from our sight. But this can only be done through the channels of industry. Industry is diligence in business, whether it be that of the merchant, farmer or professional man, and generally, it brings along with it both a wealth of gold and a wealth of learning. Habits (virtuous habits) of industry are recommended by the happiness they impart.

Nothing is to be denied to well directed labor, and nothing can be obtained without it. In order to regain the proud station we once held among the ancient States, and to fully enjoy the fruits of our unrequited labor in the country we made to "blossom like a rose," the colored man ("God's image cut ebon") must educate and become freeholders.

Habits of decency, sobriety, cleanliness and promptness can only be won by industry, but unlike hereditaments, cannot be entailed from sire to son. All these are incidents to citizenship; but the pleasures of a homeless citizen are dwarfed by this fact. Truly happy is the man whose love and care

> A few paternal acres bound,
> Content to breathe his native air
> On his own ground.

The colored man, for instance, finds himself endowed with abilities as varied, rich, durable and praise-worthy as any race or people that ever flourished on the earth. And the honored task is given us to work out our own redemption, by the propagating power of *Industry*; which is the very mother of *Creation* itself. As a laborer the colored man's arm has never been equalled. Mark him as an incorrigible reprobate and as a dangerous man in a community who looks upon diligent toil as dishonorable. Who has seen the dark face, bedewed with perspiration, the glittering blade in hand, steadily, cheerfully sweeping down the ready made, full ripe golden grain and was not by that inspired to thought and action? It is beautiful! Yet I know well that such a calling, carrying with it so much bodily exercise, is not very inviting. On every sea, in every clime, the deep laden merchant ships, teeming with the blessings of food, gold and clothing,—comforts for the back pocket and the stomach. Every honest dollar that's used in the course of trade or any other form is first leeched out of the hands of the worker. He is the prime actor whose part in the drama of life is to effectuate the unsearchable and immutable wisdom of God. He is the real agriculturist. In the order of men he is a kind of creator. God gave life, but the laborer sustains it.' Before his hand it is a withered leaf, behind him it is a Mesopotamia, garden of rejoicing, the offspring of industry and peace. Nature having responded to diligence and brought forth plenty. This is the primative occupation, and after all it is the most healthful and innocent, the noblest and the most useful.

"In agricultural sections of any country, those who own the land may be said practically to own the people. In farming countries there is nothing which can give such independence as the ownership of a good farm." When we see the millions of wealth flowing from the hands of the laborer, "the horn of plenty," and see the broad fields whitening with king cotton, the principal commodity of the South, and hear the deep bass of waterfalls accompanied by the sharp treble of thousands of spindles, we become conscious of how important it is to obtain a home for ourselves and posterity.

We are poor, because we were and are to-day the victims to the avarice of superiors in numbers and intelligence What constitutes the difference in the society make up? The answer is, so far as livlihood is concerned, opportunity. The colored man, liberated as he was, with a naked back, a penniless pocket, no monied friends, with a battery of prejudice all at work against him, he commenced life, his only stock in trade a skin tanned black and a powerful muscle, in the scramble to make money. Could it be expected then that he should succeed better or rise faster than he has by the side of the patient, industrious, clear-sighted whites who gained their fortune by inheritance, and know the value thereof? It took the white people of this country nearly four hundred (400) years to attain their present material status with land and laborers comparatively free. Yet we should not loose sight of the fact that in order to insure ourselves against any political revolution as to suffrage we *must be land owners and educated*. In this sense industry implies liberty, as it cannot be maintained without it. "Coming events cast their shadows before." I predict both a property and an educational qualification law in the near future. In Massachusetts unless you can read and write and have paid property tax you cannot vote for certain officers. North Carolina and several other States follow invariably in the wake of the Bay State. In less than ten years the South may tread in her footsteps. The South sits still and watches eagerly the North gate; then when the North enacts a great law the Sunny South immediately copies it.

The leaders of our race advance this idea with much force. One says:

"The time is at hand in this country when the men who live in the rural districts should not be content with working for shares of the crops and on rented farms, but they should make haste to identify themselves with the soil by buying lands, small farms, on which to settle their families permanently; and then if they choose to work for their wealthier neighbors who own large plantations let them do so. But they should have homes and become freeholders, to escape the proscription of the laws in certain cases, and to secure the contentment which a homestead alone can bring."

Not till this is done shall we see the hectic flush pale upon the cold cheek of race prejudice.

> "Poverty parts good company," while
> "The thousand ills that rise where money fails,
> Debts, threats and duns, bills, bailiffs, writs and jails"

often breaking up the society and steady thrift among the poor and ignorant.—Such is the case in bleeding Ireland to-day. "The grasping landlord by the law of might is not content that the tiller of the soil should reap from his fields more than will support his immediate wants of food, clothing and shelter; and thus deprived of the power to accumulate money, he is forced to plod on from year to year, as a horse in a threshing machine, without making a step of headway in the effort of purchase land upon which to provide for his own household."

Then with what earnestness should we bend our energies to the work of property getting, character-sustaining, morality and education.

It is true we have a reasonable quota of successful farmers and skilled mechanics and professional men. As the gloom of ignorance and hatred disperses, I see the *gradual* rise of our people—not sudden, like a sky-rocket—but slowly, grandly, beautifully, like the rock-ribbed, snow-capped mount, higher and higher, even with scars of the miner's spade, rising to meet the day-god in his glory. Intelligence, diligence, manhood, honesty shall be yours. With this view of the matter, I have endeavored to sophisticate no truth, nourish no delusion, allowing no fear nor selfish design to lead me to misconstrue or to put on an extra touch, but to tell the plain truth. It seems to be the delight of some to belittle all effort, of any nature whatever, made by the colored people; they have my sympathy; 'tis useless to talk history to them.

OUR AFFLICTION.

Once shackled limbs, suppressed manhood, tears from burdened souls, subdued spirits, have all fled and gone, except their lingering effect in the dark region of his ruin—gone retreating before a brighter dawn. He is gradually rising all along the line, and beginning to understand, think and act for himself, while quite a number are making a successful living. The idiotic idea, advanced by a few brainless numbskulls, that the Negro is, all things being equal, inferior to the sons of Shem and Japheth, is fading away like the morning mist before the glowing sun. The Negro may be a mere pigmy now, but just give him a fair showing, an equal opportunity, and he will prove a giant in the fight, ready, in case of emergency, to die for the South, and his country, generally. Yes, cutting and digging, teaching, preaching and building, sowing and reaping on the grand highway of progress. Therefore, these considerations bring along with them new and trying responsibilities, demanding greater efforts to obtain education and property, that we may fall in the train of their joys and comforts through the means of industry.

This is the age of farms and machinery, not of who is the whitest, blackest, or who is master by birth or color, but who is the man that meets the demands of the hour. Notwithstanding we have made some headway in spite of unfavorable circumstances, we *must* and shall look up, aim higher, and save the earnings of our labor. Morality is an industry. I am aware that education and wealth have their evil effects in certain ways, and I would to Almighty God that base men would cease to apply their ill-gotten advantage to degrade poor simple-minded colored girls, who, as soon as they begin to bloom as the lily, are sought out and hunted home in darkness with fascinating allurements and bewitching charms to destroy the young child's moral life, and then charge their own gross crimes to the whole of the Negro race. It is terrible, yet true! I appeal to the decency and justice of the neighborhoods to put it down, by mild means if possible, but if not, then by force.

My advice is, widen your fields, train your sons and daughters up in school and useful employments at *home*. I have never known any one to be defiled at *home*. Only when hired out and made to sleep in the kitchens of those who do not esteem her worthy of their guardian care and instruction. All employers are not so.

If the Negro is let alone, paid reasonable wages, and treated with equal justice, the race problem is then already solved. Justice is no problem. Respect the Negro as a citizen, and he will solve the problem for the world. It may be a problem with some men as to how they can keep the Negro down. Every Negro who succeeds in an honorable endeavor solves the *pseudo* problem. Every in fraction of the Negro's natural or constitutional rights throws back the millenium of peace and the era of good feelings. The only reasonable problem is when shall those who have wronged him make timely honorable amende to him.

The Negro has a destiny or problem to solve and it must be solved right here in the land of his captivity, in the midst of those who doubted his manhood and capacity Money and learning, embracing in their ample folds morality, can move mountains.

In Scotland Neck township, Halifax county, the colored men own 3,710 acres of land, upon which they raised last year 601 bales of cotton and 10,500 bushels of corn.

In Richmond county, N. C., the colored people own 7,720 acres, besides town lots. They own more or less in all the counties in the State. Our people of Georgia are worth, it is said, $25,000,000 in property; in Louisiana, $35,000,000.—Look at the Chesapeake Marine Railway and Dry Dock Company of Baltimore!

The Charleston *News and Courier* says: "Randall D. George, the colored man who recently bought the Reneker lands in Colleton county for $20,500 cash, has been making preparations for an accurate survey of his property. He is, it is said, the largest land owner in Col-

Seton. He is quiet, unobtrusive and business-like in his manners. George is a staunch advocate of the proposed railroad from Green Pond to Branchville. He not only signed the petition to the county commissioners, but gave $25 to the corporators to assist in preliminary work, and expresses a willingness to take $5,000 worth of stock to carry the road through to Branchville."

Under the caption of "Colored Merchants," the Savannah (Ga.) *Echo* says, and we take real pleasure in futher echoing it abroad:

"We know a colored firm in Georgia who handle about 3,000 bales of cotton per year, at a value of $150,000, and whose credit is rated in Davis' Commercial Register at from $10,000 to $20,000. In this city we have colored firms engaged in different branches of business with capitals ranging from $1,000 to $10,000, and who have annual incomes of from $900 to $5,000. To particularize would be invidious, and we only mention one instance to show that we are dealing with facts and not drawing upon our imaginations: The firm of J. H. Brown & Co., Booksellers and Stationers have an annual income of $2,000, credit rated in commercial circles at from $2,500 to $3,000, and their annual cash sales aggregate $5,000. All of the prominent cities and towns of our State have their quota of colored merchants, and taken as a class, they certainly present an irrefutable refutation of the argument that persons of color are void of business qualifications. * * * * * *

From this it seems in a few years we shall be able to stand alone.

"Many thousand years ago a tiny coral began a reef upon the ocean's bed.—Years rolled on and others came. Their fortunes united, and the structure grew. Generations came and went. Corals by the millions came, lived and died, each adding his mite to the work, till at last the waters of the grand old ocean broke in ripples around its tireless head. And now, as the traveler gazes upon the reef, hundreds of miles in extent," he can but faintly realize what great results will follow an united, determined, economical, persevering action.

"It is rising, living, doing, that brings the hearts, desire." In conclusion, the work of our elevation, and redemption is in our own hands; therefore let's worthily perform the task better than any others could do it for us, and prove to the wondering world, while many are consulting "What shall be done with the Negro," that our station is and ever shall be in the galaxy of earth's noblest, purest and best races.

AN EXTRACT FROM A SPEECH DELIVERED BY W. H. QUICK, COLORED, ON THE OCCASION OF THE "EMANCIPATION CELEBRATION," JANUARY 1st, 1883.

What remains for us to do is to struggle on, determined to conquer in the battle of life, remembering that every one of us that gets up in the world makes it easier for the rest. If you help one, that helps you. And let us all, white and colored, remember that our lots are cast in one country, and the same cause; that our destinies are identical. Let us remember, too, that the proudest title any of us can bear is that of a citizen of the American Republic—Columbia, our jewel, America, our country, from Maine to Mexico. May she live in peace, harmony and prosperity, ever flowing, while with joy in every vein, one faith for public good, strong to honor and obey. Yes, we are one body, one people. When one member suffers we all suffer; when the one prospers we all rejoice.

White and colored are embarked on one common bottom, and whether we sink or swim, we sink or swim together. This being true, we should assist by every possible means in our power in pushing old North Carolina to the very head of the sisterhood of States. As long as I have faith in the Almighty God I cannot despair of the Negro. Unlike the Boors of Denmark, the Traals of Sweeden, the Serfs of England, or the Helots of Sparta, he is convinced that industry and intelligence must govern his conduct.

When the whites and the colored understand each other better they will *like* each other better; that is, the one will trust the other further, politically. In less than ten years the political field will be thoroughly renovated. But the whites must forget their prejudice and discrimination against us because of our color, which is clean and God given.—The press must cease to magnify our faults. The press, the teacher of public opinion, is entitled to a great deal more credit than is bestowed, and is blamable where it is not charged.

Soon it will not be a strange thing to see a colored democrat and a white republican rivaling for the honored favor of the people. I mean both races will be divided pretty equally between both parties. Such a change would meet the approval of the wisest and best men of the country.

I *do not* want to see anything of ill feeling or want of confidence (a child of slavery) exhibited in the conduct of the people, white or black one toward the other. I *don't* want my eyes to behold, ever again, any unreasonable discrimination practiced against any man, thus poisoning the very air we breathe—the genius of America. I *don't* wish to see the *color line* destroying the *interest* of the black and the white man. I *don't* want to see a close *party line* drawn, and running between and dividing the two races respectively, but that noble feeling, the consumation of true statesmanship, pervading the breast of every man. I want that sentiment administered in our courts of justice; I want it enacted in our legislature:— One people, one God, one country; equality, justice and liberty for all!

CORRESPONDENCE AND ADDRESSES.

The following appeared in The Charlotte *Messenger*, a weekly newspaper by W. C. Smith, Esq., March 10th, 1888. The editor in referring to it said:

[We publish this week an article from Mr. W. H. Quick, which is lengthly, but well worth the reading. He touches two of the vital points in reference to our welfare as a race land and morals. Read his letter. ED.]

BUY LAND! BUY LAND! BUY LAND!

Dear Editor—Your editorial of the 18th ult., in the *Messenger* on the subject of homes has doubtless aroused many lethargic brethren. I love to discuss the subject, and think it ought to be made an all-absorbing topic so long as we are situated as we are.

For as a nation must have territory in order to survive the ravages of time, and to meet the increasing demands of an ever-growing population, so must a race, mingling and comminling with other races, have land and homes if it would maintain its virtue and social identity— not content to *merely exist, homeless—aimless.* There is no act, art, possession, or species of property that tends more to interest, unite, control, mould and elevate men's character, society, and even the law itself, than the subject of land.

Four (4) years in constant attendance upon the

Courts furnish me abundant opportunity to observe (and with some degree of pleasure) the earnest, honest contentions of parties—differences growing out of the nature, and condition of real estates, and rights, and benefits arising from the same.

These cases occupy two-thirds of the time of the courts And each contestant herein seems a rival lord seeing and contending on hair splitting evidence for his kingdom. Can we live honest to ourselves and just to our families and our country without properly and timely playing our part well in the drama of life as becomes freemen? A foreman worthy of his steel! No!

There is one great move needed to change our monotonous condition—not to the East, West or North nor any where else in particular, but to move from the tenant's cabin to the landlord's mansion—to premises of our own.

And there *raise* our dear little ones, (not suffering to *drag* them up as is too often the case in some towns) on home raised "hog and hominy."

Change your condition as cropper for some body else or that of a dodging, cringing, scraping, bowing domestic to that of a manly, self-supporting citizen "to the manor born." Subjects of charity, whether white or colored, are not looked upon by many as being entitled in many respects to the full measure of consideration—the same priviliges and immunities as they do those who enjoy the fruits of their labor, investment and economy.

There are unsullied virtues in the country and countless millions of wealth in her forests—rich springs of joy and health inviting and awaiting our people's coming. The wolf is not very far from the door of a whole race; for the sake of the great unknown and unknowable Father let us fight him off with strong heart and hands. Our chief strength lies in our young men and women. Can we afford to sacrifice our boys to the pit-falls of city slums any more than we should force our daughters into the embrace of the seducer? Has your little town pride dressed up in the clothes of a dude any of the elements of manhood in them?

Should our parents stop paying from $3 to $5 per acre as rent for land that they can buy for $8 or $10 per acre, our youth will remain at home to aid and bless us in our declining years, while we shall leave these shores satisfied that our life's labor will remain to be enjoyed by those that we love and those that love us in return.

Spread out before me, portrayed in living colors, upon the canvas of my mind, is the picture of a well worked field, laden with the delicacies of life. Just back of it I see a beehive, cotton factory, hear the deafening hum of loom and spindle; there among the ridges I see the farmer and owner of the premises turning the clod as the fresh earth is bursting at his feet with the swelling seed of the coming new crop as his pockets jingle with the silver saved out of his last crop which is being twisted by machinery into thread and cloth.

Then who would not be the provident owner of such a home? Who could despise such a propitious show of success? If we cannot be a manufacturer we can be more, we can draw the raw material and fleecy locks from a mere seed by dropping it into the earth.

In this way we not only make a living, and raise worthy men and women, but make up good race history also.

The soldier who with no "home and fireside" to encourage, animate and embolden him in the great battles of country has not much to fight for.

Even his Satanic Majesty over shadowing a little rough hill and hedge on a high pinnacle, in company with Christ, once bethought himself right royal heir presumptive to all the lands, wood, and waters within this limited radius of his purview, "together with all the hereditaments and appurtenances thereto belonging or in anywise appertaining," with no one to "molest or make him afraid," his first object was to win the favor and influence of Jesus Christ, he (the devil) simply told Christ that he was the owner of all the land he saw around there. He prided himself on the idea that even the son of God would bow down to a landlord. Of course he did not mean to damage Christ, but was only trying to play off as a landlord.

We are not confined to the arrogance of the prince of night for an impetus, but have an ennobling example in the person of patriachal Abraham who was only a sojourner in the land of the Heths, bought a spot while there which to him would be sacred—in order that he might establish his interest there and consequently have his rights and manhood protected while he was thus unsettled, paying to Ephron for Machpelah "four (400) hundred shekels of silver, current money with the merchants," equal to about $250 of our money, for an old field in the country that had a great cave in it. But Abraham knew how to make a man of himself, and he did it. He became "a mighty prince." Again while he was passing through the dominions of Abimelech he dug him a well and upon that account claimed equal rights and equal protection under the law of that country; he dug the well for that purpose and we see his son Isaac about 90 years afterwards coming up with an air of filial pride contending with the Philistines for the property as heir to his father and certainly he was allowed to take and enjoy it in peace.

Would Burns ever have made fame or even a name for himself or a pean to the honor of his country had he sauntered around Edinburgh? No. As the sweet muses sang in his great soul he moved into the country among the hills where he could work, think, read and write. Here Burns literay glory depended upon his first procuring him a little homestead. Some of our starched fellows would turn up their noses if they were asked to take a home in such a rural district.

There is the poet-laureate of a hardy people on a high, rocky knoll, sloping down to the river Tieth which, as it rolls in superb tranquility before his own placid eyes I see him ploughing as he sings his own immortal verse, "a man's a man for a' that" or perhaps that other melodious strain:

> "My father was a farmer on the Carrick border,
> And soberly he brought me up in decency and order.
> * * * * * * * *
> To improve both air and soil,
> I drain and decorate this plantation of willows
> Which was lately an unprofitable morass;
> But here from noise and strife, love to wander.
> Now fondly making progress of my trees,
> If it please Almighty God,
> May I often rest in the evening of my life,
> Near that transparent fountain,
> * * * * * * * *
> On these banks of the Teith,
> In this small but sweet inheritance of my fathers,
> May I and mine live in peace
> And die in joyful hope."

This is a beautiful picture of a beautiful country home Let more of us bend our energy to do likewise. Can we as individuals or as a race achieve any degree of merit or maintain the little that has been bestowed upon us by leading a nomadic, a hireling life?

As we improve ourselves in the moral, social, and material world the State improves its policy toward us.

Twenty years ago (1868), the defendant in the *State vs Taylor* appealed to the highest appellate court of this State because there was a colored man on the jury, but after some years of gradual improvement, a few months since, the defendant in the case of the *State vs Sloan* exhausted the judiciary of the great State of North Carolina because there was *not* a colored man on his jury.

We see plainly that in proportion as we come within the pale of the landlord, of acquirement and possession, our rights, service, manhood, involving the foundation elements of our citizenship, will be all the more appreciated and protected. Excuse length.—More anon.

I am yours for the good of all men.

W. H. QUICK.